Furniture
Repair
&
Restoration

Furniture
Repair
&
Restoration

Over 100 methods & projects

Len & Kay Hilts

CREATIVE HOMEOWNER PRESS™   A DIVISION OF FEDERAL MARKETING CORPORATION, PASSAIC, NJ

Manufactured in United States of America

Current printing (last digit)
10   9   8   7   6   5

Editor: Shirley M. Horowitz
Associate Editor: Gail N. Kummings
Art Director: Léone Lewensohn
Designers: Léone Lewensohn, Paul Sochacki
Additional Illustrations: Norman Nuding
Cover design: Jerry Demoney
Cover photo: David Arky
Furniture on cover: Courtesy Evergreen Antiques
                    1249 Third Avenue
                    New York, NY 10021

We wish to extend our thanks to the many designers, companies, and other contributors who allowed us to use their materials and gave us advice. Their names, addresses, and individual identifications of their contributions can be found on *page 159.*

ISBN: 0-932944-52-3 (paperback)
ISBN: 0-932944-51-5 (hardcover)
LC: 81-69640

CREATIVE HOMEOWNER PRESS®
BOOK SERIES
A DIVISION OF FEDERAL
MARKETING CORPORATION
24 PARK WAY, UPPER SADDLE RIVER, NJ 07458-2311

About the Cover

The chest on the cover is an excellent example of good factory-made furniture of the American "Golden Oak Period," circa 1880-1910. We found it in a garage where it had been stored for 16 years. Here is a summary of its history: Purchased in 1901 for a gentleman's bedroom, it served until he died in 1963. The mirror was missing; we tracked it to the family member who had antiqued it and was using it as a wall mirror. She was willing to part with it. The "safe" compartment door had been damaged when pried open during a burglary before the owner's death.

Our work list included these repair jobs: new dowels to hold the mirror lyre to the top; new casters; repair of a chipped foot; repair of the "safe" door edge and the lock; restoration of the wooden back of the mirror; new drawer guides and stops; replacement of one drawer pull; and complete refinishing. All of these processes are detailed in this book.

The restored piece should be good for a couple of generations of service. The total cost, including the purchase, restoration materials, and an allowance for work time, was around $150. The present market value of the piece is difficult to estimate, but is probably between $600 and $800 and it will rise as the piece ages.

Projects

Contents

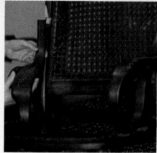

1
Look It Over and Plan the Work

We paid $3 for this 75-year-old rocker at a garage sale. After being reworked, it will be worth several hundred.

This chair, valued at $200, is hardly rare or unusual. Hundreds like it are sitting in attics awaiting restoration.

This handcarved oak blanket chest is an example of Early American furniture that still has its natural finish. Such a piece only should be cleaned.

Why get into furniture restoration? One reason is that there probably is no greater feeling of satisfaction than the one you get when you bring that newly restored chair to its place of honor in the living room.

You put it in exactly the right place, stand back — and feel good. A few months ago, that chair was battered and bruised, an embarrassment on its way to the trash collector. You thought about replacing it, but a little shopping showed that the price of a new chair of the same quality was steep — a lot steeper than you anticipated. In addition, you had a deep attachment for that old chair. After all, it had shared many years with you.

So you set out to restore it. Now the task is finished and the chair positively glows. You experience the warm feeling that comes from a job well done. You also saved a fair amount of money, which adds to your satisfaction.

Furniture restoration is rewarding in a lot of ways. You can upgrade the appearance of your home by restoring several pieces that now look dowdy. You enjoy gaining a new skill and feel real pride in your work.

One of the best rewards is that you end up with a much better collection of furniture in your home. Good furniture is hard to find today. Furniture making has undergone a number of important changes in the last several decades, as good hardwoods have become harder to get. Wood carving has virtually disappeared, and in its place are molded designs, often plastic, glued to flat surfaces. Hand rubbing and other marks of the fine furniture craftsmen have disappeared because of cost and fewer craftsmen to do this work.

New materials have come into furniture making. Plastic laminates, plastic bonded

This valuable French chest is a good example of the kind of antique whose repair should be reserved for experts. It is worth several thousand dollars.

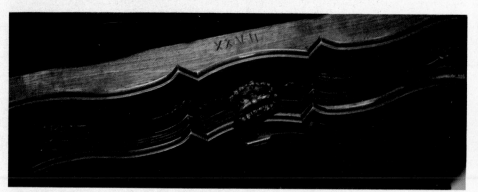

Look for these Roman numerals stamped into the drawer and the chest when you shop for good antique furniture. You don't see this notation on less valuable pieces.

to poorer grades of wood to simulate fine woods, particle board finished to look like wood — the list is long. Some of these new materials offer advantages, of course. Plastic laminates for example, make table tops that resist almost any onslaught. But overall, you receive less for your furniture dollar today, at least in traditional furniture terms.

There are other rewarding aspects, too: the sense of history that comes with salvaging an old family heirloom, or in building a collection of restored furniture belonging to a specific period.

VALUABLE ANTIQUES

One word of caution concerning valuable antiques: Make a distinction between good old furniture and very valuable antique furniture. The very valuable antique piece is a collector's item. Its value comes not only from its age and condition, but also from the fact that it probably is identified as exemplary of a style, designer or period, such as Chippendale, Hepplewhite or English Regency. Pieces such as these require very special care in order to retain their value as collector's items. It is important, for example, *not* to strip the finish from such pieces, since the original finish is an integral part of and contributes heavily to the value of the piece. Repairs to such finishes are delicate jobs, to be attempted only after you have gained considerable experience.

These days, because of their dollar value, valuable antiques are seldom *used* in a home. They are displayed, of course, but they are often worth far too much to be exposed to the dangers of everyday use.

This rough plank back helps determine a piece's age. Do not replace such materials.

GOOD OLD FURNITURE

Good old furniture, on the other hand, has real practical value after it has been restored. It, too, has money value, but not the immense price tag of the collector's piece. In all probability, a well-restored piece has a value at least equal to, and often more than, a similar piece available in the stores today. Under some circumstances, it can be worth much more than anything you can buy now. But the true value is that it pleases you, is useful, and perhaps has a history in your family.

RESTORATION ISN'T HARD

Can you restore a piece of furniture? Can you do a worthwhile job that doesn't look like the botching of an amateur? Isn't this work really a job for an expert?

Most people can restore furniture and achieve satisfactory results. That's why there are so many refinishing kits and materials on the market. People have tried them and found that they work.

The task is challenging at times, but not difficult. Mostly, you need patience and perseverance. A few skills are required but these develop quickly. A few tools are needed, but the list isn't long and the most expensive ones can be rented on a daily basis.

The usual cause of trouble for beginners is an overwhelming desire to get the job

Most pieces in antique shops are sound old furniture from 75 to 125 years old.

This shows the original condition of the golden oak dresser on the cover. More than 80 years old, the dresser had been stored in an unheated garage for 16 years.

done yesterday. This work requires time and patience. Glue needs time to dry, and you can't hurry it. Surfaces must be sanded completely, not partially. One coat of finish has to dry before the next coat goes on. This is where the patience comes in. You have to work, then wait, then work, then wait again. If you plan the work in advance, allowing time between tasks, you can avoid most problems.

Practice each technique before trying it on your project. Get the mistakes out of your system on a practice board; then work on the project and do it right. The results will be better than you expected.

HOW TO BEGIN

The first job is to take a hard look at the piece you want to restore. Assess it carefully. Some furniture is so badly damaged that a restoration is nearly impossible. Other pieces are so badly designed and/or constructed that after the restoration you wouldn't want it around.

We inherited from grandparents an old chair that had achieved heirloom status. It was *old*, for one thing. For another, it had sentimental value, so we considered bringing it back to life. As we talked about the kind of finish we would like, I sat on the chair. It had been stored in the attic for years and I had forgotten what it was like — but now I remembered. The seat was high and too wide — perhaps an inch higher than standard and two inches too deep from back to front. You couldn't sit comfortably on it for very long.

The discussion lasted long enough for me to become uncomfortable, and our decision was made. There was no point in working for weeks on a chair that we would probably never like, sentimental value or not. We quickly found another family member who wanted it (he was very tall) and went on to another more promising project.

Ground Rules

You might adopt these ground rules for deciding whether or not to tackle a project.
1. Do you like the design? If you don't, or have mixed feelings, pass it up. Unfortunately, over the years, a lot of badly designed pieces have been marketed, and the fact that a piece is 50 years old doesn't make it less ugly.
2. Can you use it now, or give it to someone who can? If not, pass it up. One incentive for doing the work is knowing that, when finished, your piece will find a welcome home and be used and admired. Without this, you may not have enough incentive to stay with the project.
3. Does the piece have many broken or missing parts? You might expect to mend some parts, but save any major rebuilding projects for later, when your skills have developed.
4. Does the piece fit into your rooms? If this is furniture that hasn't been in your home, be sure it is in scale with your other furniture. Older furniture, especially that dating back to the Victorian era, often was oversized to fit the big rooms of those old homes.

You are really asking yourself: is the piece worth restoring? It is hard to be positive and enthusiastic unless you are convinced that you will produce really worthwhile results.

This 19th century cardtable is missing a small strip of mahogany veneer.

This side chair also should be handled with care. Set into the mahogany are satinwood inserts. Note the detailing of the upholstry nails to match the style of the chair.

FIGURING OUT A REALISTIC WORK PLAN

Once you have decided the project has a future, make a work plan. This is one of those secret ingredients many people don't know about. One good way to botch a project is to start without planning each step. Sooner or later, you discover that you have just taken the step at the wrong time, like staining oak before filling it.

A good work plan guarantees that each task in the project will be done when it should be, that the proper time is allotted for each task, and that the whole job won't sink in a flurry of wasted work.

Step 1: List the Work First, make a list of what you can see has to be done. Note broken parts that must be mended, and any pieces that need to be taken apart and reglued. Examine the finish and make a judgment as to whether it can be salvaged or will have to be stripped and refinished. Check the hardware, and note any that must be refinished, repaired or replaced. Look at the drawers, at the casters, at the joints. Search for evidence of old repairs, perhaps sloppily done, that will require work.

If there is veneering, is it damaged, blistered or lifting from the surface? Is one leg shorter than the others? Are carvings damaged and in need of restoration? Is the finish damaged, perhaps by cigarette burns or deep gouges?

Step 2: Ordering the Work Be very thorough in making your list; then put the individual tasks in order. Some obviously must be done before others. Here are some guidelines.

Cleaning As a rule, the first task should be a thorough cleaning of the piece. Over the years, wax, polish, dust, smoke film and other forms of pollution tend to build up on furniture surfaces. The buildup is so gradual that you may not notice it if the piece is presently in daily use. But the dirt is there, and you can't really judge how good the finish is until it has been cleaned. In addition, cracks in the wood and other problems will show up during the cleaning. Once the piece has been cleaned, reassess the work list. You can now decide whether you can save the present finish or must strip and refinish.

Repairing Repairs should be made before any refinishing, so the next step on the work plan is to schedule repair and replacement of parts. If hardware is missing, plan the hunt for matching parts now.

This is a detail of the front of the 1850 dresser, showing the hardware and the veneer on the facing pieces. One of the drop-shaped knobs is missing and must be replaced.

The veneer on this drawer has dried, cracked and broken away. We usually try to restore veneer, but this time we'll have to replace it. The wood types must match.

Here is more veneer that has broken away and must be replaced. We also must add new casters. This piece dates to about 1852.

The back of the dresser — rough, unsanded boards — is typical of much older furniture. We keep as much of the piece as we can.

Old hardware often is hard to match. Specialty companies, which we will talk about later, can match most common old hardware, but contacting them and placing your order takes time, so put that into the work plan early. Then you may have the new hardware by the time you need it.

Regluing Is the piece wobbly because some of the glued joints have loosened? If so, the old glue is dry and has lost its holding power, so plan a complete regluing. This includes disassembling the piece, removing the old glue, and reassembling everything. Later in the book, we tell you how to do it, step by step. For now, include disassembly and regluing in your work plan.

Finishing When the work has progressed this far, you will have a completely repaired piece of furniture, with no missing or broken parts, ready for the rescue of the finish. If you are fortunate, you need only to perform repairs on the old finish to complete the restoration. See Chapter 6 for instructions on how to repair the ravages of cigarettes, misplaced drink glasses and other injuries to the finish.

If the finish is in bad shape, and cannot be salvaged by repairing, include a complete refinishing job in your plan. Schedule the stripping of the old finish, which you can do yourself or have done by a professional. In Chapter 7 on stripping,

we discuss the good and bad points of both approaches. If you decide to do it yourself, the chapter tells about the stripping

Tye Behnke at the Squaw Alley Shop in Naperville, Ill., restores an old pot metal lamp. Places like this are invaluable for the furniture restorer.

This detail of the golden oak dresser shows the carving on the mirror lyre. The lyre had been removed and antiqued before we restored and refinished it.

Detail of golden oak dresser. Note the evidence of craftsmanship in the beveled edges of the drawer. Refinish the insides as well as the outsides of drawers and cupboards.

The shop contains display boards and drawers full of old, rare hardware.

This 18th century mirror is a combination of pine, walnut, veneer and gilt. Such a combination was not uncommon, especially since pine was so plentiful.

compounds that are available and how to use them. This is a messy job that can take considerable time, so plan an appropriate place to do the work and a block of time to do it in.

Next comes the cleanup after stripping — rinsing off the stripping chemicals, drying, and finally sanding to smooth down the grain of the wood raised by the stripper. Then you can finish the piece. Chapter 8 will give the information you need about choices of finishing materials, and Chapter 9 tells how to apply them.

Step 3: Choosing a Finish What kind of a finish do you want? You have many from which you can choose.

What do you want the final color to be? For the beginner, this can be tricky. We have found that most people who don't deal with furniture every day have trouble visualizing furniture colors. They tend to think in generalities when it comes to color. Walnut, they believe, is walnut, and mahogany is mahogany. The fact is, there is a wide range of color variations within each of those categories, and you must select the specific color you want before you buy the finishing materials.

There are fashions in furniture colors just as there are fashions in clothes. Years ago, for example, mahogany finishes tended to be a deep red-brown in color. Today, mahogany furniture tends to be more of a natural brown, much lighter in color. This gives rise to the question: if you are restoring mahogany furniture, do you want the "old" red-brown look, or do you want a contemporary lighter brown? The old look is authentic, if you want the piece to look as it did originally. And it is possible that the contemporary light brown may seem out of place on this design.

Your best move is to visit some good furniture stores. Spend a few hours looking at the displays. Look at the colors. Compare the pieces on the floor, and begin to sense the color variations. It won't take long to sensitize your eyes. Then you can decide which color you want for your piece.

Next, visit the store where you purchase your finishing materials to see their displays of stains, varnishes and other materials, showing the range of colors available. You may find leaflets with color samples in them. If you have doubts, take these leaflets back to the furniture store to match the colors. This traveling from store to store takes time, but it is a good investment because if you don't like the final color you choose, the project will have been a failure.

Step 4: Finding a Work Area Furniture repair and refinishing are dusty jobs, so be prepared. You need a workroom where you can be messy in comfort. It is difficult to use a living area of your home, even if you spread papers on the floor and cover the other furniture. The major problems are dust from sanding, spills and splatters from finishing and stripping materials, and ventilation. In addition, tools must be conveniently at hand, so you need a bench or table for them.

The logical work areas are the basement, the garage, a porch, or a spare room that can be devoted to the project. You may find it best to use several work areas, depending on the task. When you sand, the air may be filled with tiny particles that can get into television sets, motors and other equipment that won't work well when full of dust. So plan to do really dusty sanding in a place where the dust won't harm anything and cleanup isn't a big problem (Minor hand sanding doesn't make much dust, but machine sanding can rapidly fill the air in a room.)

Stripping of the finish requires the use of strong chemicals and results in a lot of sloppy, hard-to-control residue. This residue can damage floors and other surfaces because it is full of active chemicals. The best place to strip furniture is in the garage or the yard, where the stripping and rinsing can be done with a minimum of concern over surroundings.

Basement work area Basements offer a logical workplace, but are not as good as many people think. All that sanding dust could do terrible things to a furnace or washing machine motor. For another, most basements have very poor ventilation. When you do a big sanding job, the fumes or dusty air has no place to go. The dust becomes concentrated — and you breathe it. Likewise, if you work in the basement with highly volatile finishing materials, such as lacquer, you will breathe in a lot of hazardous fumes.

A basement workshop, with a workbench and tool storage facilities, is probably the best place to do repairs, gluing and regluing, disassembly and assembly. Light hand sanding can be done there, too. It might be a good place for the application of some finishes — varnishes that don't give off strong fumes, for example. And perhaps, with the addition of ventilation equipment, the basement could be used for other work.

A simple but effective way to ventilate a typical basement is to open all windows and set up a good-sized electric fan to blow out through one of them. This creates cross ventilation and a good movement of air through the area to dispose of dust and fumes.

An unused bedroom can be converted into a furniture workshop if you protect the floor from spillage, arrange for good ventilation, and set up a work bench or work table for tools, clamps and other materials. If your project takes place in the winter, such a room is likely to be more comfortably heated than a basement or a garage.

Hardwoods such as oak, the fruitwoods and clear birch are used to make good unfinished furniture, which, when finished with care, become very worthwhile pieces.

2
How to Select and Use
Hand and Power Tools

HOW MANY TOOLS ARE NEEDED?

Professionals in all trades share one secret: the right tools make the job easier and quicker and do the work better. Furniture restoration is no different. It will pay you handsomely in the long run to acquire the right tools. Fortunately, it won't cost an arm and a leg to add to your present tool collection, but there will be some expense. You need to buy good tools only once, and you can amortize their cost over a large number of jobs.

If you find need for an unusual and expensive tool that you won't use often, you can rent it for a couple of days. An example might be large bar clamps, used to span big work such as a dining room table. The job might call for three or four of these — a large investment. We have found clamps such as these in most rental shops when we needed them.

Some of the tools we list may surprise you — cotton swabs, wooden toothpicks, tongue depressors, emery boards. One doesn't usually think of them as tools. But when you get down to the fine repair and refinishing work, these, along with a thin-bladed pocket knife, will probably serve you better than some expensive substitutes you could buy.

Go over the following list and note the tools you already have. Then list those you need to add to your armory. If the want list appears long, just remember that these can be bought as you need them. You don't have to get them all at once. Don't buy a doweling jig, for example, unless the present project calls for adding or replacing dowels.

TOOL SELECTION
Choosing and Using Hand Tools

Hammers Hammers are not a big item in furniture restoration, since few if any joints require nailing. Three types come in handy.

Standard claw hammers The best quality claw hammers are drop forged and have hickory handles. Look at the claw before you buy. It should have fine inside edges that will slide under the head of a nail easily, and the curve of the claw should be sufficient to provide good leverage. Claw hammers come in a variety of weights, starting at 7 ounces. The best all-around sizes are 13 or 16 ounces.

Rubber mallet The rubber mallet is one of the handiest tools to have because it enables you to pound on furniture parts without denting or marring them. It is ideal for use in knocking furniture apart before regluing and for tapping newly glued joints firmly together.

Wooden mallet A wooden mallet is not a real necessity but is handy when you chisel wood. Tapping the chisel with the wooden head saves wear and tear on the chisel handle.

Magnetic tack hammer The other hammer you might need is the magnetic tack hammer. This is a thin-nosed light hammer with a magnetic head, good for reupholstery work. The magnetic head holds the tack upright as you drive it, so that you can tack with one hand. Because of the narrow construction of the head, this hammer is good for getting into tight places where other hammers can't go, so you'll find other uses for it beyond upholstering. The head will retain its magnetism for a long period if you keep a metal washer on the face when the hammer isn't in use.

Screwdrivers You'll find mostly large screws used in furniture, notably in corners blocks and braces on chairs and tables, so you should have a good collection of large-bladed screwdrivers.

The secret in using a screwdriver is to match the width of the blade to the slot on the screw. A blade that is smaller than the slot won't provide the leverage you need to turn the screw in or out easily. A blade that is only half the size of the slot may bend under the pressure you apply or may

You will use these very handy "non-tools" regularly. Also add cotton swabs and small disposable aluminum baking dishes.

Three hammers will serve you in furniture work: a rubber mallet, a magnetic tack hammer, and a small (7½ oz.) claw hammer.

damage the slot in the screw. Your best buy is a matched set of good-quality steel screwdrivers, with handles large enough to allow a comfortable grip. There are a good many cheap screwdrivers available, but it is best to avoid these "bargains." Good ones will last longer and give much better service.

You won't need screwdrivers with Phillips heads for wooden furniture, but to work with metal units, you will need several sizes.

Nailsets In those rare instances when you use nails in furniture restoration, you want to hide all traces of them. This is done by countersinking the nailhead and then filling the hole with wood putty. To countersink a nail, use a nailset to tap the nail a sixteenth of an inch or so below the wood surface. Nailsets are more frequently used to drive out the metal pins used in some furniture in order to reinforce dowel joints.

Handsaws Most sawing in restoration is small work and requires a smooth cut. The best handsaw for the purpose is a small backsaw, a square-ended saw with fine teeth. A backsaw also can be used with a small miter box to make angular cuts.

On occasion, there are uses for a coping saw. If you need to cut a new chair splat to replace one that was broken, the coping or scroll saw would do the job. A splat, incidentally, is the wide centerpiece in the back of a wooden chair, frequently made with eye-pleasing curves. To cut a new splat, trace the design on a hardwood board of the proper thickness, then cut along the pencil line with the coping saw.

It is difficult to make a continuous smooth cut with a handheld coping saw. The job goes faster and better with an electric scroll saw or with a sabre saw. But you can use the handsaw if a motorized unit isn't available. It will take a considerable amount of sanding, however, to finish the splat edge smoothly after cutting with a handheld coping saw.

For furniture work, mount the blade in the coping saw with the teeth pointing toward the handle, so that the cutting is done on the pull stroke. This produces smoother cuts.

Wood Chisels Good, sharp wood chisels are used in a number of ways in furniture work. You'll cut recesses for the installation of hinges and other hardware, or make dovetail or mortise-and-tenon

joints with them. Have several chisels in your kit, the best widths being ¼-, ½-, and ¾-inch. Resist any temptation to use the chisels for anything but cutting wood, or you may ruin the fine cutting edges.

Use a mallet or light hammer to drive chisels when cutting, and always make a series of light, thin cuts rather than fewer but deeper cuts. The light cuts are much easier to control. Begin by making vertical cuts across the area to provide a straight finished edge. Then shave out the wood between the vertical cuts to the needed depth. Make all cuts with the grain of the wood. Have the beveled side of the chisel face up for shallow cuts, and beveled side down for making deeper cuts.

Practice using the chisel if you have never cut with one before. Clamp an old board to your workbench and try different cuts. Practice controlling the work, making just the cut you need. Keep at it until

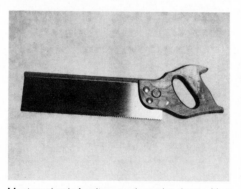

Most sawing in furniture work can be done with a backsaw, which makes a smooth, fine cut. Hold the work securely in a vise.

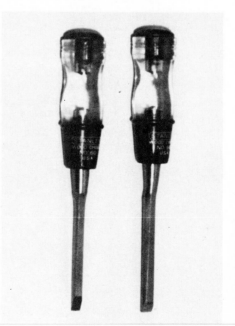

You'll regularly find uses for ¼-, ½-, and ¾-in. wood chisels. Buy ones with shanks that extend up through the handle.

you feel secure in your ability to cut the right amount at the right depth. Then you can go to your project confident of your ability to do the job. One thing about chiseling: once you have made a cut that is too deep, repair work is difficult. It is better to make a number of thin cuts, even though it takes time, than to repair a badly chewed, deep cut.

Clamps No tools are more important to the furniture restorer than clamps. Make it a basic rule from the beginning to clamp every glue job, no matter how big or how small. Then you will make neat, successful glue joints every time.

There are four basic types of clamps at your hardware store, and you'll need all of them in a variety of sizes if you do much restoring.

Hand screws These are the traditional wooden-jawed clamps furniture makers have been using for centuries. They con-

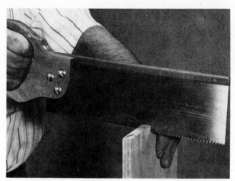

The backsaw in action being used to cut the sides of a new dovetail joint. Cut in the waste of the wood, along the guideline.

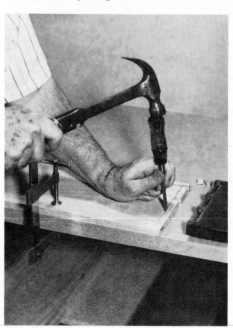

The wood chisel at work. If you plan to do much furniture work, practice with the chisel to learn how to control your cuts.

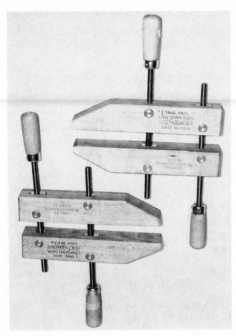

Wooden furniture clamps, called Jorgensens, are old standbys. Easy to adjust and fit, they don't bite into the wood.

These Jorgensens won't mar the wood of this dresser but will hold the base plate firmly until the glue dries.

This is a bar clamp, so called because the two clamping units fit over a metal bar. You should have bar or pipe clamps that span 4 ft. or more.

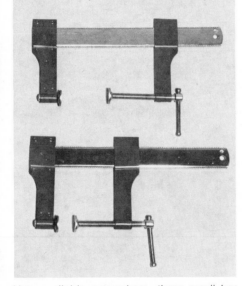

Now available everywhere, these small bar clamps have proved very handy, replacing C-clamps in much of our work.

A bar clamp is at the back of this piece and a pipe clamp at the front. In order to make a pipe clamp of any size, buy standard pipe in any length you need.

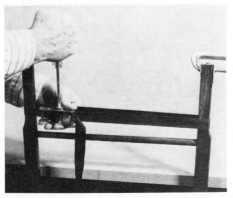

The web or strap clamp consists of a long belt and a clamping head. To tighten the web, turn an adjusting screw.

sist of two blocks of shaped hardwood, with two steel, wood-handled clamping screws running through them. To tighten the clamp, you turn the screws. Because the clamping screws are mounted in pivots, the jaws can be set at any desired angle. These come in all sizes, from miniature for modeling work, to the big ones with jaws which open to 14 inches. A good basic starter group might include a 3- or 4-inch and an 8- to 10-inch model.

Bar and pipe clamps These are called furniture clamps in some tool catalogs. They consist of two movable metal jaws, one of which has a built-in clamping screw, fitted over either a long steel bar or a long pipe. They are used to span big work such as table tops, the seat of a chair, or the side of a cabinet. You can buy them in lengths from 12 to 48 inches. We have found the longer lengths most practical, because even the 48-inch clamp can be fitted to work of 12 inches — though sometimes fitting larger clamps to smaller work is clumsy. For big gluing jobs, you may need as many as three or four at a time; two is a minimum for most shops.

Strap and web clamps Some furniture workers think these are the handiest tools in the shop. They are inexpensive and often can be made to do the work of the more costly hand screws and bar clamps. Literally, strap and web clamps are just tourniquets applied to furniture.

The clamps you buy consist of a fabric strap fitted with a metal clamp body. Put the strap around the work to be clamped, then tighten it by pulling the strap through, not unlike the way you tighten an airplane seat belt. Most clamp bodies are made so you can do the final tightening by turning a nut on the side of the body with a small wrench. Most straps are 12 to 15 feet long, so they can go around big work.

We often improvise our own strap clamps, using ordinary clothesline rope and a long screwdriver. The result is not an elegant tool, but it works. Just wrap the clothesline several times around the work to be clamped. Tie the loose ends together. Then insert the screwdriver between strands of the rope and twist to tighten, (like a tourniquet). When the rope is tight enough, tuck the handle of the screwdriver under the nearest part of the work so that the rope is held at the right tension. One word of caution: don't twist the rope too tight or it may break. Just make it tight enough to hold the glued parts together.

C-clamps The C-clamp is shaped like the letter C, with the open mouth of the letter used for clamping. The clamping surfaces are small metal pads, adjusted by turning a screw handle, which moves the lower pad. C-clamps are available with jaw openings from one to eight inches or more. It is best to buy the sizes you need for each job as required instead of trying to purchase a whole collection immediately.

C-clamps are the workhorses of the business. Note the clamp in the center, designed for clamping edge pieces as they dry.

Here, a C-clamp clamps a small leg. Note the small wooden pads used to protect the surface of the furniture.

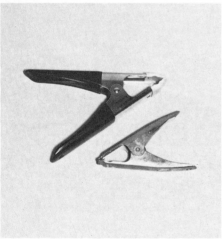

Someone took the spring clothespin and developed it into big spring clamps. They come in many sizes and are applied easily.

This drawer stop is being clamped in place with a spring clamp.

To use a wedge clamp, tap on the wedges, one after the other. The increasing width gradually drives the pieces together.

Here is one of the handiest devices you can have—the doweling jig. Use it to place opposing dowel holes perfectly.

Always insert pieces of scrap wood between the work and the metal pads of C-clamps before tightening. Otherwise the pads will make ugly dents in the surface of the furniture.

Other clamping devices Anything that can hold two pieces together while they are being glued can be called a clamp. We have used spring-type clothespins for small work and have found times when a rubber band was as good as anything else. You can buy metal spring clamps, which work the same as the spring-type clothespins but have jaw openings in sizes ranging from an inch to 3 inches. It is good to have a few of these around.

Wedge clamps Wedge clamps are used to clamp two flat pieces, such as the two halves of a cracked dresser top together while the glue dries. Although the proper tool for the job would be two bar clamps, a homemade wedge will work.

To construct the wedge, take an 18- to 24-inch length of 1x4 board, an inch or more thick, and cut it diagonally to make two long triangles. Place the work to be glued against a solid wall, such as the back rail of the workbench. Apply glue to both surfaces and fit them together. Fit the triangles you have cut together again and place them next to the work opposite the wall. Drive nails through the outer triangle to hold it in place. Then tap the wide end of the unanchored triangle with a hammer. It will slide inward, between the anchored triangle and the work, to force the glued pieces into firm contact with each other. You can see how it works in the accompanying photograph.

Dowel Jig Many pieces of furniture have parts joined by dowels — wooden pegs that fit into holes drilled in each of the joined pieces. Dowel joints are strong, neat and long-lasting, and eliminate the need for screws. To do dowel joining, you need a dowel jig. Basically each type positions the drill in the proper place on the pieces to be joined, so that the holes are perfectly aligned after drilling. It is nearly impossible to make a precise dowel joint without the jig, which is a worthwhile investment if you plan to do much furniture work. Each brand is slightly different, so follow the instructions that come with the one you buy.

Buy ready-made hardwood dowels that come grooved to take glue. After drilling the holes, coat the dowels with glue. Tap them into the holes in one piece. Then join the pieces by fitting the second piece over the dowels. Tap the pieces together and clamp until the glue dries.

Dowel centers As an alternative, you can use little metal pieces called dowel centers. These look like little bullets. To use them, drill the hole in one of the pieces to be joined; then insert a dowel center in the hole. Tap the other piece to be joined against the first one. A sharp point on the dowel center marks the spot where the second hole must be drilled. This is the inexpensive way to line up dowel holes, and it works if you are very careful. However, dowel centers are not nearly as satisfactory as the dowel jig, so we don't recommend them.

Bench vises It takes two hands to do most woodworking jobs — chiseling, for example. Unless you have a third arm, there is no way to hold the wood while you work on it. This means you should have a bench vise of some type, into which you can clamp the work. A bench vise is not only a convenience but also a safety device, since a lot of woodworking accidents occur when people attempt to work on loose pieces and a tap of the hammer causes one of the unclamped pieces to fly.

If you already have a good workbench, it probably is fitted with a bench vise. If you don't have a workbench and perhaps have no place to put one, then buy a clamp-on vise, which clamps to the edge of any sturdy table. Just be sure to put little wooden pads between the clamping areas on the vise and the tabletop to prevent marring.

Some vises have heads that swivel, allowing you to change the angle of the work by adjusting the angle of the clamp. These are the most useful for general work.

Woodworking vises are a special variety of bench vise mounted on the side of the workbench, with jaws flush with the top of the table. They are lined with wood to protect anything clamped in them, and are the most practical for furniture work. Clamp-on models are available, but swivel models are not. If you are buying your first vise and intend to work a lot with wood, the woodworking vise is best. However, you can use a bench vise to hold most wood work by padding the jaws with thin wooden boards to protect the work.

Pocket Knife A pocket knife is used dozens of times a day for scraping, mak-

ing small cuts, roughing up wooden surfaces before gluing, carving, cutting the string on packages, digging reluctant stains out of corners — the list could be endless. A small, thin-bladed knife works best. Buy a honing stone, if you don't already have one, and strop the blade on it regularly to keep it sharp.

Pliers You probably already own the standard pliers, called slip joint pliers. In addition, two other types come in handy from time to time. One is long-nosed pliers, for working in tight places. The other is end-cutting pliers, which you use to pull nails or cut off the heads of nails. Don't buy either of these immediately, because you will use them infrequently. But keep them in mind, because there are rare moments when no other tool will do.

Rules A rule, of course, is a device for measuring, and you need one constantly to measure the work. Three types are helpful in doing good furniture work: the folding rule; the steel tape rule; and the try-square, commonly known as the T-square.

The folding rule is most convenient for general measurements, especially of outside dimensions. The steel rule is handy for making inside measurements, such as the inside of a drawer or cabinet. The T-square is held against the outside of a cabinet, drawer or other square construction to show whether or not the corners are truly square.

Carpenter's Level Another measuring tool which you might use from time to time is the carpenter's level. It is used

to determine whether cabinet sides are plumb and tops are level.

Planes Once in a while you may find uses for a plane when making furniture parts, but we have found that need infrequent, so we don't recommend that you buy one.

Drills We feel the right tool for drilling holes is the electric drill — a good investment because you can perform a number of tasks in addition to drilling with it.

Choosing and Using Power Tools

Power tools do any job quicker and often better than hand tools. The costs of good power tools have come down in recent years, so they are generally affordable. We think they pay for themselves in time saved and in work quality. As with any tool, however, you must practice with a power tool to find out how to get the most out of it.

There are two classes of power tools, the portable and those that mount on a workbench or stand alone. The bench tools and stand-alone units include the wood lathe, the band saw, the drill press, the joiner, the jigsaw, the shaper, and the radial arm saw. Any or all of these are wonderful to have in a workshop, and you can find all kinds of uses for them. Each of them, however, requires a major investment in money and in workshop space — and you can do furniture restoration without them.

The portable power tools you can use in furniture restoration include the electric

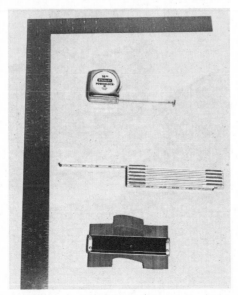
These units will handle most measuring jobs: the carpenter's square, a good steel tape, a folding rule and a contour guide.

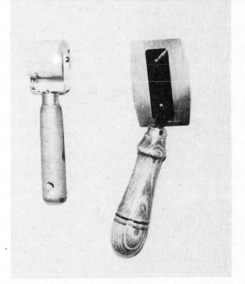
When you veneer, you'll need a veneer saw and roller. (If you have a wallpaper seam roller, use it. It is the same thing.)

drill, the sabre saw, and the electric sander. If you make furniture or have to make many replacement parts, the router is a good versatile addition to your tool collection. In overall importance, we rate the electric sander first, and then the electric drill.

Sanders Three kinds of sanders are available at most hardware and home center stores: the oscillating sander, in which the abrasive paper moves back and forth rapidly and imitates the back and forth motion of hand sanding; the orbital sander, which moves the abrasive paper in a small-diameter circle; and the belt sander, which has a continuous belt of abrasive paper or cloth that runs constantly at high speed. Some units now available are combination oscillating and orbital sanders. You control the motion of the abrasive paper by turning a switch.

Each of these sanders has its specific use. The oscillating sander is the best all-around sander for most people. Its sanding action is straight-line and relatively slow, so the novice doesn't make as many mistakes with it. The orbital sander is specifically a finishing tool, used for putting that final smooth finish on wood. It doesn't remove much material, even when used with coarse abrasive paper. The belt sander, on the other hand, cuts into wood fast, even with fine and medium abrasive papers. In restoration work, handle the belt sander carefully or you will cut deeper than you intended.

Your best buy is a combination oscillating/orbital unit. If your budget allows it, add a belt sander later.

Electric Drill An electric drill can do a lot of jobs in addition to drilling holes. It can be converted to a circular sander, or a drum sander, or a disc sander. It can be used with a wire brush to remove rust, paint and finishes. It is, with the addition of attachments, the most versatile tool you can buy.

Electric drills come in ¼-, ⅜-, and ½-inch sizes, with these numbers referring to the size of the chuck (the device that grips the drill bits and other attachments). The power rating of the drill generally varies with the size, ranging from ⅓ to 1½ horsepower. For most home workshops, the ¼-inch model is fine. If you expect to do some heavy duty work on occasion, then go up to the ⅜-inch model.

When buying a drill, features to look for include a variable speed trigger, which permits you to control the speed of the drill by squeezing the trigger, and double insulation. This allows the use of a two-prong plug because the shell and the chuck are completely insulated from the wiring.

The cheapest units have minimum horsepower, low-quality bearings and may burn out if used for heavy duty work: they are fine for light duty chores. As a rule, if you buy recognized brand names, you can as-

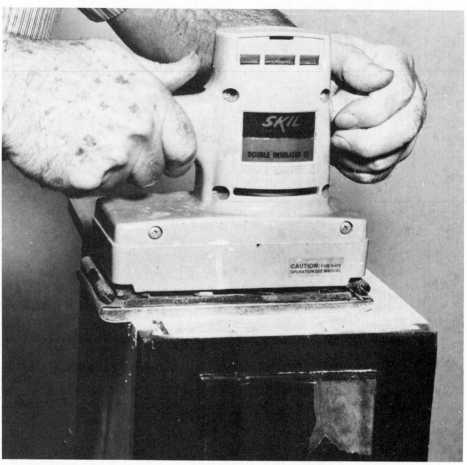

An electric sander simplifies the job of sanding. Avoid using sanding discs in a portable electric drill; always use a straight or orbital sander similar to the one shown.

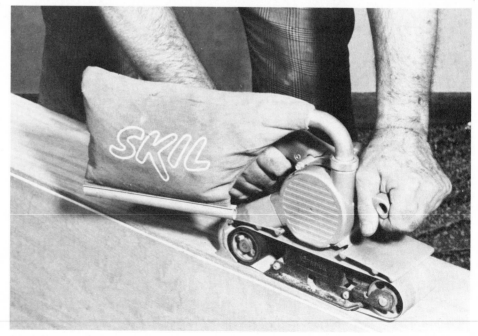

A belt sander is a fast worker, great for removing material fast. But be careful of it. You can dig trenches in the surface with it if you work too carelessly.

The sabre saw can be used to cut curved shapes, such as a new chair splat or rocker.

A circular saw is useful for straight cuts. Always use it with an edge guide.

Two very handy tools for the furniture worker—the router and the dovetail jig. Use the router for making grooves and in repair work as well as with the dovetail jig.

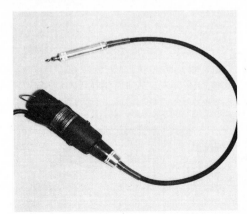

This hand grinder by Dremel has a flexible shaft and has cutters, grinders, sanding wheels and other accessories.

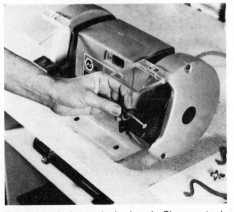

This is a grinder and wire brush. Sharpen tools on the grinder; polish hardware with the wire brush or a cloth buffing wheel.

sume that the more expensive models are made to survive heavier work. We think those units in the middle to top price range are the best buy.

Attachments Attachments add to the versatility of your drill. Good ones to consider at the start include: screw driving units; a buffing and sanding set consisting of a rubber pad, a lamb's wool buffing pad, and sanding discs; and a collection of drill bits. Bits come in small storage cases containing a range of sizes. Your collection should include wood/metal twist bits in sizes from $\frac{1}{32}$ to $\frac{1}{2}$ inch. Add to these some wood spade bits from $\frac{1}{2}$ to $1\frac{1}{2}$ inches. If you drive many screws, a set of screw-mate bits can be helpful. Use these to drill pilot holes for screws. The bit not only drills a hole of the correct depth, but also widens the top of the hole so that the screw is automatically countersunk when you drive it.

Stands A drill can be turned into a small workshop if you buy a stand for it. The stand holds the drill so that you don't

have to. You can then use grinding wheels, disc sanders and other fittings in the drill, and have both hands free to hold the work. The drill also can be converted into a small but effective drill press with the purchase of a drill press stand.

With a disc sander in the chuck, you can hold small wooden parts to the spinning sander wheel and do some very good sanding work. Many people decide not to buy a sander but to use the disc sander in the electric drill instead. This is false economy. We don't recommend using an electric drill for sanding furniture surfaces. The spinning disc is too difficult to control and you are likely to get uneven results and circular gouges. The disc in the drill is fine for sanding rungs, legs and irregular shapes, but the oscillating sander is best for flat surfaces.

Sabre Saw The sabre saw is a portable jigsaw used to make curved and interior cuts in plywood and boards up to 2 inches thick. If you have to make a new lyre-shaped splat for a chair, or new rockers for a rocking chair, the sabre saw is a good tool for the job. It is not the best tool for making long, straight cuts; those are jobs for the circular power saw.

Router The router was made for furniture work. It cuts grooves, rabbets, dovetails and dadoes. It makes cove, chamfered, beaded and other decorative edges, and is the tool to use when making inlays. You certainly can have a lot of fun with a router, and it is essential if you make your own furniture from scratch. In restoration work, however, you often can do without it. Put it on the list as a tool to buy after the more essential units — the drill, the sander, and the sabre saw.

Mini Power Tools

Space is a problem for many people, especially those who live in apartments and don't have the luxury of a basement workshop area. For them, mini power tools may be the answer. Dremel is the leading manufacturer in this field, and among the tools they offer are the Moto-Tool (small drill), a mini belt sander, a table saw, a table scroll saw, and a wood lathe. With attachments, the Moto-Tool can be turned into a drill press and a router. If you have a space problem, look these tools over. They are not intended for large or heavy-duty work, but will do most of the normal jobs in furniture restoration. They store easily and are convenient to use.

3
Fasteners, Glue and Wood

Furniture, for the most part, is a matter of wood — how to shape it, how to join it, and how to finish it. In furniture restoration, you only shape wood when making replacement parts. Your major concerns are with wood joints and the finishing of wood surfaces. In this chapter, we deal with fasteners, glue, and wood itself, as well as how to handle the problems you will encounter in restoration work.

FASTENERS
Screws

Screws are the most common fasteners used in good furniture. The majority of joints are made of shaped wood — such as mortise-and-tenons, rabbets or dovetails — and are glued. Screws rather than nails are used whenever a fastener is required. Always look for wood screws (as opposed to metal screws) when buying fasteners for furniture use.

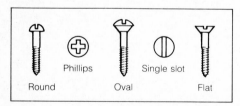

Screws, not nails, are preferred for joining wood pieces in furniture repair. Select the type most appropriate for the location.

Size Screw size numbers refer to both the gauge and the length of the screw. Gauge numbers run from 0 to 24, and refer to the diameter of the shank at its widest point. An 0-gauge screw has a shank that is about 1/16-inch in diameter, while that of a 24-gauge screw is 3/8-inch in diameter. Screws range in lengths from tiny (1/4-inch) to about 6 inches. Most stores carry screws from 2 to 16 or 18 gauge in a variety of lengths. The screws most used in

WOOD SCREWS

Woodscrews have a number of uses in furniture work. The most common is to attach table and dresser tops to frames. They also are used as joiners, replacing wood joints. In this use, they usually are countersunk and then covered with a wood plug. Always predrill holes for screws, making the hole slightly smaller than the diameter of the screw shank.

Do not drive screws into the end grain of wood, since they don't hold. Always make sure the blade of the screwdriver is as wide as the slot in the screwhead when driving screws. If the blade is narrower, you (1) may damage the screwhead or the blade, and (2) will get much less turning power. If the blade is wider than the slot, you will damage the surrounding wood.

SCREW SIZES

Screws are designated by both length and diameter. Length is designated in inches. Diameter is designated by a gauge number. Lengths available run from 1/4 inch to 6 inches. Gauges available are 0 (1/16 inch) to 24 (3/8 inch). The label on the box of screws might read 1x6, meaning the box contains 1 inch screws of No. 6 gauge. Most stores carry all standard lengths of screws in appropriate gauges. Most common gauges are Nos. 2 through 16. The heavier the work required of the screw, the larger the gauge should be.

TYPES OF SCREWHEADS

Standard slotted woodscrews come in three headstyles: flathead (flat across the top); oval head (the top is rounded and the underside of the head is beveled); and roundhead (top rounded, underside of head flat). For most furniture work, you will use flathead screws, but the others have uses, too.

Flathead	Use flathead screws when the head of the screw is to be flush with the surface. Use a countersink bit in your electric drill to drill out a place for the head, or use a screw mate bit, which both pre-drills a hole for the screw and a wider place at the top for the head. You can also countersink the head slightly below the surface.
Oval head	Oval head screws are pleasing in appearance and are easier to remove than flatheads. As a rule, the underside of the head is countersunk, and the oval top remains above the surface. Use where the screw will be seen and appearance is important.
Roundhead	Most important use for roundhead screws is in applications where you expect to remove the screw and the work is to be disassembled. They also can be countersunk covered.

furniture work range from 8 to 16 gauge, and from ¾ to 1½ inches long.

Styles Screw heads come in flat, oval and round shapes. Flat heads are used when the screw head is to be flush with the surface of the work or countersunk below the surface. Oval and round heads are used when the screw head will show on the surface of the work.

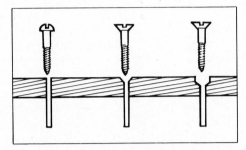

A screw head either rests on the surface (left), is set flush (center) or is countersunk (left). The countersunk opening is often filled.

When driving or removing screws, always be sure the blade of the screwdriver is the same width as the slot in the screw head.

Using Screws Much of the time in restoration work, you remove old screws and use them again. If the screw has been damaged, replace it with a new one of the same size and type. When driving a new screw into wood for the first time, always drill a pilot hole, using a drill bit two sizes smaller than the shank diameter.

Some hardwoods will split if you drive a screw in without first drilling the pilot hole. To be safe, widen the upper part of the pilot hole to accommodate the unthreaded part of the shank. This part of the hole should be the same diameter as the shank. A screw-mate drill bit does all of this in one motion. At the same time, it drills out a space for the head so that when the pilot hole is finished and the screw inserted, the screw head is flush with or countersunk below the work surface.

Screws will turn into new work easier if you lubricate them first. To do this, rub the screw on a bar of soap or wax.

Nails

Although nails aren't used in making furniture joints, they do have some uses in furniture. The nails and other fasteners you may see are finishing or casing nails, upholstery nails, tacks, dowel pins, corrugated fasteners, and staples.

The common nail has a head. Finishing and casing nails have virtually no heads and, when used, are driven below the work surface with a nail set. Then the hole is filled to hide the nail. They can be bought in lengths ranging from 1 to 3 inches, but when buying nails, look for the "penny" size number and not inches.

In England, 400 years ago, nails were sold by the penny weight. That is, you got a certain weight of nails for a penny, and the bigger the nails, the fewer you got for

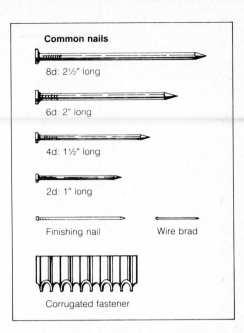

Common nails

8d: 2½" long

6d: 2" long

4d: 1½" long

2d: 1" long

Finishing nail   Wire brad

Corrugated fastener

NAILS

As a general rule, nails are for carpenters, not furniture restorers. To fasten furniture parts together, use wood joints (dovetails, etc.), dowels, and glue. When metal fasteners are needed, use screws. The two legitimate uses of nails in furniture are to hold a drawer bottom in place by driving a single small nail up through the bottom panel into the drawer back, and to pin a dowel joint. Do NOT use nails to mend broken furniture parts.

Note that in pieces made before 1895, square nails often were used, usually to reinforce glued joints or parts glued together. When restoring these pieces, reuse these nails just as they were used originally. They confirm the antiquity of the piece. If the nails have been lost or are not fit for reuse, you can buy replicas at woodworking specialty shops to replace them. If you choose not to replace them, do not use modern nails in the joint. Instead, use dowels and glue.

NAIL SIZES

Nails are sold by "penny" sizes (designated by "d"). The smallest nail is a 2d or 2 penny, which is 1 inch long. A 3d nail is 1¼ inches long. A 6d nail is 2 inches long. A 10d nail is 3 inches long.

Common nails	Typical nail with a head. In furniture, a 2d common nail will hold a drawer bottom. The thickness of the shank increases with the length.
Barbed dowel pins	These are nails without heads and with scored shanks. Used to pin a dowel in place by being driven through the dowel from the outside of the joint; then countersunk with a nailset and puttied.
Corrugated fasteners	These are small wavy steel fasteners with sharp teeth on one side. In cheap furniture, they are sometimes used to reinforce mitered joints by being driven into the wood across the joint. Can be used for some repair work.
Staples	More and more staples are showing up in furniture. They are commonly used to hold backs on dressers and chests, and to hold drawer bottoms in place. In cheap furniture, staples may be used to fasten joints, replacing glue. It is best not to use them in woodworking. They are ideal for use as replacement for tacks in upholstery work.

your penny. This system has evolved until today the penny size number refers to the nail length. A two-penny nail (abbreviated 2d) is an inch long. A three-penny nail is 1¼ inches long. Each penny number adds ¼ inch to the length. A 10d nail turns out to be 3 inches long.

Upholstery Nails Upholstery nails are made with round, ornamental heads and are used to attach upholstery fabric wherever a fastener would show — usually at the edges of upholstered chair arms and seats. There is only one size of upholstery nail, but a wide selection of plain and fancy head designs.

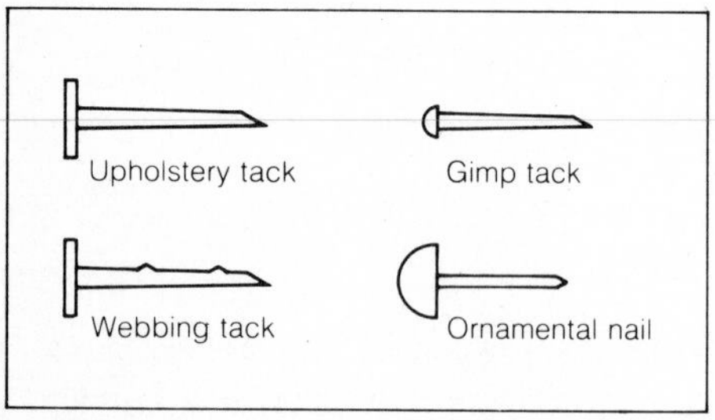

Tacks are intended for upholstery work. Head and shank styles vary according to the job for which each is designed.

Tacks Tacks are used only in upholstery work and never to hold or attach anything but upholstery materials in furniture. Standard upholstery tacks are rated in size by the ounce. That is, you buy boxes of tacks marked "1 oz." or "2 oz." Tacks in the 1-ounce box are 3/16-inch long, and those in the 2-ounce box are ¼-inch. Check the accompanying table for other lengths.

Webbing tacks are the same as standard tacks, but bigger, and are used to attach webbing in chairs and sofas.

The gimp tack, small and round-headed, is used to attach fabric coverings. The small round head is almost invisible when driven into a fabric, so gimp tacks are used when you must tack in an obvious place but don't want the heads to be seen.

Dowel Pins Dowel pins are nails with no heads. On occasion, a furniture maker will make a dowel joint and then secure it by driving a dowel pin through it. The pin is then countersunk and the hole filled. This isn't done very often, but when you are taking a chair apart for regluing you may find a dowel joint that refuses to come apart. When this occurs, inspect the area carefully for evidence of wood filler over a nail hole. If you see a small telltale circle on the surface over the dowel, you know the maker used a dowel pin.

TACK SIZES AND LENGTHS

Tacks come in three standard types: upholstery, webbing, and gimp. The upholstery tack is the commonest. Webbing tacks have barbs on their shanks to give greater holding power. Gimp tacks have small round heads and are nearly invisible when used in applying upholstery. Use tacks only for upholstery work, to tack fabric to wood frames, and never for joining wood. Be cautious when driving tacks, as they may split the wood into which they are driven. Ask for tacks by their weights. The chart below gives the weight and the length of the tack shank.

UPHOLSTERY TACKS		WEBBING TACKS		GIMP TACKS	
Size	Length	Size	Length	Size	Length
1 oz.	3/16"	12 oz.	11/16"	2 oz.	5/16"
1½ oz.	7/32"	14 oz.	¾"	2½ oz.	⅜"
2 oz.	¼"			3 oz.	7/16"
2½ oz.	5/16"			4 oz.	½"
3 oz.	⅜"			6 oz.	9/16"
4 oz.	7/16"			8 oz.	⅝"
6 oz.	½"				
8 oz.	9/16"				
10 oz.	⅝"				
12 oz.	11/16"				
14 oz.	¾"				
16 oz.	13/16"				
18 oz.	⅞"				
20 oz.	15/16"				

To remove the dowel pin, use a nail set. Tap it against the small circle of the wood filler to drive the pin through. Then use a pliers to pull the pin out. You should then be able to disassemble the dowel joint easily.

Corrugated Fasteners Corrugated fasteners are strips of corrugated metal an inch or so long, with one side sharpened like the blade of a knife. You won't find these in good furniture, but in some cheaper furniture they are used across miter joints to hold the joint together. Furniture repairers sometimes use them as a quick way to repair cracked or loose joints (not a good idea). You should never use them for any reason.

If you encounter a corrugated fastener in a piece you are restoring, take it out and rebuild the joint in correct fashion. You probably will find that the dowel or tenon of the original joint was damaged, and the repairer didn't want to take the time to make the right repair. To remove the corrugated fastener, you may have to chisel a bit of the wood away from its upper edge in order to grip the edge with a narrow-nosed pliers.

Brads Brads are small headless nails, and actually are small versions of the finishing and casing nail, with the same uses.

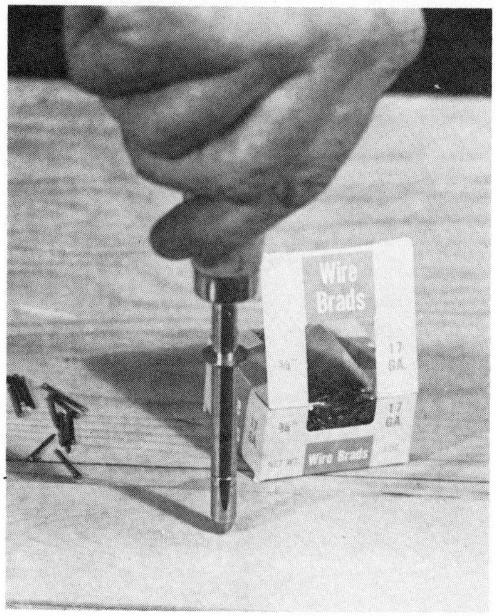

Shown here is a brad driver, a tool especially designed to drive the small fasteners. Brads are used for fastening wood trim.

Staples A staple, of course, is a piece of bent wire applied with a staple gun. Stapling with an electric staple gun is very fast, which appeals to present-day furniture manufacturers. By using staples wherever possible, they can cut labor costs. Traditional furniture buffs feel that the staple is an abomination, useful only for tacking two pieces of paper together.

The fact is that the staple is a very good fastener in certain applications, and a very bad one in others. We have found that in applying covering materials in upholstery, the electric stapling gun beats hand tacking by a mile in some places. (Tacking fabric along the bottom rail of a chair or couch is a good instance.) The staple holds better than the tack, and the work goes much faster. We part company with the traditionalists here.

Staples are a handy alternative for upholstery tacks. Do not, however, use staples to replace correct joints or wood screws.

But we agree with traditionalists on the matter of using staples to fasten wood parts together. We don't like this technique. First, to use staples in making furniture you must design the furniture for them. In designing a chest of drawers, for example, you might decide to staple the back panel in place. In good furniture, made the old-fashioned way, you would cut rabbets (grooves) on the inside face of the sides near the back. The back panel would slide into the grooves. Today, in cheaper — and even in some better — furniture, you would skip the grooving entirely, lay the back panel against the back of the chest, and staple it in place.

If the staples used are long enough, and if a sufficient number of staples are driven, then the stapled back stays in place and does its job of closing the back and bracing the whole chest. But the panel can be seen from the side because it has been stapled to the outer surface of the side pieces, and the appearance bespeaks cheaper work. We prefer the old-fashioned method because it is neater and adds value to the furniture.

The second problem with staples is that they loosen and pull out easily when used in places where they are under stress. This isn't a problem with stapled backs, but it is when staples are used to replace good wooden joints. A drawer made by stapling the sides to the front won't last long. A drawer with the sides dovetailed to the front is a strong, lasting construction.

Fasteners to Keep on Hand

Lay in a supply of fasteners because it is a nuisance to run to the store every time you need a screw. Buy an assortment of wood screws from ¾ to 1½ inches long in gauges 8, 10, and 12. If you expect to make upholstery repairs, have some No. 3 (3 oz.) and No. 4 (4 oz.) tacks on hand, along with some No. 12s. Buy other fasteners only as you need them.

GLUES AND ADHESIVES

There are more than a dozen different types of glues and adhesives available, from library paste to the new instant adhesives that will glue your fingers together if you aren't careful. Only a couple of these are suitable for furniture work. The old timers used hide and fish glues. Antique restorers who are purists still use them. Modern adhesives for furniture work include the polyvinyls, resorcinol resin and formaldehyde glues, contact cement, and the epoxies. The chart on the next page gives a good bird's eye view of glues and when to use each type.

Selecting the right glue is one half of the job. Applying it properly is the other half. But neither the right glue nor the proper application means much unless you clamp the work and give the glue all the time it needs to dry. A well-made glue joint is strong, neat and durable. A poorly made joint is sloppy looking and comes apart quickly under stress.

It may sound like gratuitous advice, but always read the label on any new adhesive you buy. Most of us have been using glues so long that we think we know how they all work, so we rush ahead to use a new glue as we used the older ones. But newer glues sometimes require different application techniques. Read the label to find out. The manufacturer wants you to get good results with his product, and his instructions are designed to help you get those results.

Gluing Techniques

In gluing, more is not better. Some people feel that if a little glue holds firmly, then a lot of glue holds even better. That's not the case. In fact, the opposite is true. Too much glue makes a weak joint, chiefly because glue in itself is not a strong substance — not nearly as strong as the wood it bonds.

If you placed two pieces of wood ⅛-inch apart, filled the space between them with glue, and let it set, you would have a weak joint that could be easily broken. On the other hand, if you applied a thin coating of glue to each of the surfaces, then clamped them firmly as they dried, you would have a joint that in many cases was stronger than the wood itself. If you tried to break the joint apart, the wood on either side of the joint would probably fracture before the joint broke.

And therein lies the secret of making a good glued joint. Apply thin coats of glue, clamp securely, and allow ample drying time.

Glue Types

Here are some of the properties of the adhesives you should use in furniture restoration.

These glues should take care of all your needs, so stock up on them. Also keep an eye on the shelves at your home center store, because chemists are working constantly to develop new formulas and techniques.

Polyvinyl Glues The white creamy glues that come in plastic squeeze bottles (Elmer's is a leading brand name) are polyvinyls. They are inexpensive, set in an hour or so, and work in just about every furniture situation. These are the choice of most furniture workers today for general gluing applications. Polyvinyls dry clear and won't stain any wood. They do have one drawback, and that is that water will soften them after they have set. Since most furniture is kept (or certainly should be kept) in a dry atmosphere, this is not a problem most of the time. But don't use a polyvinyl to glue the sides of a fishtank or to seal the edge of a bathtub.

Resorcinol and Formaldehyde Glues You mix these just before using. The resorcinols come in two parts, a resin and a powder, and the formaldehydes come as powders you mix with water. Both are good for from two to four hours after mixing, and make very durable joints. The resorcinols are waterproof but the formaldehydes are not. Follow the manufacturer's instructions on drying. Usually the time ranges from 3 to 12 hours

ADHESIVES

There are literally scores of different types of glues and adhesives available, but relatively few have direct application in furniture work. The chart below lists those you can use for furniture. The cardinal rules in making an adhesive do its job are: (1) the surfaces to be glued must be absolutely clean; (2) the adhesive should be applied as directed, and not too heavily; (3) the glued material must be clamped tightly until the glue has dried; (4) the glue must be allowed to dry completely. When waiting for glue to dry, remember that humid conditions can more than double the drying time listed on the container. The safest way is to allow the glue to dry overnight every time.

White glue	Elmer's and those polyvinyls like it: these glues are the white creamy liquids in plastic bottles. They are good for all furniture work. They can also be used on most porous materials such as cloth, paper, leather, etc. A polyvinyl has moderate resistance to moisture and should not be used on anything that will be subjected to excess moisture. (Furniture shouldn't be allowed in such areas either.) The most recent type of this glue is yellow in color, is made especially for woodwork, and is stronger than the white variety. This material dries clear, losing its yellow or white appearance.
Liquid hide and fish glues	These are the traditional furniture glues and have deserved reputations. They are strong, do not stain, and stay somewhat flexible for years — meaning that they won't get brittle and crack. These will soften in water, but aren't much affected by humidity.
Resorcinol	A syrup and powder are mixed just before use to make a resorcinol glue. Has great strength and durability, and should be used where moisture could be a problem, since it is absolutely waterproof. It will stain light colored woods, so apply with care. Drying time is long, up to 16 hours.
Epoxy	Strongest of all adhesives, it can be used for repairing metal, glass and most plastic furniture. Also good for masonry and ceramics. You mix the resin and the hardener just before use. This is the only adhesive that actually needs no clamping. It sets instead of drying, a chemical action, and will set even under water. Good to know about for special problems.
Contact cement	Two types are available, water based and chemical based. The chemical type must be used in a well-ventilated area; the water-based needs no special precautions. Contact cement comes ready to use as a thick liquid and dries in a few minutes (much like rubber cement). To use, coat both surfaces, allow each to dry, then press together. The bond is instantaneous and permanent. You can't take the pieces apart to try again. Chief use in furniture work is in applying veneers, in gluing leather to a table top, and in applying plastic laminates.

under clamps. Use both types at temperatures over 70 degrees, F. A small problem: these glues are brown in color and will stain light-colored woods.

Contact Cement This is a stronger version of the familiar rubber cement. Contact cement is used mainly to apply veneers and bond plastic laminates to wood for table and counter tops. The correct way to use a contact cement is to apply a thin coating to both surfaces and to allow both to dry. Then press the surfaces together. Be careful how you do this, since the two surfaces will stick together instantly on contact, and you won't be able to pull them apart with a tractor. Since they can't be adjusted after contact, be sure to align them before you

put them together. This is one of those techniques you should practice on old wood before trying it on your project. For specifics on how to align pieces exactly, see Chapter 10.

Chemical-based contact cements have a strong odor and must be used in well-ventilated areas. The water-based types are more expensive, but are safer to use.

The Epoxies No adhesive is tougher than an epoxy. Epoxies come in two parts, a resin and a hardener, which must be mixed just before you use the glue. By all means, read the label before mixing, because it will tell you the correct proportions of resin and hardener to use. If you mix the wrong proportions, you may end up with a sticky, nondrying mess.

Epoxy cement resists almost everything, from water to gasoline to solvents, once it has set. For this reason, you may not want to use it in regular furniture work. You may never be able to disassemble the piece again. But it can be great for making permanent repairs to metal furniture.

Note that an epoxy is the only adhesive as strong or stronger than the material it bonds. It is the one adhesive you *can* put between those two pieces of wood ⅛-inch apart and expect a strong joint. For this reason, epoxies sometimes are used as fillers when a large cavity must be filled. The dried epoxy can be machined, sanded and shaped, if necessary. For this reason, too, an epoxy is not applied in a thin coat as other glues are, and it should not be tightly clamped while setting. Clamping may squeeze out too much.

Epoxies must be used in warm temperatures, since the warmer the air around them, the faster they set. Setting time varies considerably from brand to brand, so once again, read the directions before using.

The Glue Gun

This is a plastic tool shaped like a toy pistol. You load a solid slug of glue into it, pull the trigger, and it dispenses the glue through its nozzle. The gun takes three or four minutes to warm up after you plug it in, and the glue, basically a polyethylene adhesive, makes a good bond on most materials. The glue sets firmly in about a minute.

The gun is great for spot jobs like gluing broken pieces of wicker together, so the whole chair doesn't come apart, or gluing

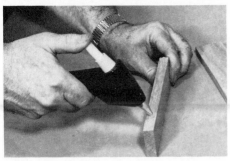

Electric glue guns can be used only in certain furniture applications. Here a gun is used to apply a bead of glue to an edge.

The glue sets in less than a minute, so the edges to be glued must be brought together quickly after the glue has been applied.

Once the edges are pressed together, the parts cannot be separated or adjusted. Hold the pieces together for a few seconds.

a part of a carving that has come loose. However, the gun is not as desirable for standard joint gluing.

The manufacturers of these guns are working to develop new glues and other materials, such as caulking compounds and joint sealants, so watch for them on your dealer's shelves.

Glue Injector

Another type of glue gun is the glue injector, similar to a medical hypodermic syringe but made of plastic. The injector enables you to inject glue deep into a loose joint in order to fix the joint without taking the furniture apart. In some cases, you can insert the long, thin tube of the injector directly into the loose joint. In others, you must drill a 1/16-inch hole near the joint to gain access. The glue injector does a good job on temporary repairs, but once furniture joints have started to loosen it is inevitable that the piece will have to be taken apart and completely reglued.

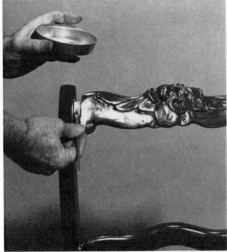

Sometimes you can reglue furniture without dismantling it. Here a brush is used to paint glue into a loose chair joint.

Glue Application

We have already talked about the basics of good glue application: apply it in thin coats; clamp it for drying; and allow sufficient drying time. Here are some other pointers to help you in making successful glue joints.

Rough vs. Smooth Glues do not adhere well to very smooth surfaces, but work best when they can grip something. For this reason, you should roughen slightly any smooth surface before applying glue.

For example, a chair rung has pulled out, and you want to glue it back in place. The surface of the rung is probably very smooth. You can make a better glue joint if you roughen the surface of the rung where the glue is to be applied. Try a few passes with coarse sandpaper or scraping a little with the blade of your pocket knife. Then brush on a thin glue coat and reinsert the rung into its hole.

Clamping Techniques Clamping, as we have said pretty often, is essential, but a careless use of clamps can create problems. Always use a pad of some kind

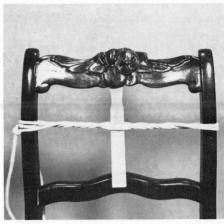

A clothesline can serve as a clamp. When wrapping the piece, use a paint paddle as the tightener, similar to a tourniquet.

Whenever a piece is glued, it must be clamped securely and left to dry as long as necessary. This is a strap clamp.

between the clamping surfaces and the face of the wood, so that you do not dent or mar the furniture. Thin little shims of wood make good pads. This advice is especially applicable when using C-clamps.

Cleanup The final joint should be neat and clean. Therefore, after setting the clamps in place, wipe away any excess glue. Watch for any later drips or runs; wipe these off, too. There is absolutely no holding value in glue on the outside of a joint. The glue does all of its work on the two butted surfaces within the joint

THE DIFFERENT KINDS OF WOOD

Nearly everyone knows that there are hardwoods and softwoods. Pine, for example, is a softwood, and oak is a hardwood. Softwoods are not as good as hardwoods for furniture because they dent and gouge more easily, and won't wear as long. Hardwoods are more difficult to work but they resist denting and gouging. The hardwoods have a more beautiful appearance (in furniture terms, at least) than the softwoods and they accept finishes better.

The most common furniture hardwoods are oak, walnut, maple, birch, cherry, mahogany, rosewood, gum and beech. The most common softwoods are pine, hemlock, fir, redwood, spruce and cedar. But in woods, as you will discover, hardness is both a matter of degree and of terminology. Maple, for example, is an extremely hard wood that will give your saw fits if you cut much of it. Mahogany also is rated as a hardwood, but it is softer and easier to work than maple.

The best furniture is made of hardwood, but you'll find a lot of attractive pieces in pine. Many Early American pieces were made in softwoods, probably because these woods were readily available and easy to work. Copies of these pieces today

also are made in these same softwoods.

In addition to the standard furniture hardwoods, there are hundreds of "exotic" woods such as avodire, ebony, lovoa, paldao and zebrawood, to name a few, that are highly prized for their rich coloring and appearance. These usually are seen in beautiful inlays and as veneers. They are very expensive and hard to find except in specialty shops. One of the interesting things you can do in restoration is to apply these exotic woods in veneer form to chests or tables, and create beautiful and unusual pieces. Veneering is complicated but can be fun. It produces excellent results. We will give you the details later.

Here is a rundown of the major furniture woods, with some notes on their uses and characteristics.

Hardwoods

Oak Tough, hard wood with a pronounced grain. If you apply a finish without first putting on a wood filler, you can feel the grain with your fingers. In older furniture it usually is filled; modern furniture often is finished without filler. Oak doesn't absorb water easily, has good bending qualities, and finishes well.

Walnut American (black) walnut is one of the premier furniture woods in this

country. Strong, with a fine texture and pleasing grain, it takes finishes nicely and wears well. It doesn't warp or shrink easily. The raw wood has a gray-brown look that turns to a rich brown on the application of a clear finish. Furniture makers often apply stain to get a warmer or darker color. If you must strip the finish from a walnut piece and want to refinish in the same color as the original, be sure to identify the color of the stain before stripping. Otherwise, you may not be able to duplicate it.

Cherry Another widely used furniture wood, cherry resists warping and shrinking. Initially a warm red-brown, it develops a richer red color as it ages, especially when exposed to sunlight. Cherry has a close, tight grain, and it doesn't need wood filler.

Maple This very strong wood is so hard that it will dull a saw used to cut it. The furniture variety comes from the sugar maple tree and is white, off-white, or amber in color. The red maple look in furniture is achieved through staining. Curly and birdseye patterns found in some maple make lovely veneered cabinet doors and tabletops. Maple has a fine grain, so it needs no filler. Its toughness makes it suitable for flooring and for wooden bowls.

Mahogany Mahogany is a very important furniture wood. It comes in three major types: West Indian, Tropical American and African. The Philippine mahoganies and lauan, sometimes incorrectly called a Philippine mahogany, are not of the same family as the others and are much softer. Mahogany is fine grained and durable, sherry brown in color. This wood doesn't absorb moisture easily, so it resists swelling, shrinking and warping. In older furniture, mahogany was frequently stained to a dark red brown; in modern furniture, the wood is used more often in natural color, or close to it.

Rosewood Most often used as a veneer, rosewood has a lovely rose red and black color, and its surface patterns create unusual configurations. Very hard and difficult to work, rosewood is close grained and can be given a very smooth finish. The wood has a lovely odor. It is a choice wood for musical instruments because its hardness apparently affects the resonance of the sound. No fillers are ever used with rosewood.

Teak Teak is another fragrant wood. It is often used for decking and rails on ships

Wood comes in two types: softwoods and hardwoods. Softwoods dent and gouge more easily than hardwoods; hardwoods are more difficult to work with. This piece is hardwood.

WOOD GRAIN SAMPLES

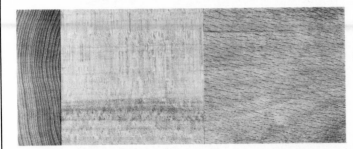

American Beech

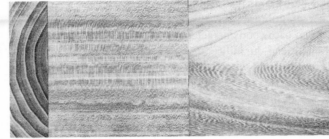

American Elm

Black Ash

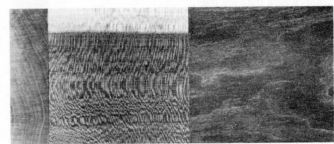

Black Cherry

Black Walnut

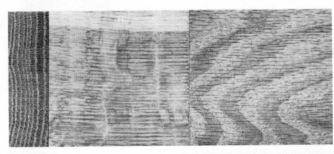

Red Oak

Sugar Maple

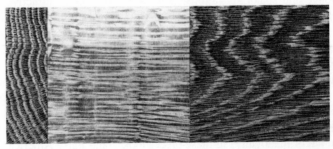

White Oak

Yellow Birch

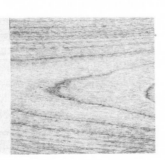

Yellow Poplar

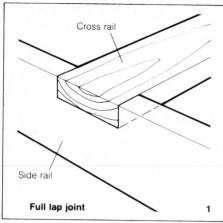

Cross rail

Side rail

Full lap joint   1

A full lap joint looks neat and finished. Only the receiving piece of wood is cut; the cross rail fits into the opening.

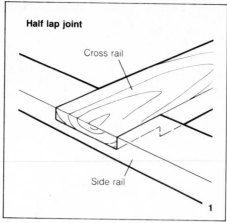

Half lap joint

Cross rail

Side rail

1

A half-lap joint mates two pieces of equal thickness. Both pieces are cut; the crossrail then fits into the mating piece.

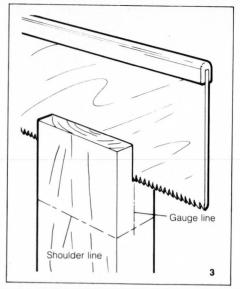

Gauge line

Shoulder line

3

Now cut the cross rail to the required depth (shoulder line). Again, cut just inside the gauge line; remove the waste wood.

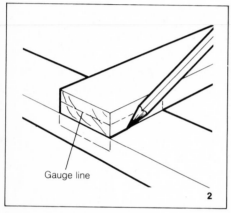

Gauge line

2

A half lap joint requires care. Mark a gauge line indicating half the thickness of the end to be cut. Then mark the width of the crossrail onto the receiving piece.

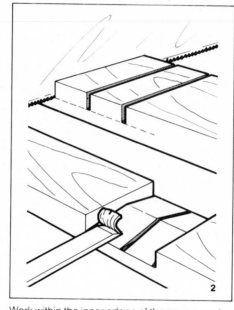

2

Work within the inner edges of the gauge marks, saw two cuts on each side and one in the center. Chisel away the waste wood.

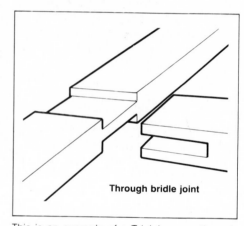

Through bridle joint

This is an example of a T-joining or a through bridle joint. Divide the edge of each board in thirds. Cut away the wood with a backsaw, coping saw or chisel.

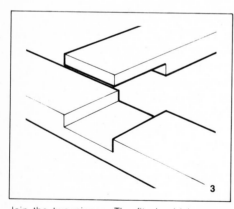

3

Join the two pieces. The fit should be snug. Then glue the two, making sure that the shoulder lines are flush. Once the glue dries, trim away any excess.

at their ends instead of their centers. For obvious reasons, this basic joint is called an *overlap*.

Two variations are very good joint types, frequently seen in furniture. One is the *full lap*, in which a notch is cut in one piece of wood to receive the other. In this type, you avoid having one piece lying on top of the other, so it is neater and stron-

ger. The other is the *half-lap*, where notches are cut half way into both pieces of wood and the wood is joined by fitting the notches together. This is also neat and strong.

The Butt Joint

When two pieces of wood are fitted together, end to end or side to side, they are said to be butted. Glue the butted sides together and you have a butt joint. Used chiefly to join boards together, as to make a larger board for a counter or tabletop, it is weak unless the butted pieces are supported.

The Dado

A dado is a groove, and the dado joint is made by cutting a groove of the right size in one piece of wood to receive the end of

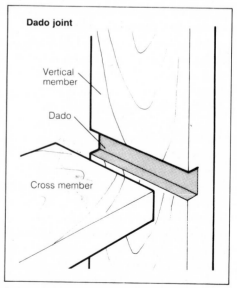

Dado joint

Vertical member

Dado

Cross member

A dado is a groove cut into a receiving piece. A second piece then slides into the groove. A dado joint is often found supporting drawer bottoms or cupboard shelves.

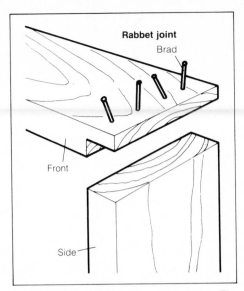

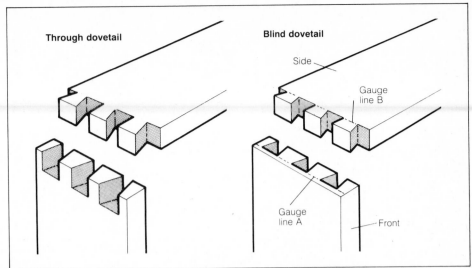

A rabbet joint combines pieces at a corner. The groove fits the mating piece. Set brads at an angle to secure the joint.

Through or blind dovetails make a strong corner joint. If you start from scratch, use a dovetail template to create the ratio of 1:6 for softwoods and 1:8 for hardwoods.

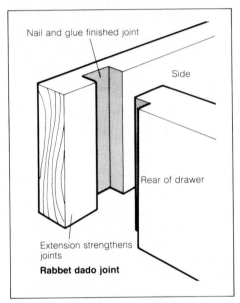

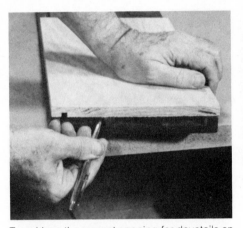

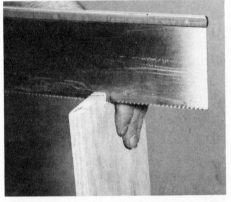

You often find a combination rabbet-dado joint holding a drawer back. The rabbet slides into the dado in each drawer side.

To achieve the correct spacing for dovetails on a new drawer side, trace the pattern on each side of the new piece of wood.

Use the backsaw to cut the sides of each dovetail to the proper depth. Hold the work in a bench vise (not visible here). The vise is essential for work like this.

another piece of wood. You can make the groove with a mallet and wood chisel or a router. This simple but strong joint often is used in furniture. Note: you will frequently run across the terms, *rabbet* and *rabbeted joints*. A rabbet is a groove or slot cut into a piece of wood, and any joint employing a groove is a rabbeted joint. For our purposes here, a rabbet is a kind of dado.

The Dovetail

The dovetail is a strong, neat joint used to join pieces of wood at right angles. A typical use in furniture is the joining of drawer sides to the drawer front.

A dovetail essentially is a set of fingers

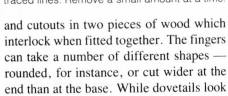

Place the old piece on the bench as a guide. Then carefully chisel out the dovetail along the traced lines. Remove a small amount at a time.

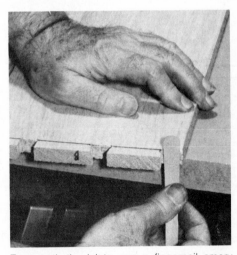

To smooth the joints, use a fingernail emery board. It is just the right size to fit into the openings and smooth the edges.

and cutouts in two pieces of wood which interlock when fitted together. The fingers can take a number of different shapes — rounded, for instance, or cut wider at the end than at the base. While dovetails look complicated, they are easy to make. The secret is to measure and mark both pieces of wood carefully, and then make all cuts exactly to your measured marks. You can make dovetails with a router, with a cop-

1 This chair back is joined to the side with a mortise and tenon joint, and the tenon is cracked. It can be repaired by making a new tenon, or by using dowels to replace the tenon.

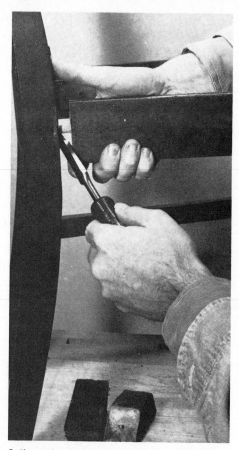

2 If you choose to replace the tenon, the first job is to disassemble the chair.

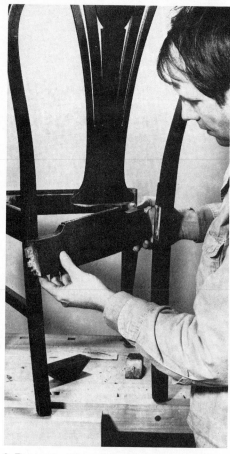

3 The back of the seat has now been removed.

4 Now the broken tenon is sawed off flush with the end of the rail.

5 We need to remove the pieces of broken tenon remaining in the mortise. The easiest way is to drill a series of holes into the mortise, using a drill bit the same size as the width of the mortise, here ⅜ in.

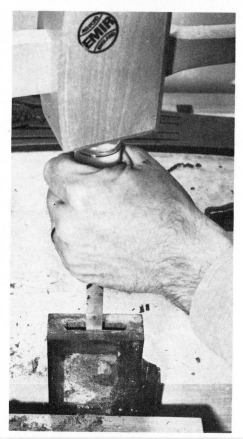

6 Using a ½ in. wood chisel, we remove the rest of the tenon. Work with the flat side of the chisel blade against the wall of the mortise.

7 To clean out the ends, use a narrower chisel (here ¼ in.) and drive the chisel down at either end of the mortise, then pry upward. This should bring up what remains of the tenon.

8 Here is the mortise with the tenon removed.

9 Cut a tenon from hardwood of the right thickness and dimensions to fit snugly into the mortise. Test fit the new tenon before gluing.

10 Now the tenon is coated with glue and driven down into the mortise.

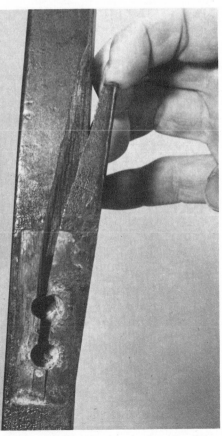

11 We found that not only was the tenon cracked, but the chair back rail was cracked through the mortise.

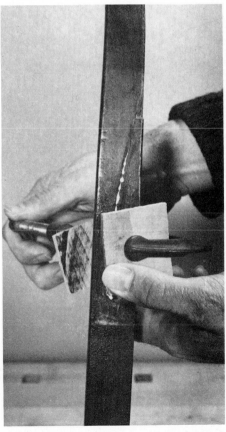

12 Repair of the crack is a simple glue-and-clamp procedure. Don't attempt to reassemble the chair until all glue has dried thoroughly.

1 The second repair method calls for the use of dowels to replace the broken tenon. The repair won't be as strong as the original work, but it can be done quicker and will be satisfactory in most uses. The first step is to make a hardwood plug and drive it into the mortise. When in place, it should be flush with the surface.

2 Now drill holes for ⅜ in. dowels. The dowels are at a slight angle here, so the dowel jig can't be used. Drill the holes down the center of the tenon plug at the necessary angle.

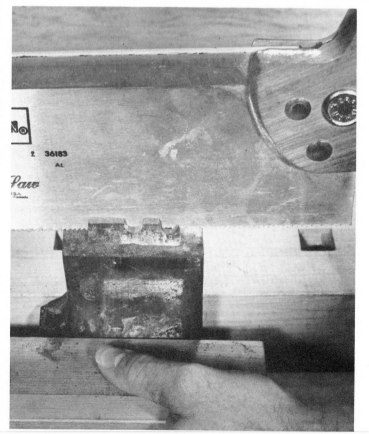

3 Use dowel centers in the holes drilled in the leg to mark the position of holes to be drilled in the back rail. Then drill the holes, coat the dowels with glue, and drive them into the holes. You can now reassemble the chair.

1 If you have a loose and worn tenon, you sometimes can avoid making a new one by expanding the old one to fit into the mortise. Cut a slot lengthwise down the tenon with a backsaw.

2 Now whittle a wedge from hardwood and drive it down into the kerf (sawcut) until the tenon has expanded sufficiently.

3 Saw off the protruding part of the wedge flush with the end of the tenon.

4 The chair can now be reassembled. Be sure to clamp tightly, forcing the repaired parts into tight contact.

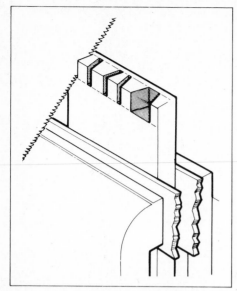

Make the initial cuts for a blind dovetail by sawing at a 45° angle with the backsaw. Do not saw past the guide marks.

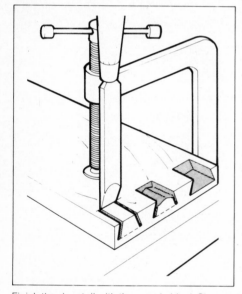

Finish the dovetail with the wood chisel. Shave a little away at a time so that you don't cut beyond the guidelines.

ing saw, or with a mallet and chisel and a backsaw.

One way to distinguish good furniture from poor is to check the way the drawers are made. In good furniture, the sides of all drawers are dovetailed to the drawer front; in cheaper furniture, the sides are lap jointed to the front and fastened with nails or staples.

The Mortise and Tenon

A tenon is a tongue, and a mortise is a slot. In the mortise-and-tenon joint, a tongue is formed at the end of one piece of wood, and a slot of the same shape is made in the other piece of wood. Then the tongue is inserted into the slot to make the joint.

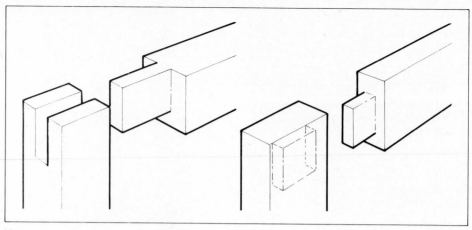

Use an open mortise-and-tenon (at left) to join pieces when the seam between the two is not visible. In a closed joint (at right) the tenon fits into the hollowed-out mortise. The tenon in both types is cut into the shorter piece, the mortise into the longer.

This is one of the most important of the furniture joints, very strong and with excellent appearance. You can cut tenons on the ends of wood pieces using a backsaw or a router. Use your wood chisels to make the mortise. Good measuring technique and careful control of the chisel are important in making a good mortise and tenon.

There are many inventive variations on these joints, but if you know the basic joining methods, you should be able to identify most when you see them. An example of a variation would be a *double tenon*. On the end to be joined, the maker forms two tenons instead of one. On the joining piece, he makes two individual mortises instead of one. In other words, two tongues and two holes or slots are made instead of one. You won't see many double tenons. The drawing above shows variations made on the basic joint.

ANALYZING THE SITUATION

You are trying to salvage a fractured chair. The side rails are joined to the back posts and front legs with mortise-and-tenon joints, a typical situation in chair construction. But whoever smashed this chair did a thorough job, and after disassembling it, you now hold a side rail in your hand with the tenon on one end broken off. The tenon is still in the mortise in the back post. What can you do? Here are some logical steps to follow. First, examine the tenon. Can it be removed from the mortise in one piece? If so, you may be able to rejoin it to the side rail and save the day. If not, carefully chisel it out of the mortise, taking care not to damage the mortise as you do so. Now examine the side rail and recognize the possible solutions. As a first step, you can cut off the fractured stump

of the tenon, using your backsaw. Now there appear to be several ways to mend the damage.

1. Buy a piece of hardwood of the proper wood and size and make a new chair rail. Cut tenons on each end of the new rail after trimming it to the right size; then fit the new tenons into the existing mortises.

2. Another and probably more practical method is to make a tenon to replace the broken one. This is best because you can reuse the original chair rail. You obviously can't cut a new tenon on the end of the old chair rail, but you can chisel a mortise into the rail to match the mortise in the back post. Then, shape a hardwood tenon to fit into both mortises to make a kind of super dowel. This method does work.

3. A third possiblity occurs: you could fill the mortise in the back post by cutting a plug of hardwood to fill it. Glue the plug in place. Now join the rail and the back post with dowels.

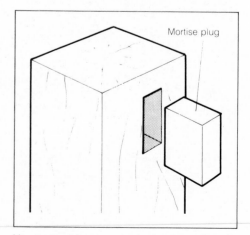

Use a chisel to remove a broken tenon from its mortise. Scrape out the old glue. Then glue in a new mortise plug.

This example describes a very common occurrence in furniture repair and provides you with two insights: (1) you must be prepared to analyze repair situations in order to consider all possible solutions; (2) you need enough woodworking skill and knowledge to make the basic joints. The joints you should learn to make are the dowel, mortise-and-tenon, the dovetail, the miter, the dado and the full and half laps.

To make these with hand tools, you will need good sharp wood chisels, a back saw and a coping saw, as well as a good small steel rule. The job is easier with power tools, including a router and an electric scroll saw. To make mitered joints by hand, you should have a miter box, a wood or metal box with slots already cut in its sides. The backsaw blade fits through these slots. The work to be cut goes into the box, and the slots guide your saw so that you make even cuts at the required angle.

The making of each of these joints is covered here in step-by-step photographs and drawings. Refer to these every time you must make a joint until you become familiar with the techniques. By all means, make some practice joints out of scrap hardwood before trying to repair a good piece of furniture. Gain some confidence in your woodworking abilities first; then go to work.

THE ART OF MAKING A DOWELED JOINT

A dowel is a round length of hardwood used to join two pieces of wood. Doweled joints are strong and, because the dowels are invisible when the joint is finished, neat in appearance.

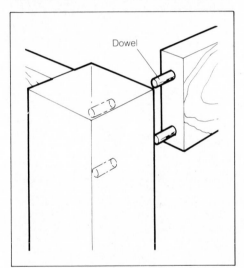

A butt joint is easily reinforced with dowels. If the dowels break, you must route out the old stubs and insert new dowels.

Dowel Joints

The dowel joint can be used in many repair situations. It often can be used to replace other more complicated joints, as was pointed out earlier in this chapter. Good dowel joints can be used at points of stress on furniture because the joints can take pressure from all sides.

Dowel joints frequently can be used to rejoin the pieces of broken and fractured parts. For instance, dowels can rejoin the two pieces of a wooden chair seat that has cracked and broken apart. Sometimes a dowel can be used to join the parts of broken rails and rungs, so that you need not go to the trouble of making an entirely new part.

If you find that a piece you want to salvage is poorly made, with weak joints or perhaps with parts held together with screws, you can increase its value and usefulness by literally remaking it. Use dowels to replace the screws and weak joints. In the same manner, you can improve the quality of a piece of inexpensive unfinished furniture by taking it apart and rejoining the poorly joined parts with dowels.

You can make your own dowels or buy them at some home centers and most woodworking specialty shops. The dowels you buy have circular grooves already cut in them to take care of the glue. You can find them in various diameters and lengths.

Advantages of a Doweling Jig

With the aid of a doweling jig, most people can make joints with precision, and end up with a professional-looking joint. We have been making doweled joints for a long time and can tell you that there is really no good substitute for a doweling jig. It makes the job simple and easy. You can use dowel centers and other ways of lining up the dowel holes, but no other method or tool does the task right every time.

The fundamental purpose of the doweling jig is to force you to drill the two needed holes in exactly the right places — precisely opposite each other — so that when you insert the dowels, the joined pieces fit exactly as you wanted them.

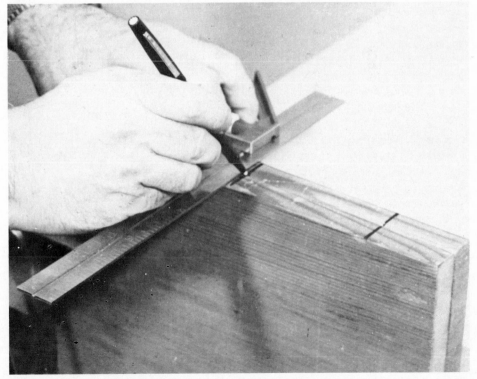

To use a dowel jig, align the two pieces to be doweled. Use a square to make lines across the positions for the dowels, marking both pieces at once.

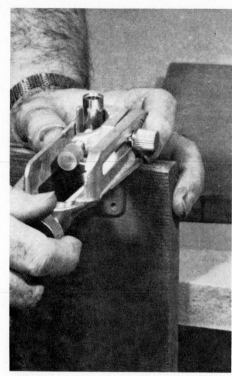

Clamp one side of the work and fit the dowel jig on it. There are a number of good jigs on the market, and each is slightly different. This jig is a Stanley.

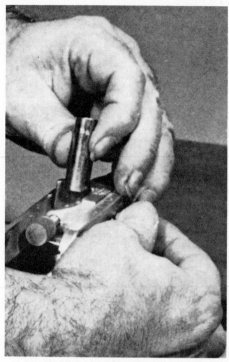

The jig comes with a set of metal tubes that serve as drill guides. Place the correct size in the jig. Sight through it to see the guide line and adjust the knobs until the jig is positioned. Then tighten the adjustment knobs.

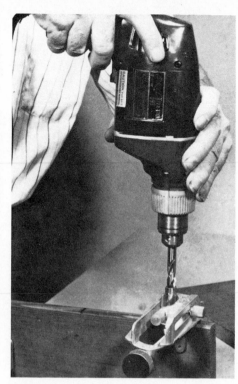

Using a drill bit of the right size, make the dowel hole by drilling down through the drill guide. If necessary, use a depth guide to control the depth of the hole.

You position the drill guide by measurement, so be careful in making these measurements. If your measurements aren't precise, the jig can't help.

Creating the Doweled Joint

Carefully follow these steps for a successful doweled joint.

Step 1: Aligning the Pieces The first step is to clamp the two pieces together, as shown in the accompanying photographs. Use a pencil and a rule to draw a straight line across both pieces, at the point where they are to be doweled. Now take the clamp off.

Step 2: Aligning the Jig Put the doweling jig on the first piece, clamping the jig in place after sighting the penciled line through it. There is a graduated marking on the jig to help you with this positioning.

Step 3: Drilling the Hole Insert your drill bit into the drill guide on the jig and drill a hole that is slightly deeper than half the length of the dowel. Repeat the process on the other piece of wood. Most dowel joints have two or three dowels, not just one, so do the same task as many times as necessary.

Step 4: Inserting the Dowels Coat each dowel with glue and insert the dowels into the holes in one of the pieces. If your

The holes have been drilled in both work pieces. Because the jig was set over the guidelines, each hole is exactly opposite its mate. Try the dowels, to make sure they fit properly.

joint has three dowels, insert all three into the same side.

Step 5: Finishing the Joint Fit the other piece over the protruding glue-coated dowels, and use your rubber mallet to tap the piece until the joint is tight. Wipe off any excess glue around the joint. Then apply a clamp to hold the joint tight until the glue dries.

After coating the dowels with glue, insert them; then tap the two workpieces with a rubber mallet to drive them together. Here rounded edges emphasize the joint. Otherwise it would be nearly invisible.

Repairing a Broken Joint

In restoration work, you may have to make new dowel joints and you also may have to repair broken dowel joints. In most repair situations, you must drill out the old broken dowel and replace it. While you *can* drill out an old dowel by eyeballing the work as you go, we don't recommend it. You can do a better job by clamping the doweling jig over the old dowel pieces, checking the position of your drill through the jig, and drilling, almost as if you were drilling for a new dowel.

Making Dowels

You can make your own dowels by buying a hardwood dowel rod of the right diameter at your home center, and cutting off dowels of the needed length. However, a dowel fits very snugly into the hole you drilled for it. So snugly, in fact, that as the dowel goes in, it may force glue to fill the bottom of the hole. The resulting hydraulic pressure can prevent the entry of the dowel.

To remedy this, put your newly made dowel in a vise and use the backsaw to cut one or two slots, 1/16 inch deep, in the dowel's side. The slots allow the excess glue to exit from the bottom of the hole as the dowel goes in. Finish making the dowel by sanding the ends to round them slightly for easier entry.

To make your own dowels, purchase hardwood doweling of the diameter you need. Clamp the doweling and cut off dowels of the length desired.

Glue must be able to escape as the dowel is inserted into its hole, so cut one or more saw slots in the side of each dowel for this purpose. Then sand the ends round.

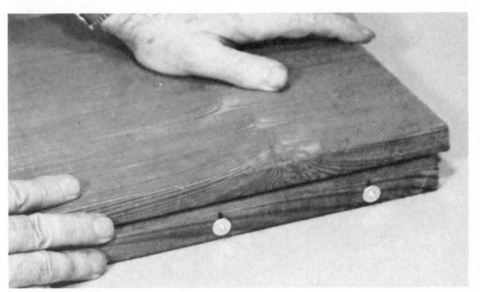

To use dowel centers, first drill dowel holes in one workpiece. Then insert the dowel centers in these holes, as shown here.

Another method for aligning dowel holes is the use of dowel centers — small metal pieces with sharp points on one end. You can buy these in sets of different sizes.

Use a rubber mallet to tap the two pieces together. The sharp points will mark the opposite piece. Center your drill bit exactly on the pinpoint mark or the dowels will not fit exactly.

SECURING MITERED CORNERS

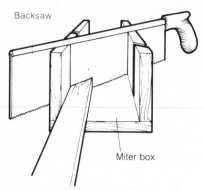

To cut an accurate mitered corner, you must use a miter box. Be sure the piece is aligned with the correct miter slot.

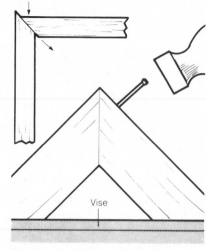

Small brads will strengthen the joint. Hold the work in a vise so the nailing doesn't shift the corner out of square.

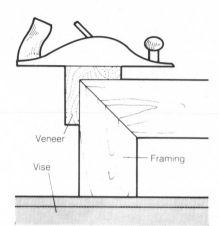

Sometimes a strip of veneer, inserted in a slot cut perpendicular to the corner, is used to secure the corner. Plane off the excess from the corner inward.

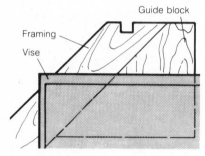

A spline in a groove can also reinforce a corner. In a vise, support the piece with a complementary guide block as you cut the groove with a router.

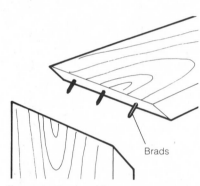

If you plan to dowel the corner, mark the positions on one piece with small brads. Press the piece against its mate to pick up an impression of the position.

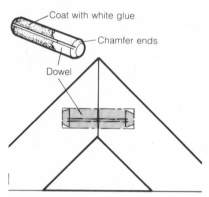

Drill the holes carefully. Cover the dowels with glue. The chamfered end allows easy insertion. The groove provides an escape route for any glue trapped below the dowel.

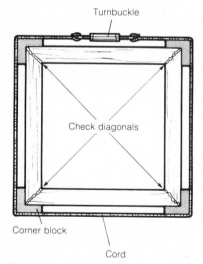

Glue the entire piece. To clamp, use a web strap or clothesline. Protect the piece at the corners. The diagonal measurements will be the same if the piece is square.

A picture frame clamp can aid in both construction and restoration projects. The exact corners and interior bracing assure perfect 45° corners every time.

SANDPAPER AND SANDING TOOLS   If you expect to get truly fine finishes on your furniture, you must learn to sand, which is easy and quick to do once you understand what furniture sanding is all about. The only roadblock is the preconceived notion most people have acquired about sanding. They think of it as a removal process. They sand to remove old finishing materials, or to remove rough wood after sawing, or to remove rust.

Sanding Equals Smoothing

Adjust your thinking now, and consider sanding as a smoothing and polishing operation. In furniture restoration, you usually don't want to remove very much of anything. You just want to make the surface as smooth as possible before any finishing material is applied. Between coats of finishing materials, you want to remove any little bumps or imperfections. Finally, after all finishing coats have been put on, you want to give your masterpiece that rich hand-rubbed look. Thus, you want to learn to sand with a delicate touch, to achieve a smooth feel and rich appearance.

Most furniture surfaces are already relatively smooth. When you run your fingers over a newly stripped furniture surface, you feel only a slight roughness and, depending on the type of wood, some raised grain. More importantly, you don't want to remove much of the surface in furniture. Old well-aged wood has acquired a patina that doesn't go very deep, and which you want to preserve. And if you are working on veneered wood, you must remember that the veneer itself is only about $1/32$-inch thick. It doesn't take much sanding with a coarse paper to cut through it and expose the wood underneath.

There are three important aspects to sanding: selecting the right abrasive paper; performing the correct sequence of sanding operations; and, using the right sanding techniques and tools.

Selecting the Sandpaper

Technically, there is no longer an item called sandpaper. Today, these gritty sheets are called abrasive sheets, because they are made of abrasive materials other than sand. Five kinds of abrasives are used: flint, garnet, silicon carbide, aluminum oxide, and emery. The cheapest papers use flint. They neither cut as fast nor

SANDPAPER

Manufacturers grade their abrasive papers by one of three methods, and there are no national standards to serve as a guide. Some give their papers a name (fine, medium, etc.); some rate them by grit number (30, 180, 400, etc.), referring to the abrasive particle size; and yet others use a numbering system (3/0, 5/0, 8/0), the oldest of all grading methods. The chart below shows all three methods in relation to each other, so that no matter which rating is used, you can buy the paper you need.

Number	Grit	Name	When to use
10/0 9/0	600, 500 400 360	Superfine	Last sanding of a new furniture finish; final sanding of fine woods; hand rubbed finish
8/0 7/0	320, 280 240	Extra fine	Same as above
6/0	200, 220	Very fine	Sand between coats of paint or varnish
5/0 4/0 3/0 2/0	180, 150 120, 100	Fine	Sand hard and softwood before and after you stain, seal, or apply a priming coat
1 0 1/0 1/2	80, 60 50	Medium	Remove deep scratches in finish; remove rust. Do shaping of parts or rough sanding
1½ 2 2½	40, 36 30	Coarse	Wood removal, shaping, rough sanding, paint removal
3 3½	24, 20	Very Coarse	To remove multiple paint coats, fast wood removal
4 4¼	18 15	Extra Coarse	Remove heavy rust, paint, varnish

last as long as the better papers. If you expect to do much sanding, it will pay you to buy better papers coated with one of the other abrasives.

Thickness   Abrasive papers come in half a dozen thicknesses. The thinner papers are good for working in tight places because these weights fold easily. However, they are not as good for use in sanding blocks or on power sanders because the paper will tear. The heavier papers feel very stiff and may crack when folded, but they stand up longer in the power and hand sanders. You should have some of each weight.

Grains   There are two kinds of papers, *open grain* and *closed-grain*. The open-grain type has only a light coating of abrasive material, made that way so that paint or other material being sanded doesn't

New sandpaper is stiff; soften it to make it last longer by running it back and forth, face up, across a table edge.

cling to the abrasive granules and clog the paper. This is the best for removing finishes. The closed-grain type has a dense coating of abrasive material and does its work more quickly. For general furniture smoothing and finishing, the closed-grain type is best. Buy some light-weight papers for sanding in and around corners, but buy mostly heavier papers for their longer mileage.

The Grit Numbers No one has ever actually standardized the method for indicating the coarseness of grit for abrasive papers. Sometimes you see papers marked with *superfine, fine, medium* and *coarse.* Other papers are marked in grit numbers ranging from 20 to 600, with 20 being the very coarse and 600 being the superfine. And still other papers use a grading system with numbers of 10/0 and 2/0.

To clarify the situation before you go to the store, check the accompanying chart, which shows the relationship between the different grading systems and tells the most common use for each type of abrasive paper. The grading method tells you nothing about paper thickness, type of abrasive, or general quality of the paper. It only specifies the size of the abrasive particles on the paper.

Waterproof Sandpaper In addition to standard abrasive papers, you can buy waterproof sandpaper. This is usually sold only in the finer grits and is made to be used with water or oil for the final rubdown in hand finishing.

Abrasive Cloths Abrasives glued to cloth last much longer than the paper versions, but are expensive and available only in a limited selection of grits. With one exception, we don't find abrasive cloths useful in furniture restoration.

The one exception is important. To sand rounded legs and rungs, and especially to sand into grooves on these rounded surfaces, you can cut strips of abrasive cloth to a convenient width, wrap the cloth around the leg or rung, and pull back and forth on the ends. This does a better job than regular abrasive papers. The narrow strip of abrasive cloth gets into the groove on a turned leg much more easily and successfully than the less flexible paper.

Sanding Blocks

A sanding block, in its simplest form, is a rectangular block of wood around which you wrap a piece of abrasive paper. A typical sanding block is about 2 inches

To make your own sanding blocks in any size or shape, you need a wood block, contact cement, a felt or foam rubber pad, and sheet sandpaper.

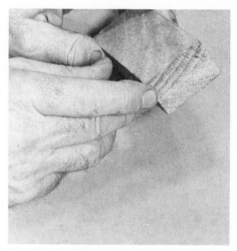

Make the block the shape needed for the work at hand. Glue pieces of wood together if necessary. The advantage of homemade blocks is their custom shape.

Coat the wood block with contact cement; allow to dry. Repeat on one side of the padding.

When the cement dries to the touch, carefully place the cemented sides together. As soon as they touch, they bond permanently.

Cut the sandpaper sheet so the piece is as wide as the sanding block and long enough to wrap around the block.

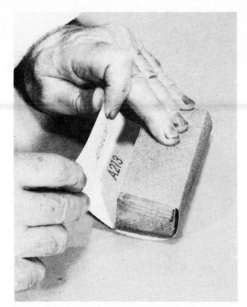

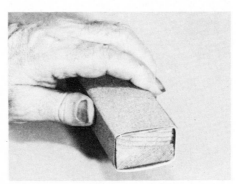

wide and 4 to 6 inches long. For smaller work, you can make smaller blocks. Holding the sides of the block, you apply one face of it to the surface to be sanded, and work the block back and forth with straight-line motions. The job is much smoother if a small felt pad is placed on

Wrap the paper around the block tightly. As paper becomes worn, shift the wrapping to expose new sanding surfaces.

Here is the finished block, ready for work. Hold the paper in place as you work, or use a rubber band as an anchor.

These are typical hand sanders that you can buy at your home center. Select models that work best for you.

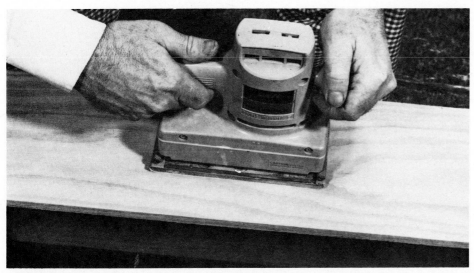

When using any type of power sander, always sand with the grain. Don't press too hard on the tool; just guide it back and forth slowly and let it do the work.

the block before the paper is wrapped around it. This cushions the paper and prevents uneven sanding.

Purchased Blocks It takes only a few minutes to make a sanding block, but you will find several types of hand sanders at your home center that are both convenient and inexpensive. All have some type of clamp to hold the abrasive paper in place, built-in felt padding, and (usually) a comfortable gripping surface that makes them easy to control.

Techniques Whether you buy one or make one, you certainly should own a sanding block and use it in the great majority of your sanding work. As a matter of principal, always use a block when sanding flat surfaces. A block is necessary when you sand up to the edge of a table top or when sanding a square runner or rung. By holding the block absolutely level on the surface, and providing even pressure on it, you keep the edge square. If you use a folded-paper pad and finger pressure, you will tend to sand too much at the very edge, and will end up with a surface that dips downward right at the edge.

Using Power Sanders

In the chapter on tools, we discussed power sanders, and pointed out that the best kind to own is an oscillating sander — one with a front-to-back sanding motion. In these sanders, the shoe on which the paper is fitted moves back and forth, traveling only a fraction of an inch but doing it quickly. The right way to use one of these is to let the sander do the work. Your job is to guide it in a straight line with the grain of the wood, to move it slowly over the surface, and to apply light pressure. In other words, don't try to use it like a hand sander, and move it back and forth by hand. Start at one end of the area to be sanded and slowly move it toward the other end. Then go back to the beginning and run the course again. Do this until the sanding is finished.

Because orbital sanders leave circular marks on the surface, we don't recommend them. Sanding disks mounted in electric drills are worse than orbital sanders because you cannot apply even pressure to the pad as it spins, and are likely to get uneven results. The pad used in the drill, however, is good for sanding rungs and other round work because only a small part of the spinning disk touches the wood at any one moment.

HOW TO SAND WOOD SURFACES FOR FINISHES

Sanding is easy to do if you are aware of the basic techniques. Follow these instructions with care.

1. Always sand with the grain of the wood, not across the grain.
2. Use a straight back and forth movement of the sanding block. Don't use a circular or irregular motion.
3. Apply even pressure to the top of the sanding block. Don't lean more heavily on the front or back of it. The pressure should be light, not forced.
4. When sanding a flat surface, be especially careful as you approach the edge. There is a tendency to lean on the block at this time, which results in heavier pressure near the edge of the work. Keep the sanding surface level and the pressure even to avoid tapering the work surface downward.
5. Tap the sawdust out of the sandpaper at regular intervals. The sawdust clogs the paper and prevents the paper from cutting properly. You can use a small brush (an old toothbrush will do).

Using a Tack Cloth

When you finish the sanding, wipe the sawdust from the surface of the work with a tack cloth. (You can buy tack cloths already made at your home center, or you can make one by moistening a cloth with a mixture of one part turpentine and three parts varnish.) The advantage of a tack cloth over a regular dust rag is that the sawdust clings to the tack cloth and doesn't fly into the air, only to settle on the work again in a few minutes.

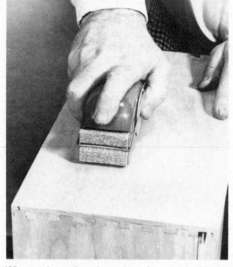
When using a hand sander, also sand with the grain. Apply even pressure. If sanding is too slow, use a coarser grade; then change to a fine grade to finish the job.

Clogged sandpaper won't cut. Use an old toothbrush to clean it out occasionally so that it continues to be abrasive.

After sanding, wipe the surface with a tack cloth to remove all the fine sanding dust. You can either buy inexpensive tack cloths or make your own.

HOW TO SAND FURNITURE FOR A FINE FINISH

Furniture sanding is a little different from ordinary sanding; in furniture sanding the objective is a polished finish. To get this polished finish, you follow a step-down procedure. You begin with a coarse paper, then step down to finer and finer papers until the surface is as smooth as you can make it.

Work Sequence

In most cases, the coarse paper to start with is rated as fine on the sandpaper chart. It would have a grit rating of anywhere from about 200 to 100, or a number rating of from 5/0 to 2/0. After sanding the entire surface with this grade of paper, move down to a very fine grade, and then to a fine grade. For the last sanding before applying the finishing material, add one more step and go over the surface with a superfine grade of paper.

The Finishing Process Let each coat of finish material dry completely (and we mean completely). Then lightly sand the surface before applying the next coat. A very fine grade works best here. Go easy on this sanding. You don't want to take off any of the finish you just applied. You only want to eliminate the tiny bumps in the surface and at the same time to roughen the surface slightly to give the next coat a "tooth" on which to cling. The tiny bumps are caused by dust particles on the surface, dust in the brush, and impurities in the finishing material itself. They come off easily. You should be able to feel them with your fingertips before sanding. After sanding, they should be gone but the new surface should still be intact.

Hand-rubbing The final hand-rubbed finish is achieved after all coats of finishing material have been applied, and they have dried hard. Then you use a superfine paper (400-600 grit) to go over the entire finish. The aim is to knock off the

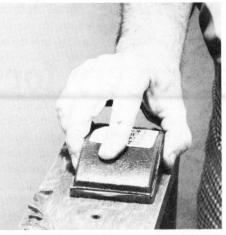

One type of hand-rubbed finish is achieved by a final sanding with superfine paper and water. Begin by sprinkling a few drops of water on the surface after the varnish has dried for several days. We use a clothes sprinkler bottle.

Next we load superfine wet-or-dry sandpaper into a hand sander and carefully sand with the grain. Do not oversand or you may remove the new finish.

After sanding, wipe the surface dry with a clean soft cloth. Complete the job by applying either a lemon oil polish or a good carnauba furniture wax.

Some say the very best hand-rubbed finish is done with oil and a superfine waterproof paper. First, sprinkle a little pumice powder (we keep ours in a salt shaker) on the surface.

Next, apply a few drops of very light oil (bicycle oil, for example, or lemon oil). Use enough to make a light abrasive paste of the pumice. If necessary, add more pumice to achieve a good consistency.

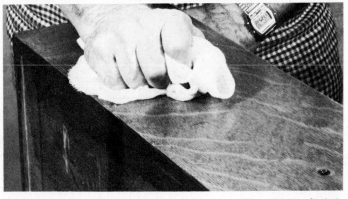

Mount a thin felt or cloth pad in a hand sander to rub the pumice and oil. Work back and forth with the grain. Do not remove the finish, but polish it; remove the gloss and tiny imperfections.

Wipe the finished surface free of oil and pumice with a clean soft cloth. Rub sufficiently to get rid of any oily feel.

glossy look that always comes with a new finish and to get rid of any last dust bumps. This hand-rubbed finish can be achieved with normal dry paper, or with waterproof paper.

Using waterproof paper, you sprinkle a little water on the surface and then sand it. You also can use a very light machine oil (racing bicycle oil is best) in place of the water. When the sanding is done, wipe the surface thoroughly with a clean dry cloth.

The last step after this final sanding is to apply a thin coat of top-quality paste carnauba wax.

Practice is Necessary

Sanding, as with all refinishing techniques, takes a little practice to perfect. But you get the hang of it in a few minutes. We especially recommend that you try the final hand-rubbed finish on practice wood before working on a newly finished piece.

As you sand and apply finish coats to the furniture, also do it to an extra board you can use for practice. Then, before you do any final sanding steps on the furniture, first do it to the practice board. This will give you confidence when you approach the furniture. The practice board takes only a few extra seconds of work, and it is worth it.

DISASSEMBLING VARIOUS TYPES OF FURNITURE

Every type of furniture piece is different in assembly. Chairs are different from cabinets, dressers from tables. The disassembly process for each type, therefore, is also different. With the general instructions below, you should be able to determine how each piece is assembled and then take it apart. There will be times when this will prove to be impossible. Then you can assume that the joint is so good that there is no need to take it apart. Move on to the next step of disassembly.

Tables

There are several types of tables. Some have aprons (those side panels just beneath the table top), and others do not. Sometimes the aprons are attached to the top by screws driven up from the bottom. Look for the screw holes in the bottom of the apron to find out. On some tables, metal corner braces are screwed to both the underside of the table top and to the inside of the apron. These are plainly visible under the table. You also may find that the top is fixed to the apron only by glue blocks. After determining how the top is attached, you should be able to take it off with little trouble.

Aprons most often are joined to table legs by means of multiple dowels, mortise-and-tenon joints, or by steel leg braces. In the latter case, look for a large lag screw on the inside face of the leg just under the table top. Use a wrench to remove the lag screw.

Tables without aprons have the legs attached to the underside of the table in a number of ways — usually by some type of metal bracing screwed to the underside of the table top. If you turn the table over, the method is self-evident and removing it presents no problem.

Dressers and Chests

Units like these are called case goods because they are built like cases. Each unit usually has a hardwood frame to which the top and sides are attached. The back is set in a rabbet (a groove in the side panels) and fixed in place with a nail. The frame is constructed so that each drawer has its own framing members. In the best pieces, there will be a dust panel (a light sheet of wood or hardboard) separating each drawer compartment and attached to the framing members.

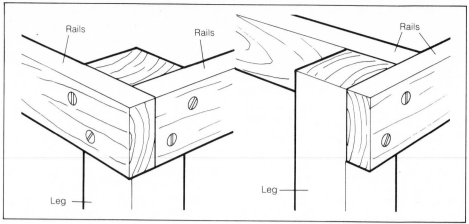

Lapped joints such as these are easy to disassemble. The screws are most often countersunk. Remove the plug over the screws and back the screws out. Then break the glue bond.

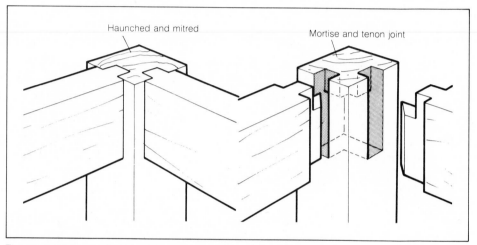

The haunched and mitered corner creates a strong joint. Often a tap or two with a rubber mallet is enough to finish breaking the glue bond. Then pull the rail from the leg.

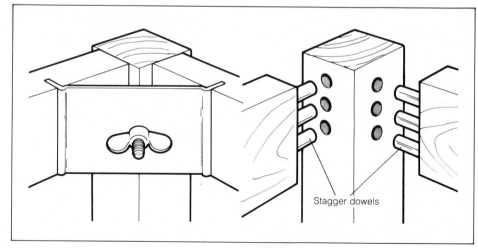

To disassemble a piece held with a hanger bolt, unscrew the bolt and separate the section. To soften stubborn glue around dowels, try a mixture of half water and half vinegar.

Some cabinet or case pieces are made without a frame. In these cases, you'll find solid wood sides joined by wood framing members called stringers.

To begin disassembly these types of units, remove the drawers and look inside. You can see the type of construction immediately — either framed or solid sides.

Look to see how the top is attached, by glue blocks to the frame, or by screws driven up through the framing into the top. Remove the glue blocks or screws and remove the top. Next, locate the nails, usually at the bottom, that hold the back in place. Remove them and slide the back panel out of its rabbets. Back panels usually are not glued in place, but sometimes an enthusiastic repairer, hoping to strengthen the piece, has glued them. Tapping the glue should loosen it, if this is the case.

Good frames are assembled using dowels or tenons, which usually can be tapped apart. Not-so-good frames may be held together with screws and/or metal corner braces. Good frames may have quite a bit of glue block reinforcement, so look for the blocks and remove them before tapping the frame apart.

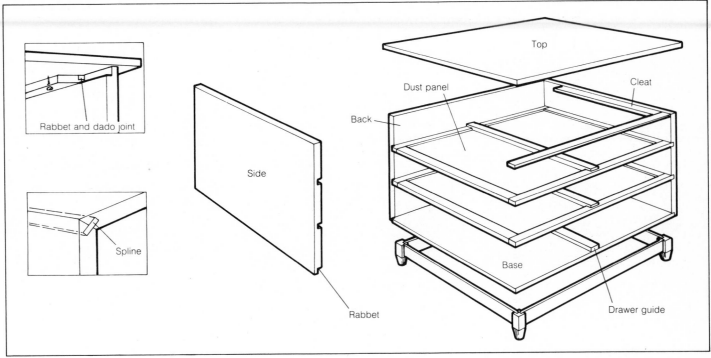

Rabbet and dado joint

Spline

Side

Rabbet

Top

Dust panel

Cleat

Back

Base

Drawer guide

Case goods are constructed around a frame or with stringers. Remove all glue blocks. Remove the top, then the bottom and the back.

PREPARING THE FURNITURE FOR REPAIRS

After reducing the piece to its component parts, spend a little time cleaning the old glue off the pieces and out of the holes. We have found that the best tool for this is the thin-bladed pocket knife. Use it to scrape the glue from exterior surfaces. Because the glue is brittle, it usually flakes away easily. Insert the blade into mortises and other

The work begins with removal of hardware, including casters; place in aluminum trays.

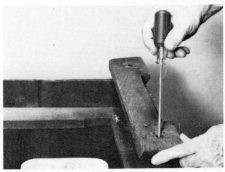

The holes under the casters were made to hold the necks of the original casters.

This marble topped dresser dates back to the 1850s. To renovate, we must reglue much of the frame, drawers, replace veneers on the front, and refinish the entire piece.

cavities to get the old glue out. Just be careful in both operations to cut or scrape away only the glue. Leave all the wood or the joint won't fit when you reglue it.

Now repair all broken parts, so that when you reassemble the piece, it will be sound. Check the list you made of parts to be repaired and locate those parts. Examine each one to see just how you can repair it, or whether it is beyond repair and needs to be replaced. In the paragraphs that follow, we will tell you how specific types of repairs can be made. Refer to these as you need them. Remember that there often are several ways to do the job; you may even be able to invent some methods yourself. The ultimate goal is to return the part to usefulness, make it look like it has never been broken, and join it to other members as successfully as it was joined when the piece was new.

The base plate wood is sound, but looks bad. These old square nails were used rarely after 1890, and not at all after 1895.

Once sanded, the original base plates are reglued to the dresser. We find that a ¾ inch brush is the easiest way to apply glue.

The square nails are now hammered into place as the baseplate is reglued. Two clamps hold the plate as the glue dries.

The upper part of the back frame had a long crack in it. Using a brush, we put glue into the full length of the crack.

The newly glued crack can now be clamped for drying. Wipe the excess glue from the surface as soon as those clamps are in place.

Now we must reglue any frame members that need it, using a brush to apply the glue that has been squeezed into the aluminum dish.

This frame member is tapped firmly but gently into the dresser with the rubber mallet. Do not damage the wood as you work.

Clamps and more clamps! Every joint we have glued must be firmly clamped, which we think is the true secret of successful gluing.

Here is another view of the frame of the dresser, showing how the joints were reglued. Clamps of various sizes were required.

HOW TO REBUILD DRAWERS

Drawers, especially large ones, take a beating in regular use and so tend to be loose and wobbly after awhile. Sometimes you simply need to take them apart and reglue them. In other cases, a bottom or one of the sides may have to be replaced. If you intend to use new hardware, the old hardware holes may have to be filled and new ones drilled. If the drawer is very old, look closely at the drawer runners, or the bottom edges of the sides, on which the drawer slides. They may have become quite worn, signalling the need for new sides.

Good, plain hardwood is fine for drawer parts. Save walnut, cherry and mahogany for places that show.

Drawer Construction

In good drawer construction, the sides are normally dovetailed to the drawer front, and the back is dovetailed to the side pieces. The drawer bottom fits into a groove in the lower parts of the sides and is held in place by small glue blocks on the bottom. To disassemble the drawer, first remove the glue blocks, then slide the bottom out. Finally, tap gently against the inside of the side panels to disengage the dovetails.

If the drawer has guides — and most big drawers should — you will see them on the bottom. The guides are two parallel strips of wood in the center of the bottom, which fit over a wooden guide rail mounted in the chest or dresser. The drawer guide causes the drawer to slide straight in and out, with no sideward motion. If you must replace the drawer bottom, be sure to reinstall the drawer guide on the new bottom.

Replacing the Drawer Bottom

Drawer bottoms today are most often made of hardboard, which is a good material for the purpose. Standard $1/16$- or $1/8$-inch hardboard is fine for small and medium-sized drawers. For very large drawers, you might need a $3/8$-inch thickness.

Measure the old bottom carefully and transfer the measurements to the hardboard. Cut the bottom out with a power saw (a saber saw is fine if you use a guide to assure a straight cut). Finish the cut edges with sandpaper. Slide the bottom into the grooves made for it, and replace the glue blocks on the bottom to hold it in place.

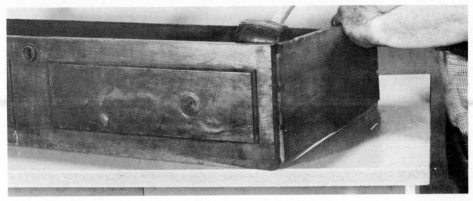

The drawers of the dresser are coming apart and need work. First they must be disassembled, using a rubber mallet.

The original dovetails on the drawer sides were hand cut and irregular in shape. They are now quite broken and worn.

The bottoms of each side are broken and severely worn; drawer bottoms are warped and cracked. We will reuse the fronts only.

Cut sides for each drawer; we used 1 inch oak. The bottom fits into a groove at the bottom of each side; cut this with a router and a ¼ inch dado bit. Trace dovetails on drawer fronts.

Cut a blind dovetail joint with a jig and a router holding a dovetail bit. Drawer side is at jig back; drawer back is in front of the jig.

A router throws a lot of chips and sawdust, so always wear safety glasses.

Sides are wider than the back because the drawer bottom must slide past the back.

Replacing the Hardware

Most hardware is attached to the drawer front by means of one or two machine screws (not wood screws), which go through holes in the wood to nuts inside the drawer. New hardware for a drawer may require a different set of holes, so you have to fill the old holes. Do this by inserting dowels of the right diameter. Sand and stain the ends of the dowels so they can't be seen.

Carefully measure the drawer front to locate the positions of the new holes. Mark the exact position by tapping a dent with the awl. This dent not only serves as a marker, but also helps the drill bit start in exactly the right spot.

Replacing a Side or Back

Usually a side or back needs to be replaced only when it is broken or the dovetail joints have become very worn. Use the old side or back as a template to cut a new one from a hardwood board of the proper thickness, probably ¼-inch. You will have to cut new dovetails in each end of the new part. Since these fit into existing dovetails, use the existing dovetails as templates; that is, use the dovetails on the front of the drawer as the pattern for cutting matching dovetails in the new side.

Step 1: Cutting the Side If the part to be replaced is a drawer side, begin by making a "blank." This is a hardwood piece of the same thickness as the side it is replacing, and of the same overall dimensions.

Step 2: Drawing the Dovetails Place the front end of this blank against the dovetails in the drawer front, into which it will lock when finished, and carefully trace the pattern. Then do the same

on the other end of the blank for the back end, tracing the dovetail pattern from the drawer back.

Step 3: Cutting the Dovetails Use the backsaw to cut the sides of each of the dovetails, making straight cuts in from each end to the depth indicated by your tracing. Then, using a sharp wood chisel, cut the bottoms of the dovetails. Sand the finished dovetails smooth. At the same time, sand the top edge of the side so that it is rounded. Test fit the new dovetails and, if necessary, use sandpaper or a small rasp for any additional trimming. The dovetail

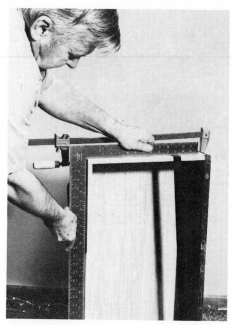

Clamp the job. Check the assembly with a big carpenter's square. For drawers, installing the bottom helps to square the work.

Use a belt sander to smooth the new wood and to sand new joints. A smooth drawer, with all corners slightly rounded, operates easily.

Drawers are assembled with new side and back panels and new bottoms made of ¼ inch hardwood plywood, ordinary plywood or Masonite.

should fit snugly, so don't cut away any more than absolutely necessary. (An emery board, incidentally, serves as a good sanding tool for finishing.)

Other Drawer Problems

If the drawer seems balky and refuses to slide in and out easily, look for any of these problems.

1. The sliding area on the bottom of the drawer may simply need lubrication. Spray it and the frame on which it rides with silicone lubricant.

2. The sides of the drawer may have swollen due to moisture absorption. Suspect this especially if the piece has been stored in a damp area. Try baking a small drawer in a warm — not hot — oven (about 120 degrees for half an hour) to get rid of the moisture. For drawers too big to go in the oven, use a heat lamp trained directly on swollen parts. The moisture may have caused swelling, which doesn't go down when the water has evaporated. In that case, sand the bottom edges and lower sides to remove the swollen wood.

3. The sliding area may be worn from overuse. Probably the best way to mend this is to make new sides, but since this seems like a lot of unnecessary work, you can try to rebuild the sliding area. To rebuild, glue a thin strip of veneer along the bottom edge, and then sand the strip thoroughly after the glue has dried. The typical veneer, after sanding, will add only about ⅟₃₅ of an inch to the bottom. If this isn't enough, add another layer.

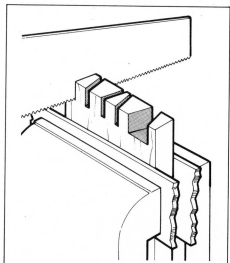

If you cut the sides of the dovetails with a backsaw, clamp the work securely in a vise. Pad sides for protection from the jaws.

HOW TO REPAIR DOWELED CHAIR RUNGS The rung on a chair, doweled into the front and back legs, may have dried out and shrunk, or been loose for a long time and become worn. You can't just reglue it, because glue alone won't make the joint tight. One way to mend it is to wrap string tightly around the dowel to increase its diameter, then coat the wrapping with glue and reinsert the dowel. However, we don't like this method.

A better technique calls for you to cut a slot down the center of the doweled end.

Use a backsaw and clamp the rung in a vise while you saw. Drive a small wedge of hardwood down into the saw cut, forcing the dowel end to expand slightly until it fits snugly into the hole. Fit the new end into the hole before applying any glue to be sure of the fit. Cut the wedge off flush with the end of the dowel, apply glue, and tap the now-expanded dowel into the hole.

BROKEN DOWEL RUNGS OR STRINGERS

Especially in chair construction, you find parts such as round stringers, rungs and rails made so that they are self-doweling. That is, each end of the piece is inserted into a hole and glued there, like a dowel. When these break, repair varies according to how the break took place.

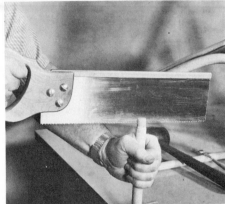

Another answer to ends of rungs that do not fit snugly into their holes is to saw cut into the middle of the end of the rung. Then you can insert a wedge into the end.

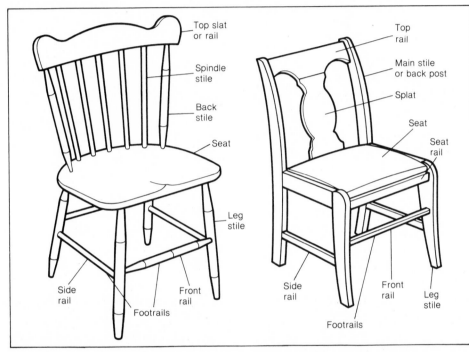

The more familiar you are with the names of parts of furniture, the more easily you will understand repair discussions. Regardless of style, the terminology is universal.

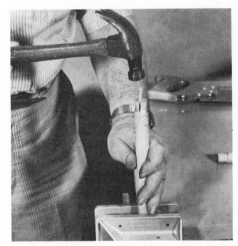

After making the saw cut, whittle a small wedge from hardwood. Tap it down into the cut, as shown. Coat with glue before insertion.

You can wrap the dowel of a loose rung with string to increase its size. This works well when you can't take the rung out of the chair to saw it. If the rung size needs to be increased only a little, use thread instead of string. To finish, coat the thread or string with glue.

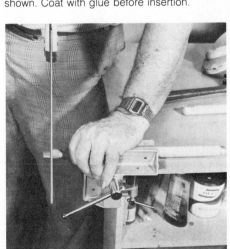

Drive the wedge in far enough to expand the size of the rung end, but not so far as to split the wood. Then cut off the part of the wedge that projects beyond the rung end.

Dowel Broken Off

In one kind of break, the part snaps off just at the hole, leaving the dowel portion in the hole. The rung itself will then have a ragged end. The repair depends on how much of the body of the rung was destroyed. If the ragged end is very near the part of the rung which served as a dowel, you are lucky. You can fix the rung by following these steps:

(1) dig the dowel scrap out of the hole;

(2) fill the hole with a hardwood plug glued in place, flush with the surface;

(3) clamp the rung in a vise to hold it while you work;

(4) use your dowel jig to drill a hole for a new hardwood dowel into the end of the rung — the diameter of the new dowel will be about half or a little bigger than the diameter of the rung;

(5) ignoring the ragged end of the rung

for now, drill dowel holes in both the rung and the piece to which it is to be joined;

(6) insert a dry dowel (no glue) in the hole;

(7) assemble the joint, making sure that the rung is in exactly the same position as it was originally;

(8) there will be some wood missing at the ragged end of the rung — measure the space between the ragged end and the chair leg to find how much wood is missing;

(9) remove the rung and use wood putty to build up the end of the rung so that it meets the face to which it is to be joined;

(10) allow the wood putty to set;

(11) sand it to the same shape as the rung;

(12) stain the putty the same shade as the rest of the furniture. When you insert the new dowel, the rung should look like new.

Alternative: Doweling A simpler method can be employed if the dowel scrap is still projecting from the hole into which it was inserted. In this case, cut off the ragged wood and then add a new dowel, as shown in the photographs.

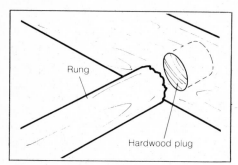

First, dig out the old dowel out of the hole in the rail. Fill this with a wood plug sanded to match the shape of the rail.

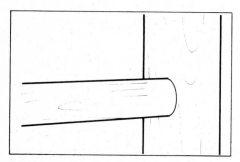

Drill holes for a new dowel that will be inserted both into the rung and into the rail. There will be an open space left between the two.

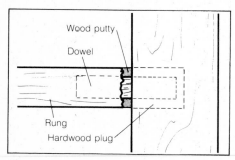

Fill the open space with wood putty or wood filler. When this dries, sand the putty to match the shape of the rung; then stain.

The rung of this chair has broken off, leaving its doweled end in the leg like a plug. The easiest repair method is doweling.

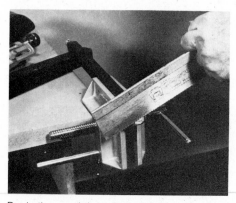

Begin the repair by using a backsaw to cut off ragged pieces of wood flush with the surface. Do this on both the leg and the rung.

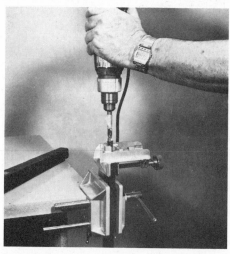

Clamp the rung, position the doweling jig on it, and drill a dowel hole. Be careful to drill in the center of the rung; use tape around the drill bit as a depth guide.

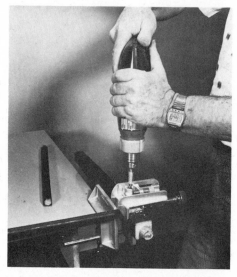

Next, drill a dowel hole in the center of the broken rung in the leg.

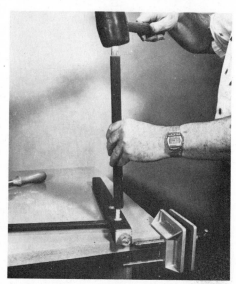

Coat a dowel with white glue. Insert it into the hole in the leg. Place the rung over it. With the rubber mallet, drive the rung tight for a strong, invisible repair.

To get glue down into a split, use a screwdriver to hold the pieces apart. Insert a small wood wedge to hold the break open.

Longitudinal Crack

Another kind of break that often occurs in self-doweled rungs is the longitudinal crack. In these breaks, a long crack develops along the length of the rung, usually continuing on into the doweled portion. More often than not, the crack is so severe that the rung comes out in two pieces. Repair, fortunately, is easy. Just glue the rung together again, exactly as it was before. If you clamp it properly during gluing, you will have a sound repair. If splinters of wood are missing, fill the gaps with wood putty. Refinish the rung to match the rest of the chair.

Replacement Rungs

Rungs and stringers can be so badly shattered that no surgery of any kind can mend them. Then the only thing to do is replace them. If the pieces to be replaced are square or rectangular or round and unshaped in any way, you should be able to buy hardwood of the approximate size and make new ones without trouble. More often than not, however, these pieces have been turned on a lathe and given some kind of shape. Then the only way to replace them is either to shape a duplicate piece on a lathe yourself or have it done by someone else.

There is nothing technically difficult about shaping a piece such as this on a lathe. It is a simple, straightforward task, a snap for someone who owns and knows how to use a wood lathe. It is probable that the rung or other piece may have to be made to match another part in shape. This, too, isn't a problem for an experienced lathe operator, using the piece to be matched as a guide. The only additional advice we can add is that the new piece should be made of the same species of wood as the one it replaces, so that you can finish it to match.

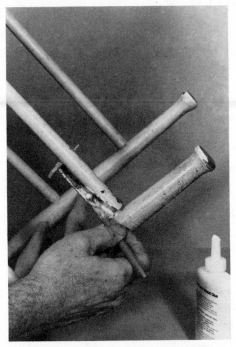

With the break still held open, paint white glue down into the crack, until all the surfaces are well covered.

This chair needs regluing. The glue is too good for the joints to be taken apart; regluing must be done with the chair assembled.

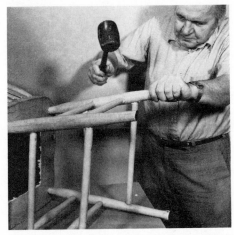

With the rungs all in position, firmly drive each rung deep into its hole, using the rubber mallet to join the two pieces.

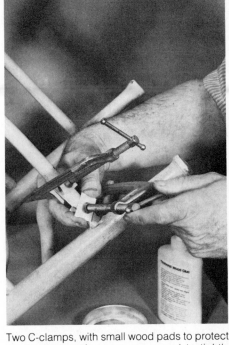

Two C-clamps, with small wood pads to protect the furniture surface, are now used to tightly clamp the pieces together.

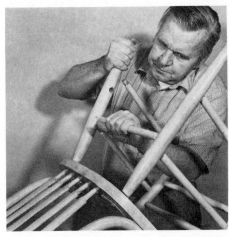

Paint glue into each of the rung holes. Use a little muscle power to get the rungs into the holes in which they belong.

Strap clamp for pressure on reglued joints; no other clamps are needed. To tighten strap ("web") clamp, turn large adjustment screw.

HOW TO REPAIR CRACKED OR BROKEN TENONS

The easiest and strongest repair is to use your backsaw to cut off the old tenon stump flush with the wood surface. Then chisel out the old tenon if necessary and make a hardwood plug to fill the mortise. Glue it into the hole. Be sure the plug is flush with the surface and not above it. Now join the parts with two or three dowels.

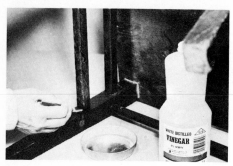

To soften joints for disassembly, paint with a vinegar-and-warm-water mixture. If still firm, the joint doesn't need regluing.

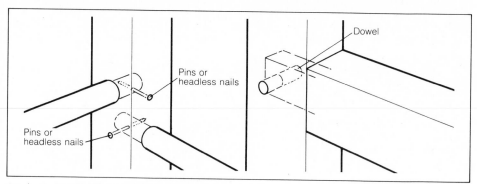

When you find it difficult to take apart a chair, you might suspect that the dowel or tenon has been locked in place with a small pin, headless nail, or a dowel. Look for a small hole, usually filled with wood filler, in the leg. Use a nailset to drive the pin out.

HOW TO REPAIR A LOOSE TENON JOINT

In a case like this, the tenon has shrunk and no longer fits snugly into the mortise. One solution is to rebuild the sides of the tenon by gluing thin shims of hardwood to it. You need very thin wood for this work; we have found small pieces of veneer to be excellent. You can buy veneers from specialty houses by mail and from some local furniture and craft shops. You also can buy thin sheets of birch at any shop dealing in model airplane supplies.

A Disassembled Piece Cut a small rectangle of veneer to the exact size of the tenon. Glue this to one side of the tenon and allow the glue to dry. Sand the joined edges to make a smooth fit. Then try the new tenon in its mortise. It should fit snugly. If the new tenon is a little too large, use coarse sandpaper to sand the tenon down. If the new tenon is a little too small, apply another shim to the other side. If you detect an up-and-down movement after inserting the tenon, you can put a tiny shim on the bottom.

An Assembled Piece In those cases where you haven't disassembled the piece, you can make a similar repair by pulling the tenon out of the mortise as far as you can, applying glue to the veneer piece and the tenon. Place the shim in the mortise next to the tenon. Tap the joint back together and clamp until the glue dries. If you think one shim may not be enough, fit the shims around the tenon and tap the joint together without glue first. If the joint seems solid, tap it apart, apply the glue, and retap it together.

When only one joint is loose, repair the tenon without disassembling the chair. A piece of wood serves as a wedge to hold joint open.

This tenon has worn too small to fit into the mortise. Cement a thin veneer shim to the side of the tenon with contact cement.

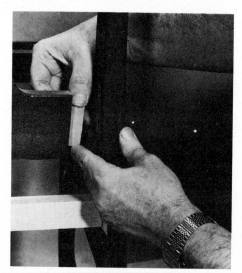

The shim, cut from a sheet of veneer, is also coated with contact cement. Let both dry for an hour. Apply the shim to the tenon.

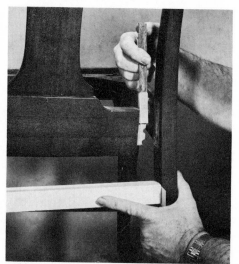

Sand the shim down until the tenon is the right size to fit snugly into the mortise. We made a small sanding block for the job.

HOW TO REPAIR CRACKED CHAIR SEATS Solid wood chair seats, cabinet sides, and table-tops sometimes end up cracked or even broken into two pieces. The best method for repairing them is to glue the separated parts back together, using a series of three or four dowels as reinforcement. In other words, create a dowel joint between the two broken parts. Apply glue along the whole length of the break. Then clamp the pieces firmly as the repair dries. This will join the two parts and make them stronger than they were before the break.

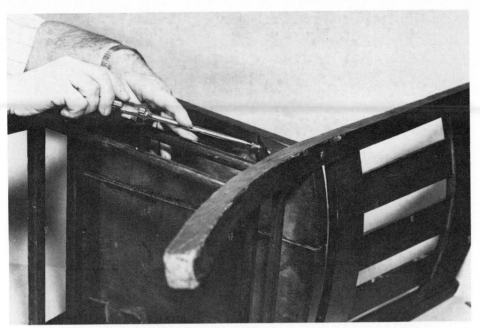

Look for screws in corner blocks, and also at the back, holding the seat to the back. Screws sometimes are hidden under wood plugs. Pry up the plug; remove the screw beneath it.

Once the screws are out, tap with your rubber mallet to knock the chair apart.

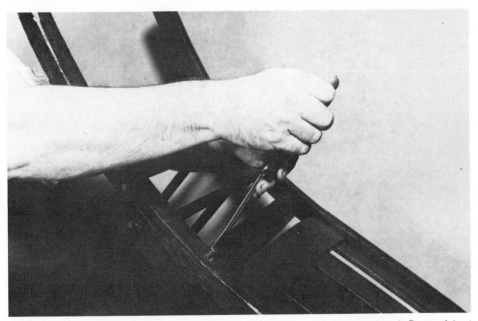

If you damage or break the plug in getting it out, you can buy a new plug to replace it. Be careful not to damage the wood frame.

The oak chair was reglued after the seat broke, and the repair didn't hold. Apply warm vinegar and water to soften the old glue.

After the glue has begun to soften, use a pen-knife to dig clots of glue out of crevices and to scrape the surfaces clean.

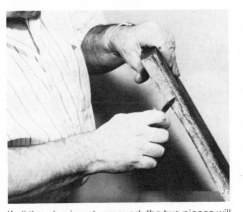

If all the glue is not removed, the two pieces will not fit together properly when they are reglued. Scrape away all excess glue.

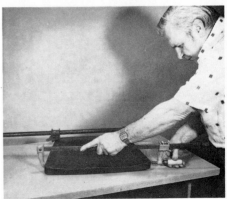

The first step in repairing this cracked oak seat is to clamp the broken pieces together exactly as they will be when doweled.

We plan to use four dowels in the repair, so we now draw marks across the crack at each point where a dowel will be used.

Draw lines across the cracked edge at each mark on the unclamped seat. Hold one piece in the vise; place doweling jig over lines.

To guarantee correct depth of dowel holes, wrap a piece of tape around the upper part of the drill bit as a depth marker.

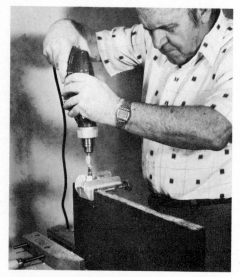

Add the depth of the hole (1 inch) to the length of the jig guide tube. Place the tape's edge this distance from the bit bottom.

Now each dowel is painted with carpenter's white glue, and is then inserted in its hole in one of the seat pieces.

Gently tap each dowel all the way into the holes with a hammer. Half of each dowel will project from the surface.

After all dowels are in place in one side, paint a generous amount of white glue on the protruding dowels and along the seat edge.

Position the other piece of the seat on the dowels. Drive it down onto the dowels. Use bar or pipe clamps to hold the two pieces firmly together. Turn the adjusting screws tight, to force the glued edges into snug, continuous contact. When dry, sand for a smooth seam.

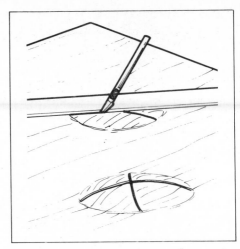

Veneer sometimes acquires a bubble in the surface. One way to repair it is to first cut an "x" in the surface with a craft knife.

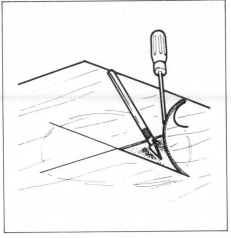

Carefully lift the edges of the bubble. (If it seems hard to lift, moisten it slightly.) Scrape away old glue; apply new adhesive.

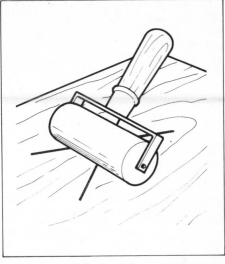

To set the patch, firmly roll the area of the blister with a veneer roller. Cover the area completely and wipe away any excess.

HOW TO REPAIR DAMAGED VENEER

The best glue to use when mending veneered pieces is the type of contact cement made for veneering. It is available wherever veneers are sold. If you can't find it, then use the contact cement you can buy at your home center. You use it by coating the two surfaces to be mated, allowing them to dry, and then fitting them together. Keep in mind that the fit must be perfect because once the pieces come together, they can't be separated.

Veneer Edge Repairs One common veneer problem is veneer on a tabletop that has lifted off of the subwood. If the veneer has lifted at the edge of the tabletop and is undamaged, the repair consists simply of regluing it to the subwood.

Veneer Surface Repairs If the repair must be made in the middle of the top, away from the edges, the problem is a little different. Veneers that have lifted off the subwood in the middle of a tabletop (or other field) seldom can be fitted down into the same place again. The veneer seems to be larger than the place from which it lifted, as if it had stretched. Such lifts-offs begin as bubbles in the veneer. Then the bubble breaks, leaving broken and lifted veneer. In your examination, you may find some veneer bubbles which haven't broken yet. These should be fixed before they can break.

Veneer bubbles To fix a bubble of veneer, use a razor-sharp craft knife guided by the steel rule, and make an X cut across the bubble. Avoid making either cut of the X directly with the grain of the wood. Use the blade of the knife to scrape away any old glue in the repair area; then carefully fit the flaps down in place. If they make a smooth fit, you can go ahead and glue them down. Use an artist's brush to apply contact cement to the underside of each flap of veneer and to the subwood. Hold the flaps up long enough for the cement to dry; press them down into place. Use a veneer or wallpaper seam roller to secure the repair.

Veneer patch If the bubble has broken before you begin the repair, the veneer flaps may be damaged and won't fit down into place properly. If that happens, use the technique described in the next paragraph for replacing missing pieces of veneer. This entails using a razor knife to cut out the damaged area, then filling the area with a patch of veneer cut to the correct shape.

Veneer that has lifted and broken, whether in the center of the table or at the end, has to be replaced by a patch of new veneer. In most cases, the veneer will have broken off after lifting from the substrate but no one will have the broken piece. If this is your situation, check the veneer still on the table to see that it adheres firmly in place. Look especially right around the edges of the break, where the patch must be made. Determine how much of it can be reglued and how much of it must be cut away.

Now buy a piece of veneer of the same wood species. Remember that the color of the veneer on the table is the result of staining, so the veneer you buy won't be the color of the tabletop. If the patch is of the same species, you will be able to stain it to the same color after the repair is finished.

Use the metal straightedge rule as a

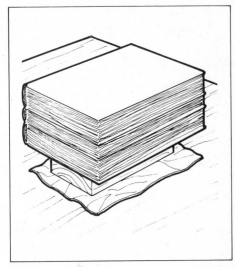

Cover the patch with kraft paper and a block slightly larger than the bubble. Weight the block with books for 24 hours.

guide and cut the edges of the veneer around the damaged area so they are straight. Make the damaged area into a simple shape — square, diamond or rectangle. Remove only as much of the old veneer as necessary.

Now cut a patch of the exact size and shape as the cut-out area. Cut and trim this piece until the fit is perfect. Coat one side of the patch and also the damaged area with contact cement, allow it to dry, and then place the patch in the damaged area.

Use a veneer roller or wallpaper seam roller to apply heavy pressure to the patch, to be sure that it is well seated and that the two glued surfaces are in good contact. Finally, stack a pile of books or other heavy items on top of the repair overnight, to hold it in place while the glue sets completely.

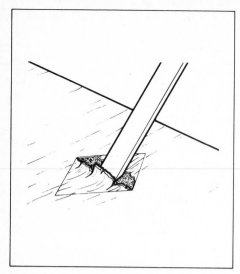

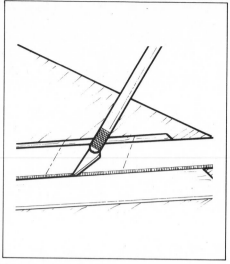

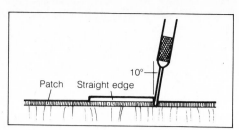

Give the patch a slightly beveled edge so that the bottom is narrower than the top.

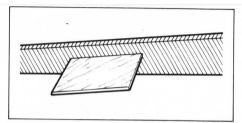

An alternative method of repair involves removing the broken veneer. Cut through to create a rectangular hole; chisel out.

From matching veneer, cut a patch that is identical to the hole in the veneered surface. A straightedge helps make straight cuts.

Try to fit the patch. Then use a file to produce the exact fit that you need.

HOW TO REPAIR BROKEN EDGES AND CORNERS

The edges and corners of furniture, and especially tabletops, often take a beating. It isn't uncommon to find whole corners broken off of solid wood tabletops, or to find a layer or two of wood missing from a tabletop made of plywood or laminated wood layers. A heavy item may fall against an edge and dent it severely. Damage of this type is most commonly found on tables, but can happen to chairs and cabinets, especially lowboys, as well.

The problem is how to fill the broken or dented area in order to restore its original shape and appearance. If the dent is relatively small, you can fill it with stick shellac. We cover that technique in a later chapter on repairing finishes. If the dent is large — ½ inch or more — it is best to make a permanent wood repair. You will have to use your own judgment on which type of repair to use.

Adhering a New Piece

If a corner is broken off a solid wood table or cabinet top and the broken part is missing, the solution is obvious. You must make a new piece of the right size and glue it in place. Here are the factors to consider as you plan the repair.

Step 1: Finding the Right Wood You will have to buy a piece of solid wood of the same species from which to cut the new corner. The new wood has to be the same thickness as the old, and the piece you buy should be larger than the missing

piece so you can cut the new corner from it.

Step 2: Preparing the Area It is not likely that the surface of the table edge where the corner broke off is even and smooth. Since it is extremely difficult to cut a new piece to match the irregularities of the fractured edge, carefully trim the broken edge until it is flat. Depending on how much wood must be trimmed away, you could use coarse sandpaper, a small plane, or a wide-bladed wood chisel. Test your work by placing a block of wood against it. The block should contact the top surface perfectly; keep trimming until it does.

Step 3: Cutting the New Corner Look at the grain of the wood on the table top, and plan to cut the new piece with the grain running in the same direction. Measure the corner carefully and, to be safe, make a paper or cardboard template of the missing piece. Breaks like this are seldom symmetrical in shape, and just measuring the area with a rule won't give you a good replacement. Cut and trim the template until it fits exactly into the damaged area; then trace it on the replacement wood you bought, observing that the grain runs with that of the top. Cut along the traced lines.

Step 4: Matching the Edge Many corners and edges are shaped in some manner. The most common designs are bevel, chamfer, cove, bead or Roman ogee. All of these shapes can be made with a router fitted with the correct bit. Make a sketch of the edge shape and take

it to your home center, where you and the salesman can select the right bit. Then go home and play with the router. Practice cutting edges on some scrap wood before doing it on the new corner. Once you have mastered use of the tool, clamp the piece to your workbench and rout the edge of the new wood patch to match the existing edge of the table.

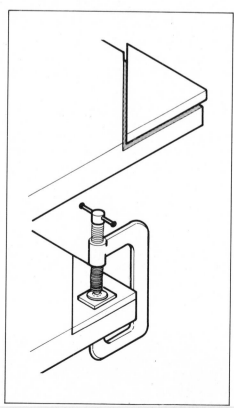

When only a layer or two of wood has broken off, cut the patch to shape and depth; glue in place and clamp until dry — at least overnight.

Step 5: Attaching the New Piece If the piece to be replaced is small, glue it into place. If it is larger, use dowels to reinforce it. Either way, clamp the repair overnight after gluing the parts together.

Step 6: Finishing the Patch Once any corner or edge repair has been made, the next problem is to finish the added piece to match the rest of the top. Sand the repaired area, including the new wood, the joint line and the area near it until it is perfectly smooth. You are now ready to stain the sanded area the exact color of the rest of the table — a task that can be pretty tricky.

The best way to achieve a good color is to finish several of scraps of the wood left over from the piece from which you cut the repair corners. Use several stains, all close to the color you believe is needed. After the stains have dried, apply a coat of the proper finishing material. Allow this to dry; then sand it lightly and compare the different colors to the tabletop. Hopefully, one will be a close match and you can go ahead with the finishing of the patch. If none are satisfactory, keep trying different stain colors until you find the right one. The success of your repair depends on how close you match it to the old tabletop.

Chipped Plywood Top

If the top is made of plywood, and only a layer or two of the plywood has broken away, follow the same procedure as for a whole solid wood corner, but do not cut away that part of the top which remains unless it is cracked or badly damaged. Use

it as the base of the repair. Trim the fractured edge smooth. Make a cardboard template of the damaged area, cut a piece of wood of the right thickness to fit into the area, and glue the new piece into place. Clamp well.

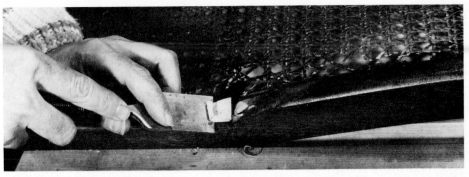

The first step is to use a broad, sharp wood chisel to remove as much wood as necessary so the repair area will be smooth and regular in shape.

Now an oversized piece of hardwood is glued in place. Be sure the wood piece is large enough so that it can be shaped to match the contours of the wood around it.

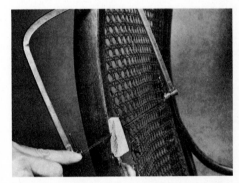

This is another view of the wood glued to the repair area. Note that it has been shaped somewhat to fit the opening.

The glue has dried and the wood piece is now ready for shaping.

Shape the new wood to match surrounding wood. One way is to cut away excess wood with a coping saw, maintaining the correct outline.

Missing pieces such as this are a common problem in furniture repair. If the chip is still around, you can just glue it back on. But since no one ever seems to save the chip, a replacement must be created.

As you get close to the final shape of the inserted wood, switch to a sharp wood chisel and carefully carve the profile.

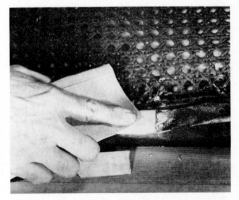

Sand the wood using coarse sandpaper on the sanding attachment of an electric drill.

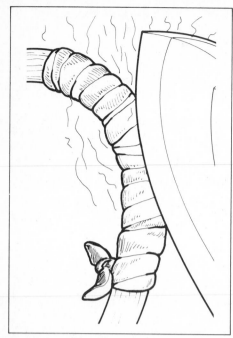

First, soften the wood. Dampen a length of cloth and wrap the area. Use a steam iron to heat. Moisten the cloth as necessary.

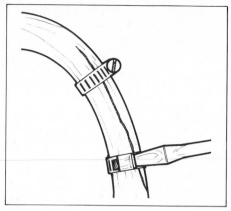

Bend the split in place and, remembering to protect the wood, clamp down. You can use either C clamps or automotive hose clamps.

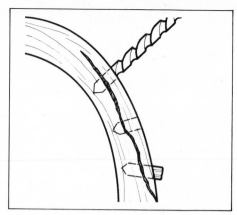

A deep slit needs ⅜-inch dowels to remain in position. The angle of the holes should not be on the same plane. Shape the tops to fit.

HOW TO REPAIR BENTWOOD FURNITURE

HOW TO REPAIR BENTWOOD FURNITURE Bentwood chairs, the runners on many rocking chairs, and other furniture with parts made by bending rather than cutting the wood, offer a particular challenge. It is difficult to make bentwood replacement parts without the steam and water facilities used to bend wood in furniture factories. In addition, bending wood is an art in itself and requires knowledge and experience. Making the equipment and learning the trade is neither cost nor time-effective for the average person, who needs only to repair a single chair or rocker. A nearby furniture maker or repairman may agree to make a new part, but for most people, such facilities aren't available.

There are a couple of options. You can try to glue the broken parts together, or you can make a replacement part that doesn't require bending.

Gluing the Split Wood

The most common use of bentwood is in light chairs and some rocking chairs. To make these, long wooden rods an inch or more in diameter are bent into continuous curves. One piece of wood may be formed into the back legs and curved back of a straight chair, or into the rockers and arms of a rocking chair. This kind of bending, while it makes very strong furniture, puts great stress along the outside of sharply curved parts. When trouble occurs, it usu-ally does so at one of these sharp curves, where the stretched outside wood fibers split away from the main body.

To repair a split like this, it is necessary to soften the wood which is standing away from the main body, then bend it down into its original position. Sometimes just gluing the softened strip down is enough, but if the tension is very high, glue may not be enough to hold it. Then insert a dowel through the strip into the main body of the wood.

Step 1: Softening the Split Wood

Begin the repair by painting water on the split wood over and over again, until it is well soaked. Or wrap a cloth soaked in water around the part for 15 to 30 minutes. You can increase the softening action by applying heat — a hot iron or a heat lamp will do it — to the wet cloth until it steams. After the wood has become pliable, bend the split wood down into its original position and clamp it until it dries. The idea is to reform the broken wood to its original shape before applying glue.

Clamping Devices Clamping this type of fracture requires some ingenuity. You can use several C-clamps, padded carefully to prevent marks on the wood, or a couple of large spring clamps. Use enough clamps to force the wood to curve properly. A 4-inch split, for example, probably should have at least three clamps to obtain the proper curve.

Step 2: Gluing the Split

Remove the clamps after the wood has dried thoroughly. Use a small brush to paint glue into the crack. Reclamp the fracture until the glue dries. As always, give the glue more than enough time to dry.

Step 3: Inserting Dowels

If you believe that the glue alone won't hold the repair together, insert a small dowel near the outer end of the repair as additional holding help. If the repair is fairly long, you should consider a dowel every two inches.

While the clamps are in place, drill through the glued-down tab into the wood under it. Use ⅜-inch dowels for the work, and don't drill all the way through the wood piece. Make each hole at a different angle to increase the holding power of the repair. Cut the dowels an inch or so longer than needed, coat them with glue, and tap them into the holes. Later, when you take the clamps off, trim the dowels flush with the surface. In this way the dowels will follow the angle of the curved surface.

Step 4: Finishing Edges

Reglued bentwood often doesn't fit smoothly back in place, so once the repair has dried, you may have to use a wood putty to fill in the edges of the repair. When the putty has dried, sand it smooth and then refinish the area.

Repair for Fractured Bentwood Arm

Another type of problem you can encoun-

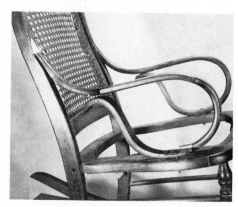

Our old rocker had two problems: the bent wood at the bottom of the arm was broken, with a chip missing from the wood at the point where the arm joins the back of the chair.

ter is broken wood at the bottom of the arm of a bentwood chair. The accompanying photographs detail one creative answer to this wood working difficulty.

1 The arm is fastened to the chair seat by means of a bolt. The wood around the bolt has been fractured, which means the repair calls for some creative woodworking.

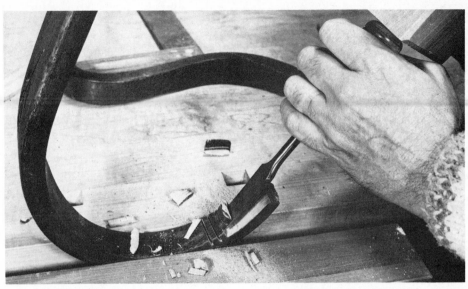

4 A wide wood chisel removes wood between the saw cuts. This creates areas on the top and bottom of the stub into which the repair wood can be fitted to form the new mortise.

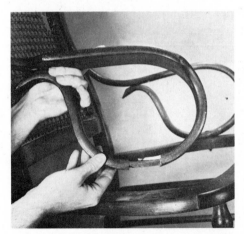

2 The arm was made in two pieces, which were joined by a mortise-and-tenon joint. The bolt holding the arm to the chair went through this joint, resulting in a weak joint that broke.

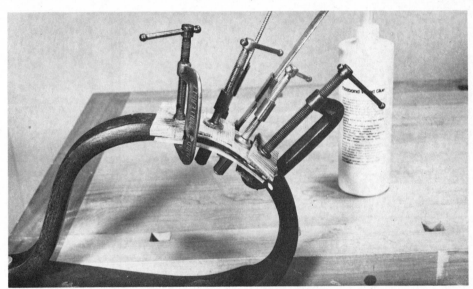

5 Now pieces of oak ⅛-inch thick are cut and inset into the areas just prepared. In this process, the arm is reassembled and the new wood is glued both to the old tenon and the newly cut sections of the arm. To bend the wood to shape, start clamping at one end and add a clamp at a time, forcing the wood to the proper curve. Oak is flexible and will take the pressure.

3 To remake arm's broken mortise, we made a series of ⅛-inch deep saw cuts, ⅛-inch apart, in top and bottom of the good wood just ahead of the broken area (saw cuts shown in top).

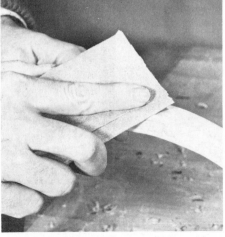

6 After the glue had dried, the repaired arm is sanded smooth. Wood filler is used to fill the edges of the repair area.

7 A new hole must be drilled to take the bolt used to hold the arm on the chair.

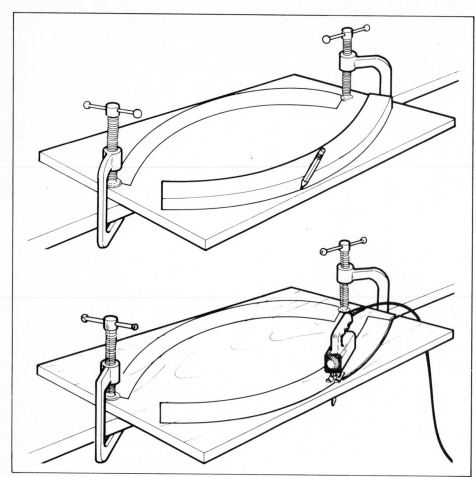

1 Most rockers are oak bent to shape under pressure during steaming. This requires special equipment and experience. By laminating curved pieces from flat stock, we made replacement rockers without bending wood. To begin trace the shape on the new wood, using the unbroken rocker as a guide.

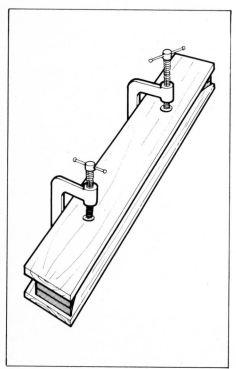

2 The rocker consists of three parts laminated together. The core is ¾-inch oak, and two side pieces are of ¼-inch oak. Clamp so core grain runs a different direction than the side pieces.

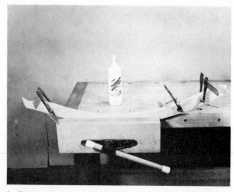

3 The core and two side pieces are glued together and tightly clamped until the glue dries. This gives us a rough new rocker that must be given a final shape.

4 The glue has dried and the rocker is ready for shaping. Use a wood chisel to level high spots and to make the rocker shape you need.

5 After cutting to the general shape you want with a wood chisel, use your drill with a sander attachment and coarse paper to continue the shaping. Change to finer grades of paper as you work until the rocker is shaped, smooth and ready for finishing.

Replacing a Rocking Chair Runner

Rocking chair runners are made in three ways. In some chairs, the runner is cut from hardwood and bent to a curved shape; in others, it is cut from hardwood in the curved shape, so no bending is required. In yet others, the runner is made by laminating three curved pieces together. If you must replace a runner, use the third method; lamination works best because it requires no bending and at the same time produces a strong unit.

Step 1: Cutting the Pieces First make a pattern from the side of the existing rocker runner or from the pieces of the broken runner. Next, trace this pattern three times on hardwood boards each of which is one-third the thickness of the runner. (Use ¼-or ⅜-inch boards for most runners). Place the pattern on each board so that the grains of the cutouts do not all run in the same direction. When the three are laminated, the criss-crossing grains will provide strength and protection against breakage.

Step 2: Gluing the Runner Coat the faces of the cutouts generously with glue and clamp them together for drying. In clamping together long pieces such as these, you can get a more even distribution of clamping pressure by placing them between long blocks of wood. Use more than just two or three clamps.

Step 3: Finishing Off When the glue has dried, remove the clamps and clamping boards and sand the new runner thoroughly. Pay special attention to the top and bottom of the runner. These should be sanded enough so that the glue lines are nearly invisible.

HOW TO REPAIR WARPED SURFACES

Large flat areas of solid wood, including table tops, drop leaves and cabinet doors, are subject to warping. Parts made of plywood are less likely to warp, but under the right conditions even they can have problems. Pieces that have no frame to support them are likely candidates. Pieces that have been finished completely on both sides have less of this trouble because the finishing material prevents absorption of moisture. Tables with unfinished undersides are an invitation to trouble. The ultimate cause of the problem is moist air, of course, and if you live in a climate that is dry all year, you don't need to worry.

Avoiding Moisture Problems

Moisture frequently causes drawer problems, but only when the moisture can get into the wood. Because drawers are hidden, they often aren't finished at all. Unfortunately, in a humid climate bare wood can act like a sponge. The moral of the story is: always finish drawers, inside and out, to reduce their ability to absorb moisture. As a matter of fact, don't save this advice for furniture restoration alone. Look at the drawers in all of your furniture, and apply a coat or two of lacquer or shellac to prevent binding, swelling and sticking.

Removing a Warp

Correcting the warp requires radical surgery and great care. If the piece is valuable, think twice before doing it. The repair may cause considerable loss of value in the antique market.

Step 1: Kerfing the Underside

Make a series of parallel saw cuts (kerfs) on the back or underside of the warped piece. Use a radial saw to make the cuts about 1½ inches apart. Set the saw to cut about ¼ inch less than the thickness of the wood. Begin the cuts an inch from one side, and make them all across the piece and for its full length.

Step 2: Removing the Warp

To get rid of the warp, place the piece on a flat surface, with the side with the kerfs in it facing upward. Dampen the wood with a fine spray from a plant sprayer, or use wet cloths. Do not drown the piece, but at the same time be sure that moisture gets down into the kerfs. Then put heavy weights all over the piece and allow it to dry. The hope is that the moisture and the weights will flatten the piece against the surface on which it rests. If at first you do not succeed, try again, using a little more moisture.

Step 3: Preventing Reoccurance

After the warp is gone, prevent its return by tapping and gluing thin shims into the saw kerfs. These should hold it flat.

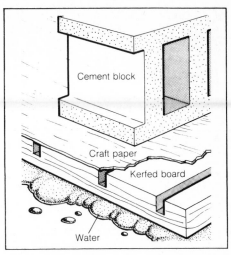

To begin the repair, cut saw kerfs in the underside of the piece. Dampen the top; then turn the piece over and force it flat.

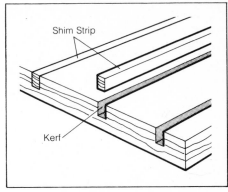

To prevent the return of the warp, insert narrow shims into the kerfs. These will force the wood to its original flat shape.

HOW TO FIX OR REPLACE CASTERS

Nothing is quite as annoying as a caster that drops out of the leg every time you roll or lift the furniture — and few furniture problems are as easy to solve. You probably won't even have to buy new casters.

Collar Caster Construction

The casters, which drop out of sockets in the bottoms of legs, are of simple construction. Understanding their construction will help you to fix them. Looking at the bottom of the leg, you see a collar around the hole. This collar has teeth that have been tapped into the wood to hold the collar in place. Up inside the leg, attached to this collar, is a tubular socket. The sides of this socket have been split into three or four wings. The stem of the caster has a slightly bulbous end, and when it is pushed all the way into this tube, it forces the wings apart. Then they close just under the bulbous end and prevent the caster from falling out.

Repairing the Caster When a caster does drop out, it usually means that these wings have become bent outward, so they no longer grip the bulbous end of the caster stem. The repair consists entirely of bending those wings back together again. To remove the socket from the leg so this can be done, pry up the collar on the bottom of the leg to loosen it. Then grip it with a pliers and pull. Use the pliers to bend the wings on the socket. Put the socket back in the hole and tap the collar into the wood. The caster now will stay in the leg.

Replacing a Caster Replacing the old casters with new ones, if that should be necessary, is equally as simple. Just pull out the old sockets and insert the new ones. Only one caution: Be sure the new sockets are the same diameter as the old ones.

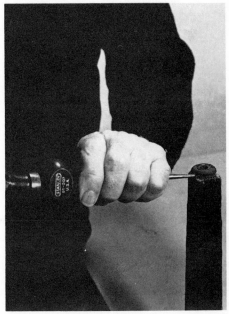

To fix casters that drop out of their sockets, lift out the socket with an awl and a hammer. The collar of the socket has teeth embedded in the leg. Drive the awl between the teeth.

Lift the socket slightly with the awl, then use a pliers to turn and lift it.

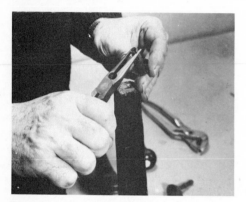

The end of the socket is slitted to form several "wings." Bent inward, these wings hold the caster up in the leg. Those shown have bent outward and no longer grip the caster. Use a pliers to bend them inward again.

Reinsert the caster socket. Drive it all the way in; the teeth on the socket collar will dig into the wood of the leg.

Put the caster back in its socket.

Plate Caster Construction

The plate caster differs from the style discussed above. It consists of a caster wheel attached to a metal plate or a metal collar. The metal plate is attached to the bottom of the leg by means of four screws, and the legs using plate casters usually are fairly large. The type that employs the metal collar is most often used on smaller legs, and the metal collar must be the right size to fit over the bottom of the leg. It is tapped in place and held there by small nails or screws.

Repair Method The major problem with a plate caster is splitting of the wood around the screws. To repair this, remove the caster and fix the split leg — usually by gluing it back together, or by gluing and inserting a dowel for added strength.

One good way to reinforce legs that have been broken in this manner is to replace the plate caster with a metal-collar caster, since the metal collar helps to prevent further splitting of the wood.

Caster Wheels

If the casters appear to be in good shape but won't roll properly, examine the wheel shaft. Rug fibers and threads often wrap around these and act as little brakes. Clean out the debris and the caster will work.

Look also for a bent shaft or bent metal sides. If you find either problem, buy new casters. Try to lubricate casters on a regular basis. We suggest silicone lubricant, or any type that doesn't contain an oil that might stain carpeting.

A plate caster is one that screws to the bottom of the furniture instead of being inserted into a socket. A small shaft fits up into a hole in the leg to hold the caster steady.

Here, the caster is in place on the bottom of our 1852 dresser. Three screws will be driven up through the plate into the leg to keep the caster in a firm, steady position.

RECONSTRUCT-ING AN OAK CHEST

This is the golden oak chest pictured on the cover before we went to work on it. The history of this piece is described in detail on page 4. This series of photographs presents the restoration work carried out on the finish, ball legs and hardware.

The dramatic difference between before restoration (above) and after (right) shows the results of careful work.

Our first job was to make a list of repairs, which included restoring this split ball leg. The original wood was long gone.

We began the repair by gluing new wood, cut to the size needed, to the leg "collar."

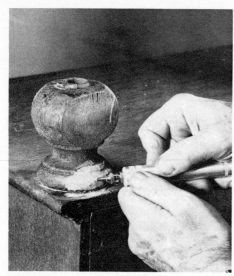

Next, using a Dremel Flex-Tool with a high-speed carving bit, we carved the new wood to match the original shape.

This is the new collar, carved and ready for sanding and staining in order to produce a smooth surface to match the existing wood.

New wood was glued to the ball of the leg, roughly cutting it to size before applying it. A pipe clamp was used as the glue dries.

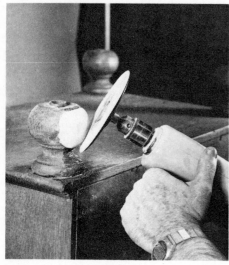

The new wood then was carved to the shape of the ball, using a sanding disc that was mounted on a portable electric drill.

This is the restored leg, stained for photographic purposes. It will get a final sanding and staining later, when we finish the chest.

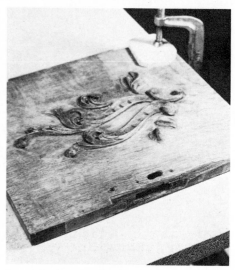

Second on the list of repairs on the oak chest is the edge of the door, which had been splintered when pried open during the burglary.

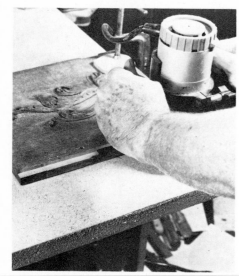

The first step in the edge repair is to cut away the splintered edge with the router, using a ¼-inch rabbetting bit.

Here you can see how the edge of the door was rabbetted. The splintered wood is gone, and is ready to receive a new piece of wood.

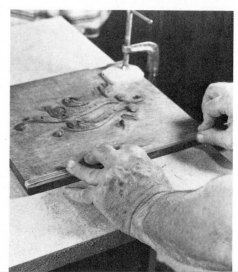

This piece of new oak, cut to fit, is fitted into the rabbeted edge. We took pains to make sure measurements and fit were exact.

This is the array of clamps used to hold the new edge as the glue dried. Spring clamps hold the piece down, while pipe and bar clamps apply pressure across the door.

A test patch of the finish indicated that the original stain was in fair condition, so we removed only the old finish, using Formby's Refinisher and steel wool pads.

This drawer has been stripped of the old finish. The old stain is sound, but it had faded, so we applied a new coat of stain to bring up the golden oak color.

It bothered us that the drawers did not have drawer guides, so we installed some by gluing on thin strips of wood.

Most of the drawer stops had disappeared, so we added new ones. You can see the refinished wood's pleasing appearance.

Refinishing the hardware came next. It was solid brass, but in bad condition. Each piece was first polished on the wire brush wheel.

If the hardware had been only dirty, we might have skipped the wire brushing and simply cleaned it with a good metal polish.

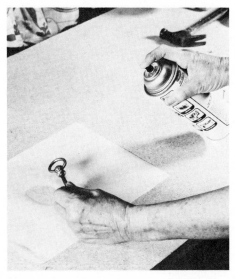

After bringing the brass to a lovely glow, we sprayed each piece with clear lacquer to protect it from dirt and hard use.

These little pieces were too small to hold in our hands for spraying, so we set them up on nails that served as steady supports.

6
Saving the Old Finish

Don't strip away the old finish on a piece of furniture unless you absolutely have to. That's the sound advice we have had time and time again from professional furniture restorers.

There are a number of good reasons be-hind this advice. For one thing, you become involved in a messy job with hazardous chemicals. For another, the final result can depend on what type of stain was used and how it affected the wood. If it was a water stain and soaked deeply but irregularly into the wood, it may be impossible to remove the stain in those areas where it went deep. In the places where it did not soak in, the stain may come off, leaving a patchy look that will be difficult to restain to an even color. Other types of stains will come off, but most professionals feel that stripped wood — and especially wood that has been stripped by harsh hot tank methods — is never quite the same.

Perhaps this is just their love for good woods coming to the fore. Or perhaps they are just more fussy than necessary. But we have come to feel the same way. We don't take off the old finish unless it is absolutely necessary.

THE BEAUTY OF AGED WOOD
Patina
One of the nice features of old furniture is the lovely patina that develops. As a piece ages, it mellows. The wood dries. The old finish deepens in color. The surface wood under the finish deepens in color. Good wood and good finishes age with grace. The entire effect is a rich, warm, mellow look. When you strip away the old finish, the mellow look disappears. No matter how good a job of refinishing is done, the new finish is still *new*, and looks it. The aging process must start all over again.

Distressed Wood
Most people say they want their furniture to look new, but in fact they don't. Furniture manufacturers know this, which is

Most furniture you buy today is distressed in some way. This chair, about two years old, was given a distressed appearance by flecking the finish with darker stain and by brushing distress marks on.

Here you can see slashing brush marks across the arm diagonally. Further distressing could have been done by striking a heavy chain a few times on different areas of the chair to make irregular dents.

why the greater majority of fine furniture offered in the show rooms today has been "distressed" to one degree or another. Distressing is a fine art that gives new furniture an old, warm look. One salesman, who described this look as "loved and lived with," came close to the truth.

Distressing Techniques Distressing consists of prematurely aging the furniture. One technique is to splatter the finish with "fly specks" of dark coloring. Look closely at furniture sold in the shops and you will see the tiny dots applied in this manner to the surface. You can do this yourself by dipping a toothbrush in dark stain, holding the brush a foot or so away from a furniture surface, and flicking the fly specks on the finish by running your finger over the bristles.

Another technique is chaining. An expert at the factory attacks the furniture with a length of chain, judiciously denting it by just the right amount. Too much denting ruins it; the right amount gives the piece that lived-with look. This is not done as often as splattering, but it is done.

A third technique is shading by means of glazing, to give the appearance of age and wear. During the finishing process, a colored glaze is applied (by hand wiping in expensive furniture, and by spraying in less-expensive pieces). The glaze is applied to edges and outer areas and carefully feathered into the lighter original finish to provide highlights. The general effect is that normal wear has worn away the darker finish — or conversely, that an accumulation of dirt has darkened some areas.

All of this is carefully and expertly done, so that the new piece takes on a simulated patina of age, but doesn't look old and beat up. This is a carefully made distinction. The furniture maker has to judge how much distressing is too much. The important point is that the maker understands his customers. They want some of the gloss and perfection of the new piece removed. They want the piece to have some of the character that comes with maturing.

The decision is very subjective, and one that is hard to give advice about. Some finishes, of course, will be in such bad condition that the decision is easy. But many will be borderline cases. Our feeling is that you should lean toward saving the finish. Make the necessary finish repairs; apply the final coat of wax or lemon oil; then put the piece into use. After a few weeks, you'll know whether the decision is right or not. You can still strip and refinish the furniture if you feel it is necessary.

Finishes That Should Look New

There are some old finishes that should have a polished look of perfection. A shellac finish, and particularly the so-called French polish finish, is typical. The Chinese lacquer finish is another of these. And so is the deep-gloss varnish finish, made with a number of coats of clear varnish and polished to a mirror finish. (This is the finish you see in TV commercials for furniture wax. The camera shows you the reflection of the user in the table top and points out that no competitive product can produce this degree of shine.)

Such finishes usually are not distressed, and the owner hopes they will be just as polished and mirror-like on their hundredth birthday as they were when new. You may be restoring such a piece. If so, you still should save the old finish if possible, but you may not want the natural distressing that has occurred. In this case, a total refinishing may be the answer.

REPAIR SEQUENCE

You should be able to make most finish repairs using one or more of the techniques presented in this chapter. To simplify your problems, look on each blemish as a separate problem, and finish one problem before going on to the next. Take care of a foggy or alligatored finish first. Then work on dents and gouges. Next, work on scratches and minor blemishes. And finally, remember that your repairs need not be absolutely perfect. A certain amount of distressing is not only allowable, but even desirable.

IDENTIFYING THE EXISTING FINISH

Ask yourself: How was it done? What materials were used? Are these materials available today? Can you successfully repair this kind of finish?

The chief reason for identifying the finish is that when you make repairs on it, you should use the same finishing material. If you apply a varnish to a lacquer, or lacquer to shellac, strange things might happen because of the incompatibility of the materials. You might get blistering, a sticky finish that never dries, or some odd colorations. What happens depends on which chemicals were used in making the finishes, but as a general rule you can assume that nothing good will come of mixing types of finishes.

Types of Finishes

In identifying the kind of finish on furniture, it helps to know a little history about the types of finishes.

Shellac Shellac was developed as a furniture finish about 1800, and for the next 50 years, just about every manufactured (as opposed to custom-made) piece of furniture was finished in shellac. Its use continued for another 70 years, but during this time, other finishes also were used. If you know the piece was made between 1800 and 1850, you can be pretty sure the finish is shellac.

Lacquer After World War I, there was a great movement to improve the manufacture of furniture— improve it, that is, from the viewpoint of the maker. Before the war, furniture assembly lines had been developed. But in the five to ten years after the war, the process was speeded up.

One of the major events in this speedup was the development first of commercial lacquer (an offshoot of ammunitions manufacture in World War I) and later of lacquer that could be sprayed on. These products cut the long drying times needed for earlier finishing materials. As a result, most of the furniture made after the mid-1920s was finished in lacquer.

Synthetics Beginning in the mid-1960s, paint chemistry took some new quantum leaps with the development of synthetic varnishes and new lacquer formulations. If your furniture piece was produced after that time, it could have one of these newer finishes.

Testing for Finish

To determine what the finish is before beginning to work on it, you can conduct tests employing two solvents, denatured alcohol and lacquer thinner.

Denatured Alcohol Paint stores carry denatured alcohol for use in thinning shellac. Find an inconspicuous spot on the furniture (the underside of a runner or rung) and clean off all wax, if you haven't already done so. Now moisten a small cotton swab or a soft cloth with denatured alcohol and rub the area. Rub for at least 10 minutes, remoistening the applicator regularly. If the finish is shellac, it will soften. You will see some of it on the applicator, and it will tend to spread over the surface you are rubbing. If it does not soften, then you know you have another kind of finish — possibly varnish or lacquer.

Lacquer Thinner Next, apply lacquer thinner in the same manner. (Be sure to use the denatured alcohol first, then the lacquer thinner. Denatured alcohol will not affect a lacquer finish, but lacquer thinner may soften shellac.) Lacquer thinner will readily soften a lacquer finish, but will not affect a varnish.

Varnish By applying these two tests you go through a process of elimination, and discover whether the finish is shellac, lacquer or neither. If the answer is neither, you probably have a varnish. Not much factory-made furniture was varnished because varnishing is a slow and delicate process, but the piece may have been custom-made, or it may have been refinished at a later date by someone like yourself who used varnish.

Bare Wood There is one other older finish to look for — bare wood finished with nothing more than linseed oil or wax. If the piece appears to have no finish coat at all, this could be what you have. Some of these pieces were stained, and some weren't. The final finish was oil or wax, applied generously and rubbed in. Many such pieces have a heavy buildup of finish, and if they haven't been cared for, an equally large collection of surface dirt that has clung to the oil or wax.

This finish presents problems. Because no new finish will adhere to the wax or oil, the old finish must be completely removed. Use mineral spirits or remove the wax, and a paint remover to take off the linseed oil. If the oil or wax has soaked into the wood to any great depth, removal may be very difficult.

Modern Finishes There is a whole spate of modern synthetic varnishes and resins, and they all have one outstanding characteristic. They are tougher than their earlier cousins and wear very well in normal, everyday use. However, some of them, such as the penetrating resins, soak down into the wood and can be nearly impossible to take off.

Because of their toughness, these finishes are much more likely to be in pretty good shape, so you probably won't have to remove them. Not much manufactured furniture is being finished in these synthetics; lacquer is still the favorite. But the paint chemists are at work on ways to get these products to dry faster. As the drying time decreases, more manufacturers will use them.

TESTING AND REPAIRING THE SOUNDNESS OF THE FINISH

Before starting to heal those visible wounds such as dents, water stains and cigarette burns, make sure that the present finish is sound. If not, it must be removed, procedures for which are discussed in the next chapter. Once in a while, you'll find a finish that looks pretty good, but actually has become dry and brittle and will flake away from the wood under any kind of pressure. Or it has absorbed dirt and skin oil and has become gummy. The latter defect is found on the arms of wood chairs. People have sat in these chairs with their hands and arms resting on the surface and their skin oil has penetrated the finish.

Brittle Finishes

To test for brittleness in a finish, draw the bottom of a spoon bowl across the surface. Press the bowl down fairly hard as you do. If the finish is adhering properly, you will see a mark left by the spoon, but the finish will stay in place. If the finish has become brittle, the pressure of the spoon bowl will cause the finish to flake and break away from the surface.

When you observe flaking, you know that the finish will have problems in the near future. Normal everyday wear will

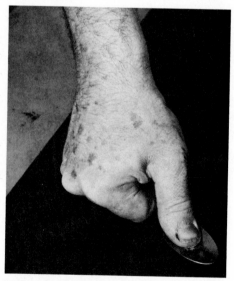

To determine the brittleness of a finish, press hard on the bowl of a spoon as you draw it across the surface. If the finish is brittle, it will crack and flake along the line you draw.

soon cause a similar flaking and you will be faced with refinishing then. The best choice is to remove the old finish now and apply a new one before the trouble starts. Sometimes only partial areas on the piece will be subject to this flaking, while the remainder is still sound. This could be caused by a tabletop being exposed to the sun for a long period, or the side of a dresser spending some years next to a heater.

How Much to Remove Ascertain just how far the brittleness extends, and remove only the dried finish on that part. Perhaps you will have to refinish the top of a table, but won't have to touch the aprons and legs. Or in the case of a dresser or chest, you may need to refinish only one side.

However, to keep the repair from being too obvious, always refinish a whole side or top, even if the brittleness occurs only on a part of it. While the newly finished section may be slightly different in color than the rest of the piece, a visitor won't usually see it. If you refinish only a part of the top or side, the difference in color may be very obvious.

Gummy Finishes

Use your fingernail to test for a gummy finish. The gummy area usually is darker than the rest of the finish, and if you scrape the dark area with your fingernail, you will plow a tiny furrow through it and pick up gum under your nail. As we said, this problem usually occurs on wood surfaces that come in contact with parts of the body.

Cleaning Away the Gum If you used mineral spirits to clean the wax from the piece, some or all of the gum may have already come off. If you didn't do it before, clean the area with mineral spirits or other wax remover now. Moisten a cloth with the solvent and rub the area clean. When the gum is all gone, you'll find the edge of the old finish. That is, the old gummy finish will come away from the wood, but at some point, the original finish is good enough to adhere. At this point, you will see the edge of the old finish.

Some refinishers sand this edge, feathering it into the bare wood, and then coat the entire segment (the chair arm, for example) with new finish. This works if the bare wood under the gummy finish hasn't discolored. If it has, and this procedure is followed, you end up with a visible discoloration under the new finish coat.

If the Wood is Affected When the wood in the clean area is darker than the rest of the arm, try to restore the color before applying a new finish coat. One way is to sand the bare area with a very fine abrasive paper, removing a tiny amount of the wood surface. If the discoloration is only on the surface, this will restore the old color. However, it also may remove some of the stain and lighten the color too much, so do this carefully: sand a little, then wipe the area clean to observe how much change is occurring.

Complete Removal Another solution is to remove the old finish from the entire arm, then refinish the arm, taking care to match the color of the other arm as closely as possible. Many people find this easier than patching, and get better results because they achieve an even color on the refinished arm.

HOW TO REMOVE STAINS AND BLEMISHES ON THE SURFACE

Some stains and blemishes don't penetrate the finish, but remain on the surface. You also may find foreign substances adhering to the surface, such as flecks of paint or glue. These can be removed by gentle scraping with the blade of a small pocket knife.

Scrape with care. You don't want to dig down into the finish, but simply want to dislodge the foreign substance. Don't apply downward pressure to the blade, but use a horizontal movement instead. Most of the time, the foreign material will flake away, leaving the finish beneath it intact.

Stubborn Substances If the substance has bonded itself to the finish and refuses to flake away, it may be removed by abrasion. Use an abrasive swab, made by wrapping fine steel wool around the end of a toothpick, or shape a very small pad of find abrasive paper for the job. Work on the blemish itself, not the entire surface of the furniture. Remember that you want to keep the finish whole, so don't rub hard enough to wear through it. Just work to remove the foreign substance. This isn't always easy, but it can be done.

Another method is to rub the area with a fine abrasive such as pumice and oil. Pour a few drops of fine bicycle oil on the blemish; then sprinkle the oil with powdered pumice. Rub the mixture over the stain with your bare finger or a small pad. Check frequently to see if the stain is disappearing, and stop rubbing as soon as it is gone. If you continue rubbing too long, you will remove the finish.

Another handy tool for making repairs in a finish is the abrasive swab — a small wad of steel wool wrapped around the toothpick.

There are dark surface stains on this table leaf. They look like old paint or similar substance. The blade of a sharp pocket knife is the best tool for removing this kind of stain. Simply scrape across the surface and lift off the stain.

HOW TO REMOVE STAINS THAT PENETRATE THE FINISH

Some of the repair techniques we are going to suggest are quite simple, while others take some practice and experience. We suggest that you practice on scrap wood with any technique. After a few sessions on the scrap material, you can undertake the actual repair on your project.

You can't always tell whether a stain

Once you have patched an area, stain it to match the existing stain. Sometimes a small artist's brush is the ideal tool for the job.

has remained on the surface or penetrated the finish. To be on the safe side, first try the scraping technique discussed under "Surface Stains" above. If that doesn't work, the stain probably has penetrated the finish and perhaps even gone into the wood itself. The only solution then is to apply mild abrasion until the stain disappears. This means removing the finish from the area.

Work the abrasive (pumice and oil, or fine sandpaper) until the stain is gone. Then examine the area to see what has happened. There are two possibilities.

Shallow Stain You have removed both the finish and the objectionable stain but have scraped down to the wood. The coloring of the wood, however, is still good. To complete the repair, clean away all abrasive material and apply a coat of the same finish (varnish, shellac, lacquer) material. Use an artist's brush for the job, and brush out the edges of the patch so that the edges won't create ridges when the

patch dries. Use several coats, and allow each to dry thoroughly before applying the next. After the final coat has dried, sand the area with superfine abrasive paper (8/0 to 10/0 grade), blending the patched area into the rest of the finish. Once you have cleaned away the abrasive residue and applied a coat of wax, the patch is finished.

Deep Stain You have removed the finish and the objectionable stain, but find that the coloring stain is also gone, and the exposed wood is its natural color. The solution is to restain the wood, then refinish the patch as described in the preceding paragraph. The tricky part is to find the right color of stain. Use a scrap of the same kind of wood, and try different colors, coating each with finish material. When the finish has dried, match these colors to the furniture, and use the closest one. Keep in mind that the old wood won't take the stain in exactly the same way as the new wood; the stain probably will be darker on the old wood.

HOW TO REMOVE CIGARETTE BURNS

A cigarette burn is an ugly thing that may or may not be a serious repair problem, depending on the depth of the burn. In the best cases, the burn damages only the finish itself. In the worst cases, the burn goes down into the wood and produces a charred trench.

Surface Burns

In this case, the repair is the same as for a surface blemish or stain. Scrape or sand away the damaged finish. If the wood under the finish has not been damaged or discolored, you can refinish the spot successfully.

Deep Burns

A deep burn extends beneath the finish.

A cigarette burned the edge of this table leaf to make a black char about ¾ in. long. To repair it, scrape with the sharp blade of a pocket knife.

The wood near the surface usually is charred black, and the charred wood must be removed.

Step 1: Removing the Char Use your pocket knife blade to carefully scrape the char away. Keep at it until undamaged wood appears. (You also can use a little hand grinder for this work, with an abrasive wheel in the chuck.)

Step 2: Filling in the Area When you have removed the char, you will have an indentation, sometimes fairly deep. The remainder of the repair consists of filling this indentation and then refinishing the surface. If the indentation is shallow, you may be able to use varnish, shellac or lacquer as the filler. If it is deep, you

should use stick shellac, stick lacquer or other filler.

A shallow dent To fill the shallow dent, paint coat after coat of the finish material (the same material the piece is now finished with) into the indentation. Use an artist's brush, and allow each coat to dry before applying the next one. This is a slow process, and you could apply several dozen layers, but the result is worth the effort. Note that this works best when all the blackened area has been removed. If any black remains, it may show through the patch.

A deep dent To fill a deep indentation, use the same techniques as for any dent or gouge, described below.

The scraping takes longer than you might think. The surface char comes off easily. Then, keep scraping until all signs of black discoloration are gone. In most cases, a little stain restores the color after scraping. If the char is very deep, use stick shellac to fill the crater.

WORKING ON THE 1852 DRESSER This marble-topped 1852 dresser requires extensive restoration work. Much of the frame needs regluing, some of the drawers need to be rebuilt, veneers on the front must be replaced, and the entire piece needs to be refinished.

1 The work begins with the removal of the hardware. These drawers are in excellent condition.

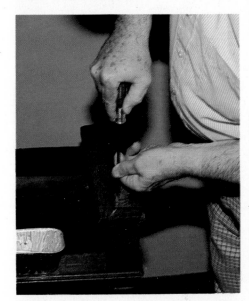

2 Next we took off the casters. There is a hole under each, indicating that these were not the ones used when the dresser was new. The hole accommodated the neck of the original. We will try to find substitutes for the old ones.

3 One of the most important problems that this dresser has is the missing veneer strips along the sides of the drawer openings. We must find replacement veneer that is of the same kind of wood.

4 Before restoration can begin we must disassemble the dresser. After removing the screws beneath the marble top, we can lift off the section. The marble pieces need minimal work.

Project continued on next page

5 Inspect a piece carefully so you do not overlook necessary repairs. These small drawers and their glides need only to be refinished. Some drawer stops, however, will have to be reglued or replaced.

6 The base plates look bad. Should we replace them? We decide that the wood is sound, and only the appearance is bad. It is important in restoration to retain as much of the original wood as possible, hence the decision to sand and replace these base plates. Note the old square nails, a good clue to age. These nails were not used much after 1890, and not at all after 1895.

7 The old square nails have been left in and are now hammered into place as the base plate is glued back on the dresser.

8 Now we reglue those frame members which need it, using a brush to apply the glue that has been squeezed into the aluminum dish.

9 We need a variety of clamps to glue the dresser joints together. Notice the small wood pads that protect the finish of the dresser from the jaws of the clamps.

10 Clamps and more clamps — every joint we have glued is firmly clamped, the real secret of successful gluing.

REPAIRING BROKEN VENEER

The most common repair of veneered surfaces is replacement of areas, usually near an edge, where the veneer has broken away. You seldom have the old pieces to reglue. Instead, you must use new veneer.

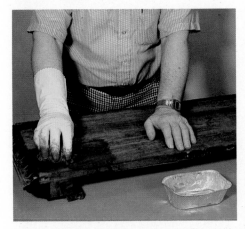

1 Buy veneer of the same wood. To aid in matching the new and old wood, we first strip the finish off the area to be repaired so we can see the actual color of the old veneer.

2 Stripped of its old finish, the veneer near the repair area shows its true color — the color we must attempt to match. Note that while we stripped away the varnish, we used refinisher and thus did not remove the stain.

3 We applied stain to a corner of the new veneer to match it to the old. As you can see, the color is a very close match.

4 The broken area has irregular edges which must be trimmed away. Using a metal straightedge and a small craft knife, we trim the patch to a rectangular shape.

5 The old veneer within the rectangular cut is removed by lifting with a sharp wood chisel.

Project continued on next page

6 The repair area is now ready for new veneer. It is a clean rectangle in shape and all the old veneer has been removed.

7 The next step is to cut a small cardboard pattern. Cut and fit until the cardboard is an exact fit in the repair area. Use the pattern to cut out the patch. Move it around the veneer sheet until you find an area where the grain of the new veneer closely matches that of the veneer remaining on the old surface. Now use a straightedge and either a veneer saw or a craft knife to cut out the patch, carefully following the cardboard pattern as you cut.

8 Check the veneer patch for size by placing it in the repair area. When it is perfect, coat the area to be repaired and the underside of the veneer patch with contact cement. Allow both to dry for at least an hour.

9 After the contact cement has dried for at least an hour and is no longer sticky, place the patch in the repair area and roll it down. Apply plenty of pressure as you roll.

10 After the contact cement has set for a couple of hours, you can apply stain to the patch and the area around it. This is a demonstration project. If you were working on this table insert, you would have stripped the entire surface, and now would stain the whole surface so that the color would be even all over.

11 The patch is difficult to see. To hide it further, a second light application of stain might be necessary after the first has dried. Finish by lightly sanding, then applying varnish or lacquer.

12 Another common veneer problem is when the veneer lifts from the base wood, as it has here. This table leaf was soaked during a flood and now must be restored.

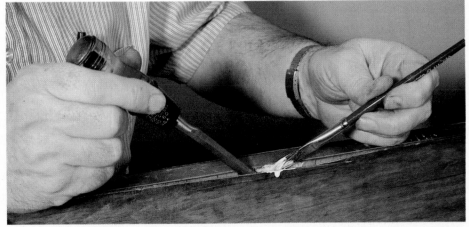

13 Examination shows the veneer to be lifted for only an inch or so in from the edge. The repair consists of working white glue into the opening. Use a brush. Hold the work vertical and apply plenty of glue so that it can run to the depth needed.

14 The final step is to clamp the repair area, using two long, flat boards and C-clamps. Tighten the clamps as much as possible. Wipe off all glue which is squeezed out with a damp cloth. Don't allow any to remain on the surface as it will interfere with later refinishing.

15 Once in a while, veneer will bubble up in the center of a veneered piece. Many times, a simple repair can be achieved by applying a hot iron to the bubble. Place a dry wash cloth on the bubble and press the iron to the area. Be careful not to hold it too long, as it may affect the finish.

REMOVING STAINS BY BLEACHING

In those cases where the objectionable stain penetrated both the finish and the wood, you must sand or cut away wood to get rid of it. This will leave an indentation that you don't want. In the case of a deep stain, bleaching may come in handy, because instead of destroying wood to eliminate the deep stain, you may be able to bleach it out and save the wood.

SAFETY PROCEDURES

You can use several bleaches— common household bleach, full-strength ammonia or oxalic acid. They are all hazardous to some degree, so take precautions. Always wear rubber gloves, and always wear safety glasses. This may be a nuisance, but it makes very good sense. You could burn your skin or lose your eyesight if any of the bleach accidently splashes, and even experienced hands have accidental spills and splashes.

We don't recommend ammonia because its strong odor can overcome you. We do recommend a regular chlorinated household bleach. If that doesn't work, you can progress to oxalic acid, keeping in mind that it is strong and can do damage to both you and your furniture. Use it accordingly. Follow the instructions on the label to make the oxalic acid solution— and follow them exactly.

GUIDELINES

Here are some things you must know when bleaching.

1. The surface to be bleached should be free of all wax and other foreign substances, including the finish coat, so that the bleach can penetrate evenly.
2. Once the bleaching is finished, the bleached area must be neutralized and all residue removed. Otherwise the bleach will act on your new finish. Mix a cup of borax in a quart of hot water, allow the mixture to cool, and apply it to the bleached area with a cotton swab. Blot the area with absorbent paper; then apply clear water with the swab to rinse. Blot again, and allow the area to dry for at least 24 hours.
3. If any of the bleach ever comes in contact with your skin, rinse it with clear water. Don't wait. Do it instantly. The longer the bleach stays on the skin, the greater the danger of burning.
4. If any bleach splashes into your eyes—

1 The black marks on this surface were caused by water. They are in the wood, not just in the finish. To get rid of them, you need these materials for bleaching: a two-part wood bleach you can buy at your home center; some vinegar; a lot of cotton swabs; and three little cups. The cups we use came from a photo developing kit and are numbered. This makes it easy to remember where each chemical is.

2 Begin by applying Chemical A from the kit, as directed. Remember that these are powerful and dangerous chemicals. Wear rubber gloves and eye protection (in case of accidental splashing) and follow the manufacturer's directions exactly as written.

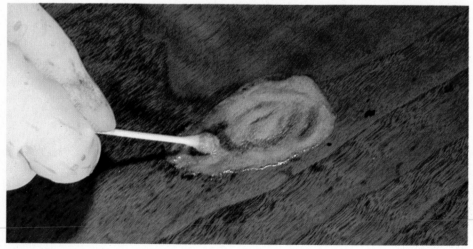

3 After the specified time, use a cotton swab to apply Chemical B from the kit. There will be a white foaming action.

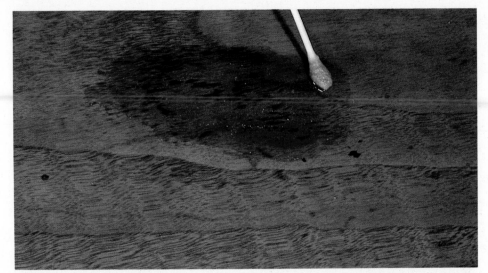

4 As a final treatment, apply vinegar and water to the spot to neutralize the other chemicals. Use a mixture of two parts water and one part vinegar. After a few minutes, blot up the vinegar and allow the spot to dry.

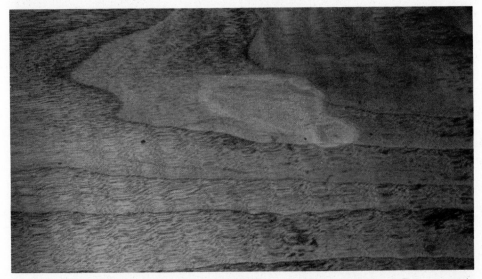

5 Here is the spot after drying. You can see that the black marks have disappeared. There was stain on this surface and it, too, is gone. Your first refinishing step will be to stain this spot first to bring its color level up. Allow it to dry, then apply a coat of stain to the whole top.

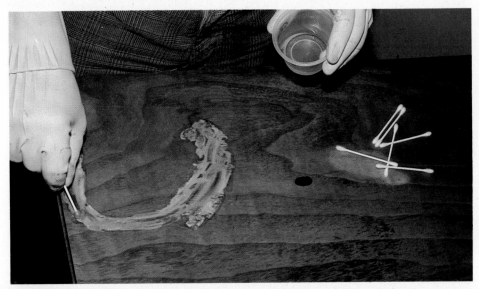

6 We think a flower pot made this semicircular mark. We used the bleach here, too, and on some other spots on the top. It worked nicely wherever it was used.

even the tiniest drop— wash them out immediately with clear water in an eye cup. Then go directly to your doctor or hospital emergency room. Do not take any chances. The danger may be slight, but *you* can't judge it. Let a professional take care of it.

5. Do not sand any wood that has been bleached until the bleach has been neutralized and rinsed away. This is because the sanding dust will contain fine particles of the bleach that you will inhale— and you certainly don't want a powerful bleach at work in your nasal passages and lungs.

6. If any bleach gets inside of your rubber gloves or splashes on your clothing, take the glove or clothing off quickly and rinse the skin area with clear water. The fabric may make the danger of burn greater by holding the bleach against the skin like a poultice.

Bleach in Stripping

The use of bleach to lighten the color of wood in a small area has been described. Bleach also is used to lighten the wood color of furniture that has been stripped of the old finish. It can get rid of stain that the stripping did not remove, and it can lighten the color of wood that may have been darkened in the stripping process. However, bleaching an entire piece of furniture is quite different from bleaching a small patch. The job is a lot bigger, and you use much more bleach. Because you handle so much bleach, the big job is more hazardous.

7 Here are the newly bleached areas. Bleaching also can be used to remove stains which have soaked deeply into the wood.

Project continued on next page

8 Now the top is ready for refinishing. First sand thoroughly. Since it is already reasonably smooth, use a fine paper and don't sand too much.

9 Following sanding, wipe the surface clean with a tack rag. Lean on the rag so that it digs the sanding dust out of the grain.

10 We decided to use a gelled stain here. Gelled stains are the easiest to apply and control. Use clean cheesecloth as an applicator.

11 Apply the stain like shoe polish. Use a thin coat and spread it pretty well by rubbing it out. You can keep the color even simply by not applying too much in any one spot. If a place looks too dark, rub it out with a clean cheesecloth pad, removing excess stain. Wait fifteen minutes after covering the whole surface; then wipe again to pick up stain which has not been absorbed. Allow the surface to dry overnight. If you want it a shade darker, apply another coat the next day.

STAINING AND FINISHING A RESTORED PIECE

Once a piece is completely restored, it is time to work on the finish. There are several methods to use, but the order remains basically the same. You must remove the old finish, restain (if necessary), refinish and hand rub.

1 Using a furniture refinisher (Formby, Hope, Squaw Alley brands) and 0000 steel wool, we strip away the old finish, leaving the original stain and the wood's patina.

2 After taking off the old finish, the piece is sanded with fine paper. Old wood is dry and sands quickly, so don't overdo it. Watch the surface as you work to check progress.

3 Remove all traces of sanding dust by wiping with a tack rag. Press hard to get all dust out of the wood grain, and keep wiping until the tack rag stays clean when you wipe an area.

4 We chose a liquid wiping stain for this job but could have used a jelled stain. The first step is to apply a light coat of stain to each part of the piece and allow it to stand for ten minutes.

5 Next, wipe the stain thoroughly to expose the grain of the wood and achieve the proper color. Allow the stain to dry overnight before putting on the final finish.

Project continued on next page

6

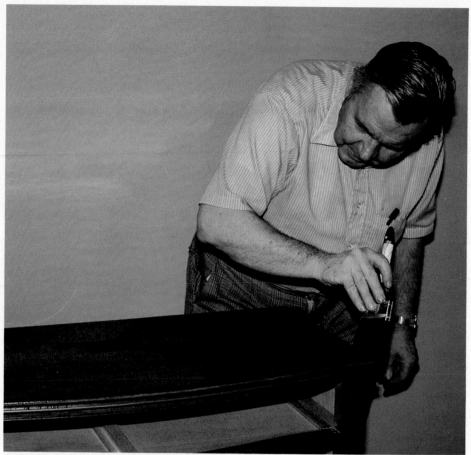

7

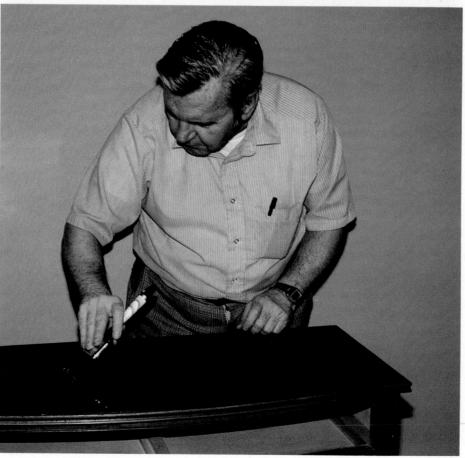

8

6 Sand the surface before applying varnish. This should be a light treatment. Then clean away the dust with a tack cloth.

7 With light on opposite side of the surface, you can observe how the varnish is going down, and spot areas your brush has missed.

8 Varnish is laid down with the brush, not brushed out. You want a good coat, fairly heavy, evenly applied across the surface.

9 There are two ways to achieve that lovely hand-rubbed final finish. The first is to use pumice and light oil rubbed with a felt pad. On this drawer, which has three coats of clear polyurethane varnish, we have sprinkled pumice, and are now adding a few drops of light oil.

10 With a felt pad mounted in the hand sander, the pumice and oil mixture is rubbed over the surface. This treatment will knock off any dust bumps, level the finish, and get rid of any gloss. Pumice is a mild abrasive but don't over rub or you may cut through the finish.

12 The second method of hand rubbing is with wet-and-dry sandpaper (400 to 600 grit) and water. A sprinkling bottle used for dampening clothes for ironing is handy for applying the water.

11 After rubbing the surface out, wipe it thoroughly with a soft cloth to clean up all remnants of the pumice and oil. When you finish, you should feel no oil on the surface, which should be extremely smooth and have a soft, warm color.

13 Rub sufficiently to produce a completely smooth, gloss-free surface, using light hand pressure. Be sure to keep an even pressure on the sander. Finally, wipe the surface dry and finish with a lemon oil or paste wax treatment.

RESTORING AN OLD SETH THOMAS CLOCK

This old Seth Thomas clock has been sitting in a sunny window for years. Heat and light had reduced the finish to a maze of tiny cracks and alligatoring. The top appeared to have no finish at all.

1 Before attempting to refinish, we must determine what kind of finish is on it. The testing procedure is to try a small area first with denatured alcohol, then with lacquer thinner. Alcohol here is applied with a cotton swab.

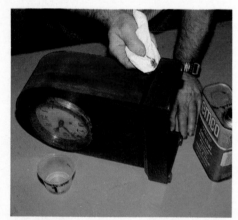

2 After about two minutes, the finish appears to be softening. A cheesecloth pad is rubbed across the area to test it.

3 The denatured alcohol has softened the finish, which indicates that the finish is shellac. If it had been lacquer or varnish, the denatured alcohol would not have affected it.

4 Reamalgamation is a technique for repairing scratches and alligatored surfaces in shellac and lacquer finishes. Here, the old clock is reamalgamated by saturating the surface with denatured alcohol and keeping it wet for a few minutes, until the old finish melts. The alcohol is applied by means of a soft pad.

5 As we apply the denatured alcohol to the top of the clock an interesting event occurs. The top looked like bare wood. Now, however, the old finish reappears as alcohol is applied to it.

6 The line between the dried out finish and the reamalgamated area is clearly visible. The clock is beginning to look more like its old self.

7 The reamalgamation is continued on the front of the clock. Reamalgamation is useful for eliminating scratches on shellac and varnished surfaces. Gently treat the scratch with solvent, using a cotton swab to first soften and then spread the finish.

8 We have decided that time (some 75 years) and the reamalgamation have resulted in a finish that is too thin. We decide to apply a new shellac finish. We first sand the old finish with fine paper to remove any blemishes.

9 Shellac will fill sandpaper quickly so keep a toothbrush handy to clean the paper frequently.

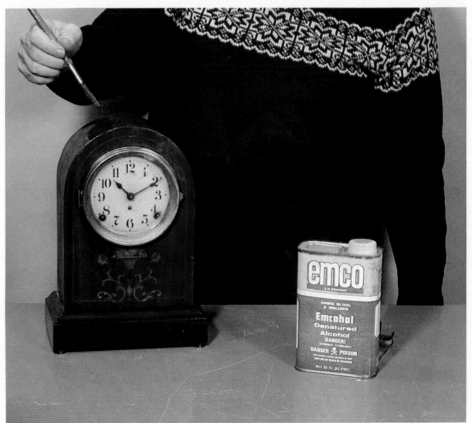

10 When shellacking, use a top quality brush and gently lay the coating on. Don't brush it out, as you would with paint. Here, a 3-pound cut of shellac is used straight from the can, and we plan on 4 coats. If you use a 1 or 2-pound cut, increase the number of coats.

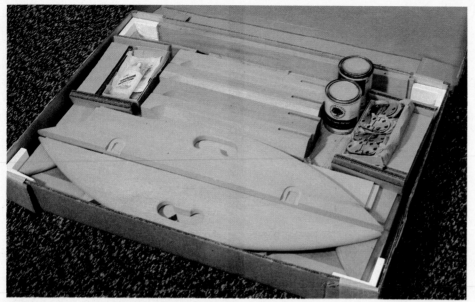

1 Furniture kits arrive at your house neatly packed in cartons. This one is the Heathkit Butler's Table, and the box contains all wood parts, hardware, stain and varnish, beautifully detailed plan and instruction sheets, and even such items as drill bits, drill bit depth gauge, and sandpaper.

2 The most important task in finishing finewood kits (this one is in solid mahogany) is the sanding. Each face of each piece must be thoroughly sanded, first with 220 grit and then with 280 grit sandpaper. This can be done by hand, but it would be a long job. The sander we used is a "finish" sander, made especially for furniture finishing. It is small, square in shape, and orbits at 10,000 rpm. You can use a regular oscillating sander for most of the work.

3 To sand the small grooves on the front corners of the legs, we made a sanding block and did the job by hand. The sanding block is a piece of wood that fits the grooves.

4 All of the table joints are mortise-and-tenon. After you have finished sanding all parts, the base is assembled dry. During this assembly, you probably will have to sand the tenons a bit to make them fit. Note that we have placed a soft bath towel on the workbench to protect the sanded parts as we work.

HOW TO BUILD A PIECE OF UNFINISHED FURNITURE

In recent years, unfinished furniture kits featuring fine designs and hardwood construction have become more and more popular. The kits come complete with all the tools and with instructions. All that is required is patience and care to create a fine piece of furniture for the home.

5 Sand each tenon carefully so as not to change its shape or the face of the adjoining wood, then fit it into its mortise.

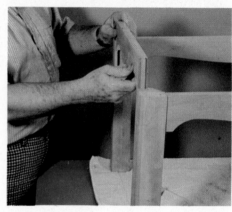

6 Assemble the table base without glue. Here the last side rail goes into place after the tenon was sanded to fit.

7 Now each leg and rail is numbered, so that when they are reassembled for gluing, you will get each tenon in the mortise.

8 To glue the pieces of the base together, a thin bead of glue is applied to the side walls of each mortise. No glue is put on the tenons. Be careful not to use too much glue, and do not allow it to get on the surface of the wood.

9 The rail is fitted into the mortise after glue was applied. If necessary, tap the rail in place with a rubber mallet. If any glue squeezes out, wipe it immediately with a well-dampened cloth. A better way is to allow the squeezed out glue to dry, and then trim it away with a single-edge razor blade. The best way is to use only enough glue so that none squeezes out.

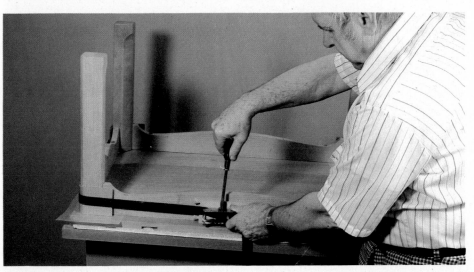

10 When the base has been assembled and glued, place it on an absolutely level surface and apply a web clamp. Let the glue dry overnight.

11 Now place the table top face down on the towel on the workbench and position the base (with the glue now dried) in the center. Measure the distance from the edge of the top to each rail to be sure the location is correct.

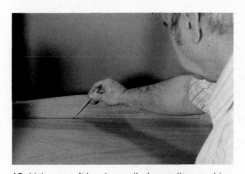

12 Using a soft lead pencil, draw a line marking the inside dimensions of the base on the table top. Be careful not to move the base during this operation or you will have to stop and remeasure its position.

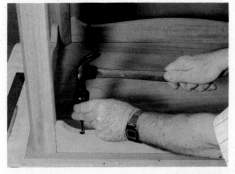

13 Now insert a scribe, a long nail or any other sharp, thin tool in each of the screw holes in each rail. Tap the scribe enough to make an indentation in the table top.

14 Lubricate the screws by rubbing each in a bar of face soap before driving. Place the tip of the bit in each indentation on the table top, with the depth gauge in place. Holding the depth gauge with a pliers, drill straight down as deep as the gauge will permit. When the drilling is finished, you have pre-drilled the holes for the screws which will hold the top on the base.

15 Next place the side leaves of the table on the bench beside the top and fit the brass hinges into the cutouts. The fit will be snug and you may have to try a hinge several times to find a cutout that is right for it.

16 Once all hinges have been located, use the scribe to scratch a number on the back of each, and pencil a corresponding number on the wood of the cutout.

17 Again using the depth gauge on the drill bit, drill a hole for each hinge screw. There are 6 holes per hinge, and 8 hinges.

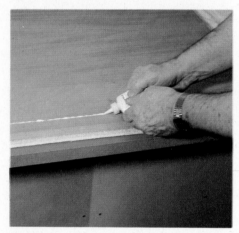

18 Remove the base from the top and with the top still on the work bench, place a thin line of glue around the table about ⅜ in. from the pencil line you drew. The glue bead should be thin, continuous and the correct distance from the guide line.

19 Now the screws are driven through the holes in the side rails and into the holes which had been drilled into the top earlier. These screws must be turned tight to pull the top into close contact with the base.

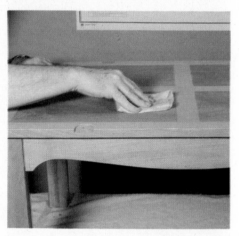

20 Whenever you prepare to apply finishing material to any part which has been sanded, wipe the entire piece with a tack cloth to eliminate all dust. To be thorough, wipe it twice, using different tack cloths. You will be surprised at how much dust comes off on the second wiping.

21 The paste stain is wiped on with a clean, soft, lint-free cloth. Stain an area about a foot square at a time. Wipe the stain on, rub it in for no more than 30 seconds, then use a clean cloth to wipe any excess stain from the area.

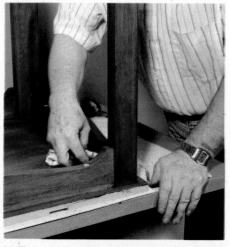

22 The staining has progressed nicely. We found it handy to have a small brush to work stain into corners and grooves. A cloth around the end of the brush handle is used for wiping these areas after staining.

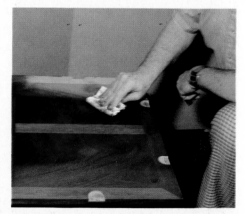

23 After the base has been stained, turn the table over and begin work on the top. The procedure is the same as before. If the color of the piece is not as dark as you want, apply a second coat of stain before varnishing, but only after the first coat has dried. A good feature of paste stains is the color control they provide. You keep applying stain until you get the color you want.

HOW TO REPAIR DENTS AND GOUGES

Most of the time, the best way to repair a serious dent or gouge is to fill it. There are a number of filler formulations now available for use on wood, and each type has its advantages and disadvantages.

TYPES OF FILLERS

The first disadvantage you will discover is one of terminology. Every formulation has its own name, they all sound alike, and none tell you very much about what's in the can. So you must read each label. The names include such terms as wood dough, wood filler, wood patch or water putty. Most are premixed and ready to use, but a few are powders that you must mix with water. There seem to be two basic formulations among the ready-mixed varieties, one based on acetone and the other on latex. There are variations within these formulas, too.

What Type Do You Use?

Wood dough, wood filler and water putty are best used in areas that aren't visible, or in furniture which is to be painted. Stick shellac or lacquer is best on furniture which is lacquered, shellacked or varnished, and where the repair is in a visible spot. Wood dough is best for deep holes (screw holes, for example), while wood filler is best for shallow dents. Both can be used to fill cracks. Whatever filler you employ, use a color that is close to the furniture finish to start with. Don't depend on later coloring to match the finish.

Wood Dough

Marketed under names such as Plastic Wood and Duratite, wood dough is made by mixing sawdust and a cellulose acetate cement. It dries quickly, can be sanded and drilled, and can be softened by lacquer thinner. Don't forget this if you are working on a lacquered piece. The dough will soften a lacquer finish if in contact with it for very long. Also, don't apply the thinner for these formulations to the surface of a patch on a lacquer surface. You will mess up the finish.

Wood dough comes in a variety of colors, and most of the brands can be stained after they have dried. It is handy stuff for filling old screw holes, building up small sections of corners which have broken off, filling deep dents, and repairing carvings on furniture. After a little practice, you become familiar with its characteristics and can use it effectively.

How to Use It As it dries, wood dough shrinks. If you fill a deep dent (¼- to ½-inch) with it, the dough will shrink during drying and leave a depression. For deep dents, apply two or three layers, allowing each to dry before putting on the next one. Always apply a little extra in the last application, so that the top is slightly rounded. Some of this will shrink. The rest is sanded down once the dough has dried.

Some of the wood doughs cannot be spread very thin or feathered at the edges of a patch. Others are creamy mixtures and will feather very well. Those that don't feather are better for filling holes; those that do feather can be used in shallow surface dents.

Wood Fillers

We are applying this name to the latex fillers. Read the labels to find products with a latex formulation. These are smooth mixtures of the consistency of cream cheese. They spread easily, feather nicely and are shrink resistant, which means they shrink less than the wood dough products.

Disguising the Patch None of the fillers exhibit a wood grain, and when used to repair furniture with a prominent grain, they will be visible. After sanding, you can disguise the repair by drawing a simulated grain across the patch with a crayon or with artist's colors and a very fine brush. Join the grain lines on either side of the patch, so that they appear continuous. Then give the patch a coat of stain, if needed, and a coat of final finish.

Most fillers come in a variety of wood and furniture colors, so you may be able to buy the exact shade you need. They also can be stained if the exact color isn't available. However, you should always test a patch of the filler with stain before applying it to your project. All fillers take stain differently from wood, and you probably will have to use a slightly different color of stain on the filler than on wood to achieve a match with the surrounding area.

Water Putty

You buy water putty in powder form and mix it with water to a creamy consistency. The mixture hardens quickly with very little shrinkage. There are dry powdered colors you can add to it, to match the wood being repaired. It, too, has no grain appearance and will show when used to repair prominently grained wood.

One excellent use for this product is as a filler after you have repaired fractured wood. Apply the putty to the edges of the crack and use it to replace any missing wood shreds. You can rebuild the broken part to its original shape and, after refinishing, you probably won't be able to see the fracture.

Stick Shellac

This is a specialty filler product, not sold everywhere. Woodworking and craft supply houses have it. What you buy are small sticks of colored hard shellac. There also are stick lacquers and stick sealing waxes available. These sticks melt when heated, and the softened material is used to fill holes and dents.

Color Choices The lacquer and the shellac can be purchased in both opaque and transparent forms, and you should be able to buy a color very close to the one you need. The best way is to buy sets of a dozen or so colors in both transparent and opaque. The sealing wax comes only in the opaque. We like stick shellac but many refinishers prefer stick lacquer.

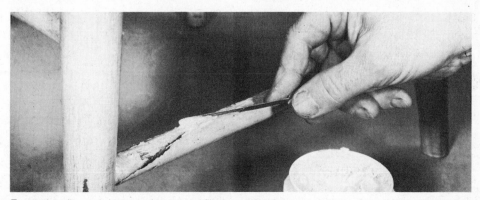

To repair splits and dents, try latex wood filler — probably the easiest repair product on the market. It accepts stain well, does not shrink much, and can be sanded when dry.

REPAIRING A DENT USING STICK SHELLAC

We always advocate practicing with any material before using it on your project, and stick shellac is no different. You can learn its characteristics and then use it to your best advantage.

Step 1: Preparing the Surface To repair a deep dent, clean out the bottom of the dent first. If the bottom is smooth, scratch it a little with the knife blade, to give the shellac a rough surface to which to adhere.

Step 2: Heating the Stick Then hold the shellac stick directly over the dent and apply a hot knife blade or soldering iron to it. The shellac will melt and drop into the dent. Allow enough shellac drip to more than fill the hole, so that the repair is a little rounded.

Step 3: Smoothing the Patch When the dent has filled, use a small flexible spatula, heated in a flame to smooth the surface. To heat the blade, use the flame from a gas stove or Sterno canned heat. Don't use a candle because carbon will gather on the blade and will discolor the patch.

Step 4: Trimming the Patch After the shellac has cooled, use a single-edge razor blade or a very sharp wide-bladed chisel to carefully trim the rounded top down to the level of the surface. The last step is to buff the surface with an 8/0 or 10/0 sandpaper.

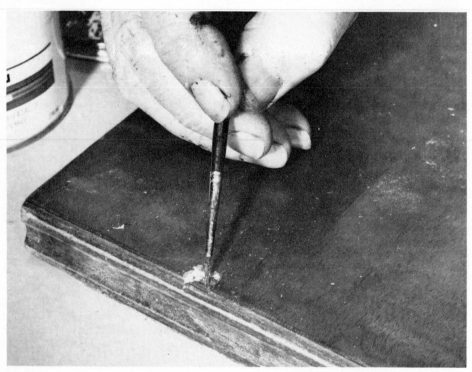

Because the wood at the bottom of the gouge is white, we begin by dabbing it with stain the approximate color of the surface. This is necessary because the stick shellac is transparent.

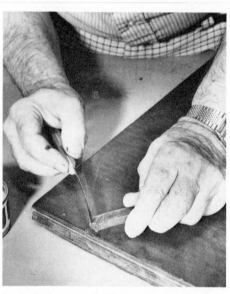

Apply the hot spatula blade to the stick of shellac as you hold it over the repair. Allow the shellac to drip into the repair or lift some of the soft shellac with the blade.

Select the color closest to the color of the finish. Light a can of Sterno or use an alcohol lamp to heat the blade of a spatula. (Do not heat by candle flame, as this will deposit carbon on the blade which will discolor the stick shellac.)

Use the spatula blade to smooth out the shellac. On an edge repair, also use it to shape the shellac to the same shape as the edge.

You will have to hold the spatula blade in the flame of the Sterno several times during the shaping to reheat it. When the blade cools, it will not work the shellac, which hardens quickly.

Keep heating the knife and smoothing the surface of the stick shellac as long as necessary. You want the surface of the patch smooth and level with the area surrounding it.

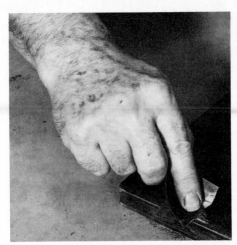

Finally, finish the job by sanding the surface of the patch with a 400 grit sandpaper. You can apply lacquer, varnish or shellac over the patch if necessary.

HOW TO STEAM A SHALLOW DENT

Sometimes a shallow dent can be steamed out of the wood, or even made to swell back to the original shape by an application of water. This technique is particularly useful if the dent is located in the middle of a table top.

Water Swelling

Apply water to the dent with an eye dropper and let the water soak into the wood. If the wood is porous and swells when wet, it may now swell enough to eliminate the dent. If the bottom of the dent is covered with unbroken lacquer or varnish, use a pin to prick the surfaces in a number of places. This allows the water to get to the wood.

Steam Swelling

Steam usually does a better job of swelling the wood than water alone. To steam a dent, apply water to the dent as in the previous paragraph. Then place a very moist cloth on the dent and touch the tip of a hot iron to it. Hold the iron in place long enough to create steam not only in the cloth but also down into the wood. This should cause swelling of the wood. One application may raise the dent, but you probably will have to repeat the procedure several times. One problem this technique sometimes creates is "blooming," a white area where water has soaked into the finish. This problem is solved in the same way as the removal of water rings, which is described next.

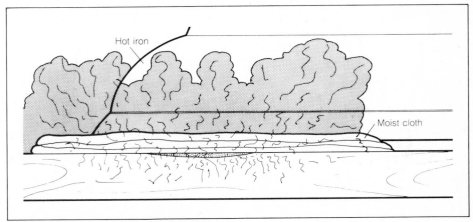

Hot iron

Moist cloth

One way to fix a shallow dent is to steam it. Apply water to the dent; cover with a moist cloth. Touch the cloth with the iron so that the steam can get down into the wood.

HOW TO REPAIR WATER RINGS ON FINISHES

A guest places a glass on a lovely table top, and later you find a white ring where the bottom of the glass rested. It is a discouraging sight. The whiteness is called "blooming," which occurs because the finish absorbs the moisture from the bottom of the glass. Lacquer and shellac finishes bloom readily. Some varnishes will bloom, but not as easily. Blooming also shows up as a milky look on the finish of furniture that has been stored in a moist place.

Most blooming takes place on the surface of the finish and doesn't go very deep. To get rid of blooming, you must remove that tiny fraction of the surface of the finish which has clouded. The best way is by means of a mild abrasive. Any of the following, rubbed gently into the bloom until it disappears, will work:

(1) rottenstone mixed with mineral spirits;
(2) pumice and fine oil;
(3) fine 4/0 grade steel wool;
(4) powdered dentifrice;
(5) cigar ashes used as an abrasive.

If the bloom goes very deep, the rubbing will take some time, and you might have to switch to a harsher abrasive — to a 3/0 steel wool, for example. But longer rubbing with a mild abrasive is better than quicker rubbing with a harsh abrasive, because you will do less damage to the surface. You want the repair to be as unnoticeable as possible.

FIXING A SMALL BLEMISH OR AN ALLIGATORED FINISH

The technique involved in repairing lacquer and shellac finishes is called "reamalgamation." In it, a solvent is applied to the finish to cause the finish to soften and spread over the surface. The two most important uses of this technique are in the repair of small finish blemishes and in the restoration of finishes that have alligatored.

Small Blemishes

If you have repaired a cigarette burn on a table top, the last step in the repair process is to refinish the surface. If the finish is either lacquer or shellac, you can reamalgamate instead of applying a new coat of finish material to the repaired area. The advantage of reamalgamation is that you don't need to worry about color matching the old finish, because in this process, you literally "melt" the old finish on the surface adjacent to the repair, and cause it to flow over the repair.

Alligatoring

When furniture has been exposed to the sun for a long time, the surface may craze — become criss-crossed with cracks so that it looks something like the hide of an alligator. Such finishes can be restored by reamalgamation because the crazing disappears when the finish is made to reflow over the surface.

Solvents

Reamalgamation for lacquer and shellac is the same, except that the solvent is different in each case. With lacquer, use lacquer thinner. With shellac, use denatured alcohol.

Pretesting the Finish

If your lacquered furniture has ever been refinished — given a new coat of clear lacquer — you may have a situation in which the top coat is clear and the subcoat is colored. In some cases, a clear coat may have been applied over a color coat at the factory. When you have two different coats like this, reamalgamation may cause streaking as the two lacquers blend. Once streaking has occurred, it cannot be corrected and you will have to remove the entire finish and start over. For this reason, test reamalgamation on a hidden area before going to work on visible surfaces.

Step 1: Preparing the Surface In each case, begin by making sure the finish is free of all wax and dirt. To prevent streaking and to permit the solvent to stay in place while it softens the surface, reamalgamation should be done on a horizontal surface. The solvent will run on a vertical surface and become uneven.

Step 2: Applying the Solvent Then apply the solvent, using either a brush or a soft pad. Brush application is the easiest. Use the brush gently to avoid excessive brush marks. Minor ones will

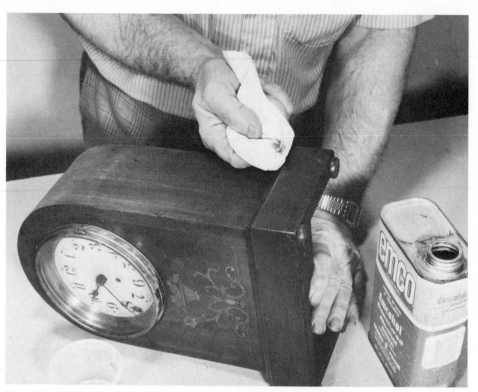

Before reamalgamating a piece, identify the finish on which you are working. First use denatured alcohol to test for shellac; then use lacquer thinner to test for lacquer.

Apply the solvent with a brush or a soft pad. The finish will soften and spread out. The dark line on this clock marks the difference between treated and untreated sections.

level out during the drying process. Make continuous applications, keeping the surface wet until the softening starts. At that point, the finish material will begin to flow over the surface. When you see an even film over the whole surface, stop applying the solvent and allow the finish to dry. Make the last application in the same direction as the grain of the wood.

Step 3: Finishing the Job To complete the reamalgamation, apply a new coat of shellac or lacquer over the entire finish, allow it to dry, and then rub it down with 4/0 steel wool or 8/0 sandpaper.

Step 4: Buffing the Surface
Although these surfaces dry to the touch in a short time, they should be allowed to set completely before the final buffing. To be safe, wait until the next day. Then buff with very fine steel wool.

Hints and Cautions
When the surface is soft, it can easily pick up lint and dust. For that reason, use lint-free cloths and work in an area where dust is not a problem. Both shellac and lacquer dry quickly, so the surfaces do not have to be protected for long.

For reamalgamation of shellac, use only pure denatured alcohol. Some alcohols are cut with water, and the water in these mixtures will cause the surface to turn white. In addition, work with shellac on a day when the humidity is low or in an air conditioned room, since high humidity also can cause blooming.

WHAT TO DO WITH A FOGGY FINISH Old furniture, and especially old furniture that has been stored for a long time, sometimes looks as though there were a haze over its surfaces. This haze may remain even after thorough cleaning. There are dozens of reasons for this, from absorption of moisture to exposure to the sun. Whatever the reason, the haze must be removed. Sometimes you can do it, and sometimes you can't. If you can't, then the best procedure is to strip the old finish away and apply a new one.

Fog on Lacquer Try reamalgamation, or try applying a new coat of clear lacquer, which will have the same effect as reamalgamation.

Fog on Shellac Try reamalgamation or a new coat of white shellac.

Fog on Varnish Rub the surface down with fine steel wool, on the theory that the problem is on the surface itself and that the finish under the surface is still sound. After the rubdown, apply paste wax to a small area and observe how the finish looks. If the fog remains, you can assume that the fogging has gone deep and that a new finish is required. See chapters 7, 8 and 9 for instruction.

HOW TO REPAIR SCRATCHES ON THE SURFACE There are two kinds of scratches that can plague you in furniture restoration. The first is the deep scratch, usually caused by something sharp dragged over the surface. The second is a collection of fine scratches, commonly caused by normal daily use, which create a matte or dull area on the surface.

Lacquered or Shellacked Finishes
Reamalgamation can cure both problems on furniture that is lacquered or shellacked. If the deep scratch goes through the finish to the wood, and has caused some of the finish material to flake away, you might apply a thin coat of new finish material to the scratch. Use an artist's brush and carefully place the clear lacquer or shellac in the scratch without getting any on the surrounding surface. Allow this to dry. Then reamalgamate. The new material will serve as a filler during the reamalgamation process, and reamalgamation will cause the colored finish material to flow over it and blend in with the rest of the surface.

Varnished Finishes
Fine scratches on varnished surfaces often can be removed by buffing with 8/0 or 10/0 sandpaper. Deep scratches are tougher to handle, since varnish can't be reamalgamated. You may be able to use the artist's brush to paint a number of coats of varnish in the scratch, gradually building it up to the same level as the surrounding surface. Finish the repair by rubbing it with fine sandpaper.

Much of the success of this repair depends on the color of the varnish. The original varnish may have been colored, or it may have discolored since application. Begin the repair with clear varnish and observe what happens. You may have to switch to a colored varnish, and then the problem becomes one of selecting the right color. We suggest you increase the intensity of color slightly with each succeeding coat and keep careful watch over the result.

A surface covered with scratches need not be totally refinished. Before you take drastic measures, try reamalgamation. Apply new varnish to the scratch. Then reamalgamate.

7
Stripping Off the Old Finish

Furniture stripping is the process of removing all of the old finish from a damaged piece of furniture. You do it as a last resort, when you have decided that there is no way to save the existing finish. Stripping is a messy business, one that many people prefer not to do. If you are one of these, look up a professional furniture stripper who will do the work for you. The prices for professional stripping usually are not high, especially if you consider the investment in time and materials required if you were to do it yourself.

PROFESSIONAL STRIPPING

Before you go shopping for a professional, you should know something about the different processes used, and how they could affect your furniture.

Bath Stripping

There are three basic methods used by professionals: hot tank, cold tank and hand stripping.

Hot Tank In the hot tank method, the furniture is dipped into a tank filled with a hot solution of caustic soda. It is held under just long enough for the chemical to dissolve the finish. The piece then is removed from the tank and rinsed. Any remaining caustic soda is neutralized in a muriatic acid bath, which is followed by a final rinse. Then the piece is allowed to dry.

The hot process is rough on furniture. Glue often is softened and veneers that weren't loose before may peel off. We suggest that you allow only solid wood furniture to be stripped by this method. If the piece has any plywood, veneering, or inlays, keep it out of the hot tank. The fact that the glue holding the furniture together may be softened during the process isn't bad if you planned on regluing. You may be saved some of the disassembly work.

Cold Tank In the cold tank method, your furniture is dipped into a cold solvent, methylene chloride. This chemical does not attack glues, so plywood, veneers and inlays are safe in it.

Disadvantages of Hot and Cold Tank In both bath processes, the chemicals are powerful and they have an effect

This highchair from about 1910 has about three thick coats of enamel. All three have chipped off in places. We used standard water-based paint stripper to take off the paint.

on the wood. When you get the furniture back, you will probably find the wood surfaces rough, the result of wood grain raised by the chemical. The surface fibers will have absorbed moisture and lifted away from the underlying wood fibers. This means plenty of sanding to make the wood smooth before applying any stain or new finish.

You may be surprised to find that either the wood is a gray color, or that it still has much of the original stain on the wood. Stripping chemicals will remove any oil stains, but may not do much to analine or water stains. These latter soak deeply into the wood on application, and usually only part of them come off. In those cases where the stain does come off, the wood may not have returned to its original color. Instead it may now have a gray look. When you apply new stain and finish, you will have to take this into account, because the wood will darken quite rapidly.

Hand Stripping

The professionals who hand strip furniture do the job with the same chemicals and tools that you would use. The difference is that they perform the labor and you pay the money. Hand stripping is more expensive than tank stripping, but more restorers think the additional expense of hand stripping is a good investment. There is less opportunity for serious damage to the furniture, and the wood is left a brighter color, so is easier to refinish in a light tone.

Our opinion is this: hand stripping is the best for most furniture. Do it yourself or have it done for you. We think the finish you get after a hand stripping job is significantly better than the one achieved after tank stripping. In addition, the furniture piece will suffer less.

Recommendations for Hiring Out the Job

Stop and talk to several professional strippers nearby. Look at samples of their work and check their pricing. Describe the furniture you want to bring in. Discuss problems such as veneers, inlays, glues and wood color. Listen to what they recommend as to how to refinish furniture stripped by their methods. They probably have been around furniture for a considerable time and can give useful information. But they will be biased about which are the best methods of stripping; listen, ask questions, and keep your own counsel. You would get another viewpoint by talking to a professional furniture finisher or repairer; if you have the time, do that too.

HAND STRIPPING

There are three methods of hand stripping. You can burn a finish off, sand it off, or take it off chemically.

Burning

Burning involves the use of a propane torch, an electric paint remover or a heat lamp to soften the finish, and a scraper to scrape away the softened finish. Burning is frequently used to remove paint from houses, and takes practice. You apply the heat until the finish blisters and softens, then quickly scrape the softened area. Care must be taken, especially with the open flame of the torch, not to let the materials on the surface catch fire. They will, if you hold the torch on them too long.

With burning, you can get down to the original wood easily, and there is no chemical discoloration. Burning will not affect a stain that has soaked into wood, but this technique will remove anything that is a coating on the wood's surface, including stains. Burning will remove some varnishes, which are not affected by chemicals. But burning furniture surfaces is clumsy work. Table tops and dresser sides aren't bad, but you'll find it difficult to handle intricate pieces, such as rungs, stretchers or small frame members.

Sanding

Sanding, by hand or by means of a power sander, will take off any finish. It can be a long and arduous task, and creates a cloud of hazardous dust made up of tiny particles of finish. You *must* wear a mask and goggles when doing this kind of work, or run the real risk of serious lung damage. There is risk for the furniture, too, since it is easy to remove surface wood unintentionally and to round corners and edges that shouldn't be rounded.

Chemical Stripping

Taking all factors into consideration, we believe the best method is chemical removal. It is sloppy, and you must take precautions because you are dealing with strong chemicals. However, on balance — considering the hazards, the work methods, and the eventual results — chemical stripping seems to be best.

The basic chemical in today's stripping mixtures is methylene chloride. Others that may be added (depending on the brand) are toluene, methyl alcohol or methanol, mineral spirits and triethyl-ammonium phosphate. These mixtures are hazardous and should be used with great care.

HOW TO SAFELY USE CHEMICAL STRIPPERS First, these mixtures are flammable. Do not use them in a basement work area where there is a furnace with a pilot light, a gas water heater or anything else with an open flame. And you absolutely should not smoke while using them. They are not only flammable, but when methylene chloride burns it makes deadly phosgene gas. By inhaling the fumes of a stripper through a cigarette, you could poison yourself.

Second, they are caustic and prolonged contact with the skin will cause burning. They will cause serious injury if splashed in the eyes.

Third, the vapor produced by these mixtures is hazardous, and we advise you to avoid any prolonged breathing of it. Always work in a well-ventilated area, preferably with one fan to exhaust fumes from the room and one to blow fresh air in.

Fourth, the government says that persons having (or suspected of having) heart trouble or any pulmonary disorder should consult with a physician before using these products.

This is a frightening list and may discourage you from doing your own stripping. We don't like to take a negative or scary approach to anything, but in a case like this, the hazards seem serious enough to merit it. In the past, there has been too much emphasis on "it's easy to do with our product," and not enough emphasis on the dangers of the products. The bottom line is this: if you know enough about the dangers, and know how to guard against them, then you are more likely to use the product safely and effectively. The potential risks are real.

Taking Precautions

Where to Work An important element in safe stripping is your choice of a work area. Because of the vapor problem, the safest place is outside in the yard, or in the garage with the door open. In these areas the ventilation problem is solved, and so is the problem of working near open flame. The basement is bad place to work, and so is a closed room in the house.

What to Wear You must protect yourself from splashes of the chemical. Just being careful while and how you work isn't enough, because accidental spills and splashes can be expected. Wear rubber gloves, preferably the long type that also protect your wrists. Wear safety glasses to keep splashes out of your eyes. Wear a rubber or plastic bib-type apron, so that chemicals splashed on your front won't soak into your clothes. Do *not* wear canvas or cloth shoes.

How to Proceed Begin by reading the manufacturer's instructions carefully. Read every word on the label, and read any brochures available at the store. In this book, we give generalized instruction only. The label gives specific instructions for that specific product. Since all products have somewhat different formulations, these specific instructions are the ones to follow. The manufacturer wants you to get safe, satisfactory results from the product, and the instructions were written to achieve that end.

Set Up a Work Area

Take the piece of furniture to the work area and arrange everything so you can work conveniently. For example, to avoid stooping or getting down on your knees, put the furniture on supports such as sawhorses. There is much less chance for an accident. Arrange a table or bench to hold chemicals. The materials should be conveniently placed, but not so close to the work that you might bump. Clear away anything you might trip or stumble over. Make sure everything you need — chemicals, cloths, steel wool, scraping tools — is there and ready to go. Arrange for sufficient light; you do not want to have to peer so closely your nose ends up in the chemical.

HOW TO STRIP OFF THE OLD FINISH

Once the work area and tools have been set up, the work will proceed quickly. However, even before beginning the work, you will discover a major advantage of chemical stripping: the tools and materials needed either are inexpensive, or are likely to be those you already have on hand.

Tools and Materials

You will need the following materials to strip a piece of furniture: two wide-mouthed cans; a wide bladed paint scraper; a 3- or 4-inch paint brush or a cloth pad; toweling burlap or steel wool; an awl or other sharp pointed tool; and sandpaper of graduated grades.

A Word about Scrapers Scrapers are flat steel blades with handles. Scraper

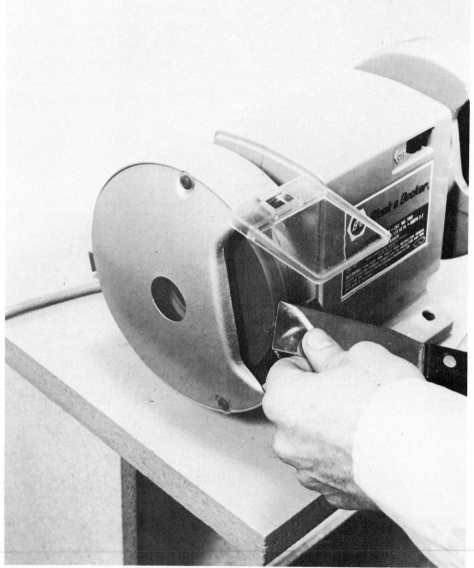

Square corners on a scraper have a tendency to dig into wood softened by a paint stripper. Round corners prevent unsightly gouges.

Before stripping furniture, make a scraper that minimizes gouging. Buy a standard paint scraper and grind the corners round with a grinding wheel.

blades are stiff, while spatula and other applicator blades are very flexible. Other than that, these look alike. The best blade for scraping is wide. We have found 4-inch blades to be the easiest to handle. You may want a second 1-inch scraper for smaller areas such as legs. We have also found that the outer corners of scraper blades are sharp points. When the stripping chemical softens the finish, it also softens the wood under it slightly. It is very easy, when scraping up the sludge, to dig into the surface of the wood with the scraper and make cuts you must repair later.

To avoid this, we use a grinding wheel to grind the very sharp corners down, rounding them slightly. The rounded corners won't gouge the wood surface. They also won't get into corners quite as well for scraping. So we grind the corners of the large scraper only, and leave the corners of the smaller scraper sharp.

Step 1: Applying the Stripper

Pour some of the stripper from the original can into a clean coffee or other wide-mouthed can. Be sure that the furniture is solidly placed and level, so it won't tip as you work. Now use a 3- or 4-inch paint brush or a cloth pad to apply a heavy coat of the stripping chemical on one surface of the furniture. Do not brush this out as if it were paint. You want a heavy coat to stay on the surface so the chemicals can work on the finish.

Step 2: Scraping the Residue

Allow the chemical to stand until the finish bubbles and wrinkles, or until it is soft. This will probably be 10 to 20 minutes. Some finishes, such as varnishes and epoxies, don't bubble. They just get soft. Test these with your scraper after about 5 minutes, and begin scraping them as soon as they have softened. Don't wait until the surface has dried. Scrape paints and enamels after they have wrinkled.

In some cases, especially old and very thick coats of enamel, you may have to repeat the process several times before getting down to bare wood.

Step 3: Cleaning the Surface

Have a wide-mouthed can available. As you scrape away the surface material, deposit it in the can. Don't allow this residue, which is chemically active, to drop to the floor, or to fall on your clothing or

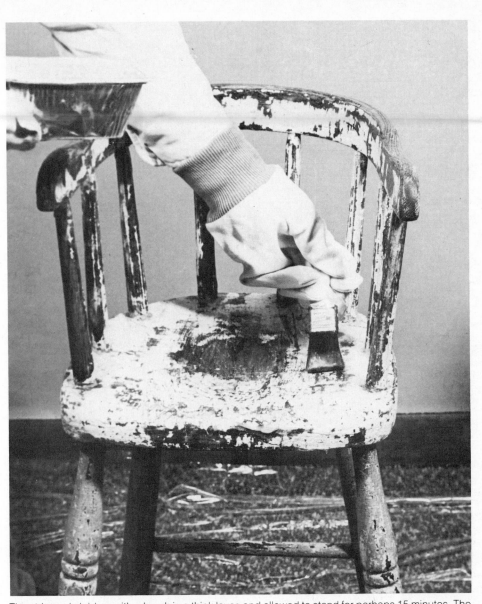

The stripper is laid on with a brush in a thick layer, and allowed to stand for perhaps 15 minutes. The material will cause the paint to blister and wrinkle.

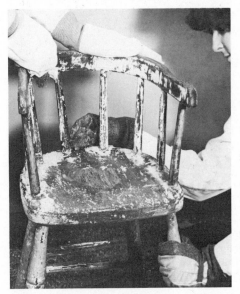

After the stripper has worked on a layer, and after scraping, use steel wool to remove the paint and break up the next layer.

Slowly the old paint comes off. Under the white, there is a light brown and a darker brown coat, which are difficult to see here.

When the old paint is gone, the chair is ready for a good sanding. The seat and back are of oak; the rest is unidentifiable.

A wiping down with the tack cloth follows sanding. Because of the visible dings and dents, no distressing will be needed.

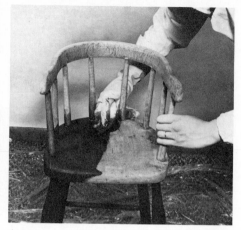

A dark oak stain has been chosen for this piece because it has a nice appearance and because it will minimize the distressing.

The stain has made each of the woods a different color. Apply second coats to the lighter woods. To lighten the seat, wipe it with paint thinner to remove some stain.

shoes. When all of the softened finish has been scraped off, use a piece of old toweling soaked in cool water to wash the surface clean.

Water is an enemy of wood, and for good furniture this rinse may not be a good idea. It may raise the grain or cause water stains. For furniture of this type, after scraping off the old finish, rub the surface with a dry coarse cloth (burlap or toweling) or go over it with steel wool. Use an awl or other sharp pointed instrument to clean any residue out of corners, cracks and joints. Clean out carvings.

Step 4: Completing the Scraping

Now turn the furniture, and follow the procedure for the next side. Complete each side before moving on to the next. When all sides have been scraped clean, allow the piece to dry for 24 hours.

Step 5: Follow Up

Allow the furniture to dry for 24 hours. Examine it. You'll probably find areas where some finish remains, and there will be bits of old finish clinging here and there. Use an awl or ice pick to dig any remaining finish out of corners and crevices. Then sand the entire piece with medium grade sandpaper. Wear your mask for this job, since the dust may contain dried chemicals.

Don't use steel wool for this job. Steel wool, and especially fine grades of steel wool, can have a polishing effect on hardwood, literally closing the pores to future stains you may want to put on. Use sandpaper, beginning with the medium grade. Before you apply the finish, you'll want to sand again with finer grades to achieve the greatest smoothness.

RESTORING OR RETAINING THE CURRENT STAIN

You won't know in advance what kind of a problem you will encounter in regard to the coloring stain on your furniture once the finish is off. There are a dozen different kinds of stain that may have been used. Some of these will come off with the finish, leaving you with clean wood. Some absolutely will not come off at all. And some will come off partly, leaving splotches.

If the wood is clean, there is no problem. If the stain was untouched by the remover, there also is no problem — at least not if you intend to restore the piece to the same color it had before. A new finish coat can be applied over the old stain wih no trouble.

Splotchy Stain

If the wood is now splotchy, with some unstained areas and some lighter or darker than others, you have a problem.

New Stain One solution is to apply new stain of the same color right over the old. This may work but also may create some new problems. If you decide to try it, test the idea first on a hidden area. Look at what happens to the darkly stained areas. Are they now too dark? Can you achieve an even tone over both the stained and unstained areas? Sometimes you can, depending on the wood and the original stain.

Bleaching The more common solution to this problem is to bleach the stain out of the wood. We discussed bleaching in the previous chapter, where it was suggested for use in repairing finishes. The bleaching of a whole piece of furniture, or at least large parts of it, is essentially the same operation, but on a much larger scale.

We have worked out a method that we think is less difficult than most. Keep the furniture right there in the work area where it was stripped. Fill a typical window spray bottle with common household bleach. Spray this bleach on the entire piece. Spray again and allow to dry. Keep repeating the process until the stains have disappeared. What should happen is that after each spraying, the stains become a little lighter in color.

Once the bleaching is finished, rinse all surfaces with clear water to get rid of all chemicals. We don't like all this liquid bleach and water on furniture, because it almost always produces raised grain. But this method appears to be the only solution to the splotchy stain problem if restaining doesn't work.

RECENT PRODUCT SOLUTIONS
Formby Products

Homer Formby is well known for his line of furniture finishing products. A third-generation refinisher of fine furniture, he thought about the stripping problem and reasoned that in the great majority of cases, there was no problem with the stain, only with the deteriorated finish. So why not simply take off the finish and retain the original stain, and then apply a new finish over the old stain? This would make a lot of refinishing much quicker and easier.

Having decided that there was no reason to completely strip most furniture to the bare wood, Formby developed his "Furniture Refinisher." The label says that the product dissolves varnish, lacquer and shellac without stripping the wood. The material is applied with fine grade steel wool pads, which are rubbed into an area about a foot square until the finish in that area is dissolved and picked up by the pad. The routine continues until the finish of the entire piece has been removed. During this process, the original stain remains intact, so that the restoration is completed by simply applying a new finish coat. There is no need to deal with stain problems.

The idea is good. It should be noted that the refinisher is a methylene chloride product and should be used with the same care as any other such product. It should also be noted that stains that were applied to the surface may be removed along with the finish. The final result depends on what stains were originally used.

This method assumes, of course, that you want the furniture restored to the original color. If you don't, then you have to use a paint remover or stripper as we described earlier. Formby's refinisher does not work well on paint, polyurethane varnishes or other synthetic finishes.

Hope Company Products

A similar product is put out by The Hope Company, of St. Louis, Mo. We like both this material and the Formby one because they are somewhat easier to handle than true stripping products, and they can in some cases cut down on the work time.

A more modern solution to the stripping problem is a product such as this one by Formby. These remove the old finish but, in most cases, leave the stain intact.

8
Sanding, Filling and Staining

By this time, all the repair, stripping and other preliminary work is behind you. You are ready to put the new finish on the piece of furniture you have chosen to restore. What next?

First, you sand the piece in preparation for the new finish. Next, you may apply a filler if you decide it is needed. Then the piece is stained to the color you want. And finally, several coats of the chosen finishing material are applied.

Each of these steps requires the use of certain materials. Since you will have to choose among a variety of these at the store, we will discuss each step and the materials themselves, and give you some parameters for making your decisions if you haven't already done so. At the same time, we will discuss how to use these materials.

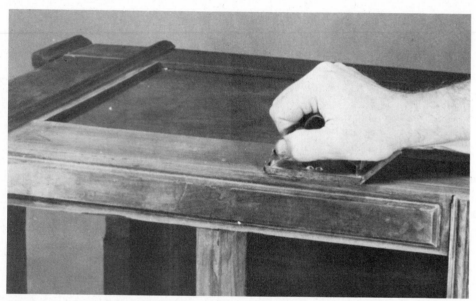

Once repairs and stripping are done, sand the piece. First, level repaired areas. Then eliminate scratches and raised grain to achieve a satin smooth finish.

HOW TO SAND THE STRIPPED WOOD SURFACE By this time, the surface wood of your furniture has been worked over pretty thoroughly, having undergone repairs, stripping, and possibly bleaching. In medical terms, the piece you have been working on is now out of surgery, and has been moved to the Intensive Card Ward. It is at this point that restoration really begins. The grain of the wood may be raised; there may be scars of repairs to be hidden; the color of the wood may be something very different from that the wood had originally. Your task now is to build a new, attractive finish.

We discussed sanding in some detail in Chapter 4, which you should read again to remind yourself about such tools as sanding blocks and grades of paper. Right now, run your hands over the surface to discover how much sanding must be done. Plan to sand in two or more steps; three is a good average.

Step 1: Initial Sanding

Begin by sanding all surfaces with a paper rated at grit 120 (3/0 to 4/0). During this first sanding, pay particular attention to repaired cracks, working to make them as smooth as you can. Also sand the areas near glued joints, especially if any of the glue oozed out and dried on exposed areas. If you don't remove all of the glue, the excess will become very obvious as soon as you apply the stain. If necessary, use a pocket knife to scrape away any glue you can see and then sand the spot thoroughly. If the stain is to be even on all surfaces, you can't leave any vestiges of glue.

After this sanding has been completed, wipe the piece down with a tack cloth; then run your hands over the surfaces again. You should be able to feel the difference — and you should know where you must apply a little extra pressure.

Step 2: The Second Phase

Move up to a finer grade of paper. If you plan to settle on two sandings, do this at about a grit 180 (5/0) paper. If you plan three steps, move first to a grit 150, then to a grit 180. Keep in mind these goals: elimination of any raised grain; elimination of scars made during repairs; achievement of a satin smooth surface.

Caution: Do Not Oversand It is possible to make the surface too smooth for the new finish. This is why we recommend abrasive paper only up to a fineness of grit 180. If you sand with very fine papers or scrub with very fine steel wool, it is possible to go beyond sanding many hardwoods, and to actually polish them to an extremely smooth, tight finish. Such a tight finish will not accept stains and can cause problems from this point on, unless you intend the final finish to be natural wood finished only in lemon oil or wax.

We learned this the hard way early in our refinishing career. We used very fine steel wool during the stripping operation on the legs of an upholstered chair. Later, when it came time to apply stain, we had a terrible time, and ended up by applying a colored varnish. The final result was not what we envisioned.

As a general rule, papers up to 180 or 200 (at the most) are for smoothing wood. Papers from 200 to 420 are for sanding between coats, where you want to eliminate dust and other specks, but not to remove much of the material. Papers of 360 to 400 are excellent for that final hand polishing of the finish. Papers above 400 can be used on the final finish, too. They also are recommended for polishing of bare woods.

The softer the wood, the less likely you are to polish it to a hard finish through heavy sanding with fine abrasives. Just remember that when you have finished sanding, the surface must be open and receptive to the stain you apply, not sealed against it.

Step 3: Deliberately Raising the Grain

If you intend to use a water stain, you can expect the stain to cause a slight swelling in the wood. This will raise the grain and create a rough surface. But since you will have applied the stain, you won't want to do much sanding. One way professionals alleviate this problem is to raise the grain

Marble tops often are dull, stained and pitted. Refinish with wet-or-dry sandpaper in grits 120 to 600 and an orbital or oscillating sander. First, sprinkle water on the surface.

Start with the 120 grit paper in the sander and work it back and forth over the marble under fair pressure. Keep sprinkling water every few minutes to keep the surface wet. A white paste will form as the marble dust mixes with the water. Keep an eye on the scratches and pits on the marble surface, and as they disappear, change to finer sandpaper grits. The final polish should be done with a 400 grit or finer paper.

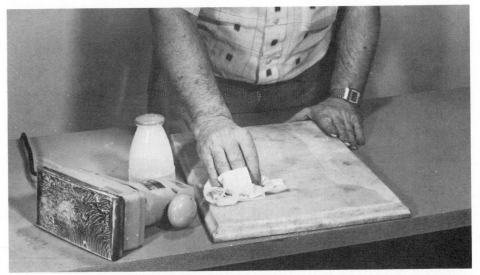

Wipe the marble clean occasionally to see how you are progressing. The process may take half an hour or more, depending on the depths of the pits and scratches. When the marble is smooth and beautiful, wash off all the white paste, allow the stone to dry, and apply a good marble polish.

To raise the grain of an open-faced wood deliberately, first apply water, as shown here. The raised grain is then sanded smooth.

deliberately and sand again before applying the water stain. Note that this problem arises only with the use of water stains, not with others.

To raise the grain, spray the sanded piece with enough water to soak the surface. Allow the piece to dry. During the drying period, the grain will raise. Resand the piece to knock down the raised grain. Later, when you apply the water stain, the grain will raise only slightly and cause few problems.

Sanding Softer Woods A curious thing happens when you sand softer woods. The surface becomes smooth and then begins to fuzz. This fuzz will interfere with the stain later on. To avoid this, sand the fuzz off by first spraying or brushing on a thin coat of sanding sealer. The sanding sealers you buy are a type of lacquer. You can make your own by using a thin shellac. Whichever type used, the sealer stiffens the fuzz, which can then be sanded away. This method produces a very smooth surface. It also may seal the pores of the wood (which you do not want) if you apply too heavy a coat.

If you intend to use a penetrating stain, this sealing might cause uneven penetration, depending on how much filling it creates. If, however, you intend to use a surface stain, this creates no problems, and in fact makes a good base for the stain.

HOW AND WHEN TO USE WOOD FILLERS

To get a very smooth finish on furniture, the surface wood must be very smooth. Because this isn't possible on open-grained woods such as oak and chestnut, furniture makers for centuries, have used fillers on these woods. The purpose of the filler is to fill the little craters and valleys on the surface, leveling it completely before the final finish coat is applied. Fillers are not used on woods with naturally smooth surfaces.

In recent years, furniture buyers have begun to appreciate the natural look in furniture. Thus when they buy oak or chestnut furniture, they no longer expect it to be smooth. They want to see the rough grain. In your restoration work, if the piece you are working on is made of an open-grained wood, you have a choice. You can use filler and produce a final finish that is smooth and glossy — which it probably was in the first place — or you can skip the filler and give it a natural finish by applying only stain and the final finish. If you choose to fill the surface, there are two ways to apply the filler.

APPLYING STAIN AND FILLER
When you are filling open-pore wood or repairing minor scratches in the surface of the wood, you will do the filling either before or after the application of the stain. The choice is dependent upon the makeup of the two materials. Some fillers and stains will combine badly unless applied in a certain sequence.

Application directions will appear on the packages. The directions will be specific about the sequence of application. As a guideline, however, remember the following: most fillers will be dissolved by the solvent in alcohol stain. If you are using an alcohol stain, use the stain first and then apply the filler. If you are using a water-base stain, fill the wood before you stain.

Filler that is left on the surface of the wood (not actually filling pores or scratches), may inhibit the absorption of the stain by the wood. The surface should be carefully wiped clean before staining.

Filler that is applied after the wood has been stained must be "dyed to match" the finish of the wood. Filler is sold in either a white or cream color and will accept color. There is a stain (dye) sold that is specifically formulated to color the filler.

Method 1: Filling with Lacquer or Varnish
Apply coat after coat of the finish material (lacquer or varnish), and sand between each coat. During the sanding, you remove the finishing material from the high spots and leave the material in the low spots. Eventually, the low spots will be built up to create a glassy smooth finish. This type of finish can be done without staining, so that the original color of the wood is retained, or you can stain before applying the first finishing coat. If you do, be careful not to sand too much or you may take off some of the stain and cause uneven coloring.

Method 2: Using a Wood Filler
The second method is the most common. A wood filler is brushed on the finish, then scraped off. The scraping leaves filler in the low spots.

Most refinishers recommend a paste filler containing silex, which is finely powdered quartz. There also are the liquid sanding sealers, mentioned before in connection with sanding softer woods. These can be used as fillers, too. They spray or brush on to replace many of the coats if you intend to build the surface to a glass-smooth finish.

Step 1: Preparing the Filler You buy wood filler in cans. It is neutral cream in color and very thick. Thin it with turpentine or paint thinner until it is the consistency of thick cream. Color it by adding pigments right after thinning.

Most furniture finishers like the filler to be just a shade darker than the wood stain. An unusual treatment, called the "silver fox," calls for the use of a dark stain on the wood and a white or very light colored filler. You can apply filler either before or after you stain, depending on the result you want. If you stain afterward, you get a consistent color across the surface. If you stain before you fill, the stain will remain darker than the wood and provide an interesting texture.

Step 2: Applying the Filler After thinning and tinting the filler, brush it on the surface. Apply the first coat by brushing with the grain, and use the brush to scrub or work it into the crevices in the surface. Now apply a second coat before the first has dried. Make this a full coat; brush across the grain, to leave a heavy coat of filler on the wood.

Step 3: Scraping Away the Excess The most difficult part of applying filler is selecting the right moment to

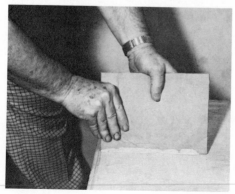

Wood filler is a creamy paste which you paint over an open-grained wood to fill the grain. Allow it to stand until it suddenly loses its gloss.

scrape the excess filler from the surface. Watch the filler closely. For some minutes after you stop brushing, it looks wet. Quite suddenly, it turns dull. This is your signal to start scraping. If you scrape too soon, the filler will come out of the surface. If you wait too long, the filler becomes too dry to scrape.

The scraper can be any kind of a tool with a stiff straight edge. A wide-bladed drywall knife is good. So is a stiff piece of cardboard. Work at a slight angle across the grain as you scrape, removing all of the filler you can from the surface. The idea, of course, is to leave all the filler in the rough spots on the surface.

Step 4: Burnishing the Surface

When you have done all you can with the scraper, burnish the surface by rubbing across the grain with a big piece of burlap or other very rough cloth. Then allow the surface to dry overnight.

Step 5: Sanding On some surfaces, you may have to apply filler in several coats to achieve perfect smoothness. After the filler has dried, sand any rough spots. Keep sanding until the surface feels smooth under your hand, but don't apply a lot of pressure or use coarse abrasives. Just keep working, lightly and steadily, until the surface feels ready for the final finish coat.

The moment the shiny look of the wood filler disappears, wipe or scrape it from the surface, working across the grain. If you wipe, use a coarse cloth like burlap. If you scrape, just draw the scraper, such as a piece of cardboard, across the grain. After the filler has dried, sand it smooth and then apply a stain.

SELECTING AND USING WOOD STAINS

No doubt about it, staining can be the biggest trouble-maker for part-time and beginning refinishers. Many novices feel that there are too many kinds of stain on the market, and too many possible ways to do the job. It is difficult to know when the stain you apply is the right color, because the color changes as the stain dries. Every stain looks different on different woods. Some stains are difficult to apply because they easily produce overlap marks; others are runny or result in uneven color when they aren't put on exactly as they should be.

THE PURPOSE OF THE STAINING PROCESS

The reason for applying stain is to color the wood. We have become accustomed to certain wood colors in furniture that are different from the natural color — and, in fact, have come to believe the colors we see so often are the natural colors. Some woods are so beautiful in their natural colors that we believe they shouldn't be stained. Walnut is one of these. Mahogany is another. However, wood color is a matter of very personal taste, so staining sometimes is found even on these lovely woods.

Wood is colored either to enhance its appearance or to make it appear to be a different wood. Plain hardwoods often are stained to simulate walnut, cherry or mahogany. Using this innocent deception, you can improve the appearance of otherwise undistinguished furniture.

FINDING A SUITABLE STAIN

The reason that there are so many different staining products available is that there has been an ongoing search for ways to color wood for the past several hundred years. Each new staining product has been produced to: (1) give better color; (2) give better control of the process; (3) speed up the process by faster drying; or (4) to overcome some deficiency of existing products.

Water stains, for example, are dyes dissolved in water and applied to the wood. They provide good, warm coloring. However, because they contain water, they may cause the wood to swell, raising the grain. This means that your once-smooth surface is no longer smooth and must be sanded again. But when you sand, you disturb the even level of color and may expose unstained wood. To combat this, NGR (Non-Grain Raising) stains were developed. These contain the same dyes, but employ a solvent other than water. Both types continue to be sold, which helps confuse the newcomer to the field.

The plain fact is that many stains remain in use and are still on the market because

professionals learned to use them, to like them and to believe that they are the best. These professionals won't use the newer products because they can do so well with the old ones. The problem is that these older stains are good only in the hands of an experienced person who has used them over and over, knows how to get good results and knows their deficiencies. The newcomer has none of this experience, but following the professional's good advice, obtains these stains for his own furniture — and gets into trouble. The professional fails to realize that his marvelous results come from a combination of product and experience, and that the newcomer is missing half of that formula.

Types of Stains

With this is mind, we are going to do a brief rundown of some of the stains you might encounter, but are going to discuss the application of only those stains you can use with some degree of ease and assurance. Since the objective of staining is to color the wood to your satisfaction, we think you should use the product and technique most likely to achieve that end with a minimum of trouble. Purists in the field of restoration will be offended by this approach because, to many, the object of restoration is to "restore" the piece to its original condition, and not just to refinish it. We think there are three stains that are easy to use, provide few problems, offer good control, and produce the kind of results you want. These are pigmented oil wiping stains; water stains; and paste or jelly stains. There are others that you should recognize, although they are difficult for a beginner to use confidently.

Alcohol Stains These are alcohol-based colorings that produce good cooler colors tinged with green, rather than the warmer tones brought about by most stains. Some workers like them because they dry very quickly, but they also produce overlap marks if you aren't extremely careful. Unless you are trying to set a record for finishing furniture, don't use them.

Pigmented Oil Stains Watch the terminology here. You will find good pigmented oil *wiping* stains everywhere, and these are excellent for your use. They are different from pigmented oil stains, an older type that was brushed on and allowed to dry. No wiping was employed. An even color sometimes was hard to achieve except by an expert. There also were unpigmented oil stains, which are applied in the same way and have the same hazards. The key word is *wiping*. As you buy, watch for it on the label.

Padding Stains Padding stains are very special. The name is applied to certain products put on existing finishes to enhance their appearance. Antique dealers, for example, might use padding stains to "freshen" up a new acquisition before putting it on the display floor. Most padding stains are simply thinned shellac or lacquer mixed with a dry coloring powder. They are wiped into the finish almost like a furniture polish to cover minor blemishes and revive the old finish. You can try this technique yourself on an old piece of furniture. You might find the result good enough so that refinishing isn't necessary.

Varnish Stains These aren't really stains at all, but are colored varnishes (or lacquers) that are applied as both stain and final coat. If you want to do a quick refinishing job on some furniture in the children's room, for example, these might serve. Remember, however, that the color is in the finish, and any surface damage will immediately expose the bare wood under the finish. Because of this, a piece finished in this manner can deteriorate in appearance very quickly.

Water Stains These stains are made by mixing a dye in water. You brush the colored water on the surface and continue to add more color with each application until you get the color you want. These stains are good because you have almost perfect control of the color. They don't show overlap marks, and you can mix up any color you want. Water stains do raise the grain of the wood, however, and call for additional sanding or for preraising of the grain. See "Deliberately Raising the Grain" (above) for details.

Water stains are not as available as many others, and your dealer might have to order them for you. They are slow to apply because you may have to brush on three or four applications to reach the desired color, and must allow 24 hours for drying between applications.

NGR (Non-Grain Raising) Stains Once water stains were developed, somebody figured out that the grain raising problem could be eliminated if you dissolved the dye in some base other than water. The result was NGR stains, which brush on, won't raise the grain, and provide good coloring. They are not, however, as easy to control as water stains, and you can get a darker color than you want by too heavy an application. Practice with NGR stains before applying them.

Penetrating Oil Stains These are found on every dealer's shelves. They are pigmented oil stains that are brushed on and allowed to stand for 15 minutes or so, then wiped with a pad. Excess stain is removed during the wiping, but some stain penetrates the surface of the wood. It is easy to get a smooth, even tone with these stains, and you can control color to some degree by wiping earlier or later than 15 minutes. We think these are easy to use, raise few problems, and offer good results.

Paste and Jelly Stains These are the newest addition to the field, and we think they are great. They are applied with a soft pad, like shoe polish. You have complete color control with them and absolutely no mess. The stain can't splash or splatter. You just rub it on, rub until the surface is even in color, and let it dry. We think these come as close to a foolproof stain as you can find.

Such stains may have been around before, but they received a big boost from Bartley (makers of fine unfinished furniture kits), Homer Formby (noted for his full line of furniture finishing products) and others selling directly to consumers rather than to professionals. Because the consumer audience is inexperienced, each of these companies had to tailor a product that would provide top-notch results with minimal opportunities for failure.

APPLICATION METHODS

There are slight differences from brand to brand in all of the products in each of these three categories, so we can't give you specifics of application. Read the label of the product you buy and follow the instructions exactly. As always, make a practice run on scrap wood to get the feel of the product before working on your project.

In general, the steps for a wiping stain are:

(1) brush it on;
(2) allow it to stand for a recommended period;
(3) wipe it off;
(4) allow it to dry

With water stains, you brush on several applications getting a deeper color each time, until you arrive at the desired shade. With paste and jelly stains, you apply like shoe polish with a pad, and can apply more than one coat if you want deeper tones.

In all cases, the stain must dry completely before you apply the finish coat. Sand lightly to remove any dust or other imperfections, but don't sand so much that you break through the stain to the wood underneath.

Stains come in many varieties. Select the one that will give you the best results.

Because of ease of application and quality results, we prefer paste and jelly stains.

9
Applying the Final Finish

After long preparation, you are now ready to select and apply the final finish. There are half a dozen or more finishes from which you might choose, and you may already know what you want to use. But before we go on to the subject of the chapter—how to apply a final finish—we will review the preparation of the surfaces and the selection of the finish. You may want to change your mind about the finish, or rework some of the preparatory steps.

STATUS OF YOUR PROJECT
At this point, the piece of furniture you are working on is in one of these conditions:
(1) naked, either because it is new unfinished furniture or because you stripped it of the old finish; or,
(2) stained or stained and filled; you have applied stain and (if necessary) filler to the previously stripped surface; or,
(3) partially finished—you have not completely removed the old finish because it was not in bad condition, and you have made whatever repairs were necessary—now you are going to add a new finish coat over the old to complete your work.

Naked Unfinished Furniture
If you have new naked unfinished furniture, read this chapter to learn about the finishes that are available, but do not do anything until you turn ahead to the chapter on unfinished furniture. Unfinished furniture has some specific problems you should consider before applying the final finish.

Stripped, Unstained Furniture
If your furniture piece is now stained, you are striving for a final color that really will

When the time comes to select a final finish, you have a number of materials to choose from. This chapter covers the advantages and disadvantages of the various types available.

be a combination of the color of the stain plus the effect of the final finish coat. You probably realize by now that the final finishing material usually produces a color deeper than that of the stain alone. If the final finishing material has any color of its own, the ultimate color will be even deeper. This is why we have recommended from the beginning that you conduct tests as you proceed.

Testing for Color These tests take time, but they are simple enough. All you have to do is stain and finish a small sample of wood of the same species as the furniture. Every species reacts characteristically to stains and finishes. A walnut stain on walnut, for example, produces a deep, warm walnut color. The same stain on oak, pine or mahogany produces a different color. And then, when a finish coat is applied, the color may change again.

The point to keep uppermost in your mind is that no matter how beautifully you have repaired the piece, you will either love or hate it next month, depending on whether or not the final color and finish

pleases you. And since you already have invested a good many hours in this project, you should be willing to spend a few more at this time to guarantee a pleasing result.

Partially Finished Furniture
If you are now applying a new final finish coat over an existing finish to refurbish it, the major thing to remember is that the new finish must be compatible with the old. It is safest to apply a new finish of the same material: lacquer on lacquer, varnish on varnish, and so on. This will eliminate any unexpected chemical reactions or adhesion problems that could affect the finish immediately or over time.

RECONSIDERING THE FINAL FINISH
This is the time to review your decision on how to finish the piece, and here are considerations to take into account.
1. Do you want to duplicate the finish that was on the piece, or put on something different? The original finish may have

been lacquer. You can relacquer it, or finish it in varnish.

2. Are you concerned about special problems? For example, if the piece is a table that will be in regular use, you might want to apply a surface finish that will resist blooming. Shellac and lacquer bloom quickly if a wet glass is put on them. Varnishes, and especially varnishes designed for bar tops, resist these white blooming marks.

3. Do you prefer a glossy or a satin surface? You can buy gloss, semi-gloss and satin in most finishes (but not shellac). You also can control the gloss during the final sanding and hand rubbing operations.

4. Do you want a deep transparent finish, the result of many coats of clear finish? If so, you can choose among lacquer, shellac, varnish, plastic.

As we said much earlier, the secret is to know what look you want to achieve in order to choose a new finish that will please you. With this ultimate look firmly in mind, read through these pages and decide (or confirm the earlier decision) how to achieve the final appearance you want. Dream a little. See the finished piece in your mind. Then work to make the fantasy a reality.

The goal, at this time, is to have a piece of furniture that is sound, well-glued, evenly colored, and smooth of surface. Any imperfections will show suddenly after the first coat of finish is applied, and although additional sanding at that time will correct them, it is better if you can avoid this last-minute correction work.

THE FINISHES AVAILABLE

The following is a list of ways in which you can refinish furniture. Some are common, and some are obsolete; all are listed because they can still be found on some furniture pieces:

Natural varnish
Synthetic varnish
Sprayed lacquer
Brushed lacquer
Penetrating resin
Tung oil
Shellac
Wax
Hand-rubbed oil
French polish
Enamel
Antique glazing
Plastic

Each of these finishing methods has a reason for its use and popularity. Some, like the wax and the hand-rubbed oil finishes, were once very popular but are no longer in general use. Some, like the French polish, produce a very pleasing result but aren't used because they require a great amount of labor. Some are very durable, while others tend to be fragile.

A French polish is a very specialized finish. The highly reflective surface is the result of layer after layer of shellac and oil.

In general, the finishes most common today are sprayed lacquer (by furniture manufacturers), and synthetic varnish and tung oil (favored by refinishers). Enamel has always been desirable on certain kinds of furniture, and antique glazing, which employs latex enamel and a glaze, has enjoyed popularity among do-it-yourselfers for the past ten years. The plastic finishes, which come in clear and colored formulations, seem to find use mostly in modern and contemporary furniture, but not so much on traditional pieces. The penetrating resins, which have been around for a number of years and are very easy to use, offer some outstanding benefits and have a number of loyal fans.

Varnishes

Varnish has long been considered the best finish for fine furniture by furniture finishers. Because it was always slow in drying and required careful application by brush, it never was popular with furniture manufacturers.

Natural Varnishes The natural varnishes used for many years were a combination of oil and natural resin, and the different names you may have heard — spar varnish, bartop varnish, church pew varnish, gymnasium varnish, piano varnish — really were references to the percentage of oil used in the formulation. The more oil in the mixture, the more durable

and flexible it was. But an increase in oil also increased the drying time.

Thus, varnishes intended for tough use, such as spar and bartop mixtures, had more oil and had to be given long drying periods. Varnishes that needed to be hard or intended for a beautiful hand-rubbed finish were made with less oil. They dried quicker and harder, but were more brittle and scratched easily.

Synthetic Varnishes Then paint chemists discovered how to incorporate manmade resins into varnish formulations, and everything changed. Manufacturers were able to control hardness, flexibility, drying times and so on, to produce formulations that would satisfy the special needs of the spar maker, the piano maker, the furniture maker and the church pew maker. You can still find natural varnishes in specialty stores if you are intent on duplicating the finish of an old and valued piece, but the great majority of available varnishes are made with manmade resins, and generally are referred to as synthetic varnishes. There are four basic synthetic varnish formulations: alkyd, phenolic, urethane, and plastic.

Alkyd varnish The alkyds are available in glossy and satin (matte) finishes. This formulation is excellent for producing good hand-rubbed finishes. The varnish tends to be somewhat yellow in color and darkens any wood to which it is applied. Nor does it brush on as easily as a urethane finish. You will find some formulations that combine alkyd and vinyl, to produce increased flexibility. Drying time is relatively slow and varies from maker to maker.

Phenolic varnish Usually available only in glossy finishes, the phenolics have

Many people don't take the time to do it, but we have found that applying a finish to all surfaces of a drawer, inside and out, makes sense. It seals the drawer against moisture and cuts down on swelling and cracking.

the reputation for being tough and weather resistant. For this reason, they are extensively used in exterior applications around the home and on boats. Phenolic varnishes are quite yellow when applied, tend to darken wood, and they get yellower as they age on the wood. This means that you must start with a lighter stain to achieve the color you want, and you should be prepared for further darkening over the years. Drying time is on the slow side.

Urethane varnish The urethane combinations are probably the best for furniture work. They are the easiest to brush on, and faster drying than either the alkyds or the phenolics. They are the clearest (least yellow) of the varnishes and don't darken after application. They do, however, darken the wood to which they are applied, so be sure to color-test them over the stain you are using. They rub out to a handsome finish, and are available in gloss, semi-gloss, satin and flat. You can find spraying versions of urethane varnishes if you intend to spray instead of brushing the finish on. Drying times vary considerably with the brand, so check the label and follow application instructions carefully.

In our opinion, the urethane varnishes are the best for furniture finishing. They are easy to apply, rub out nicely for a beautiful final finish, resist water, alcohol and general wear, and look good. You can achieve either a deep gloss finish or a satin finish without difficulty.

Vinyl varnish Most furniture people won't call a vinyl finish a varnish. Instead, they refer to it as a plastic finish. The vinyls certainly have totally different characteristics than the three varnishes already mentioned. For one thing, they dry in 15 minutes. They are absolutely clear and don't change color after application. They have good resistance to water and alcohol, but they suffer from abrasion so you don't hand rub them at the end of the finishing process. Vinyls can be brushed on or sprayed on, come in gloss and semi-gloss, and generally are thought of as fine finishes for wall paneling.

HOW TO APPLY A VARNISH FINISH

The first rule in applying any modern varnish is: Read the label first! The second rule is: *No matter what we tell you here, follow the instructions on the label.*

The reason for these rules is every formulation today is different in some degree from its neighbor on the shelf. Since no two are exactly alike, every varnish can require special rules of application. We can only give you generalized instructions. The manufacturer is extremely interested in helping you obtain good results with his product, so his instructions generally are the best.

APPLICATION GUIDELINES

The main points of difference to watch for between sets of instructions are (1) thinning procedures; (2) drying times; (3) brushing procedures.

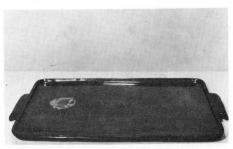

This is a solid mahogany tray that someone has left a very hot, wet pot on. Our job is to attempt to restore the surface.

The first step is to test the finish, using first denatured alcohol, then lacquer thinner, to find out what type of finish was used. Neither of these chemicals affected this, so we believe the tray probably is varnished.

We tried finish remover on the bad spot but it didn't work. The finish appears to be a heavy coating of polyurethane varnish. Our only choice now is to sand out the bad spot as far as necessary to remove any discolored wood. Fortunately, not much sanding was required, so the surface of the wood remains unharmed.

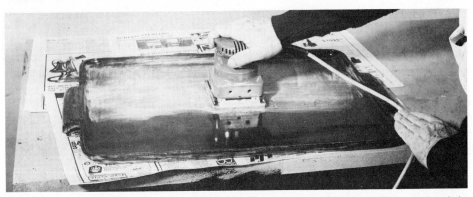

The old varnish had a glossy surface. As a result, we had to sand both sides of the tray to break the gloss so that there would be enough tooth for a new coat to catch hold.

Next, we applied a coat of varnish to the damaged area. When this dried, the entire tray was varnished to fully restore the tray.

Thinners

There once was a time when one could use turpentine to thin just about any coating material but this is not so with today's formulations. You might ruin the mixture by thinning it, or you might thin with something that isn't compatible with the formulation. *Read the label.* If it tells you to use the varnish straight from the can, do so. If the label provides the name of a thinner to use, follow the directions for such thinning. If no thinner is suggested, be safe and don't attempt to thin the mixture.

Drying Time

Drying times vary strictly because of the chemical formulation, but watch out for very special drying instructions about when you can apply a second coat. With some varnishes, you can apply a second coat after 4 to 6 hours of drying. If you do not get around to putting on the second coat in those 2 hours, then you must wait 24 hours before applying the next coat. This might sound odd, but it happens because the second coat produces a bonding action 4 to 6 hours after the application of the first coat — which is good. After 6 hours, however, the first coat becomes too hard to permit the bonding action, so you must wait until drying is complete to apply the second coat. And then you must do a light scuff sanding before putting on the second coat, to create "tooth" for the new coating to grab.

Unless special drying instructions are indicated, varnish should be allowed to dry thoroughly between coats. The instructions on the can tell exactly how long. Usually, 24 hours between coats is a safe time, but this can depend on the humidity in your work area. If the air is humid, you should leave the work set for 36 hours to ensure a safe drying time.

Varnish is laid down, not brushed out. The material then smooths out by itself. A light opposite you helps highlight missed areas.

The drying of modern varnishes is a two-step procedure. They dry and harden in the first step; they cure in the second step. During the latter part of the drying period, the varnishes look dry and feel dry. That's when they are curing. If you apply a new coat too soon, you slow down this curing process. As a general rule, allow the longest practical time for drying to get the best results. It doesn't hurt to extend the time to 48 hours or more.

Technique

The object in applying varnish is to "lay down" a coat rather than to brush it on, and you will be more successful if you think in those terms. Always work on a horizontal surface when possible. This means you will have to varnish a dresser top first; wait until it dries to turn the piece and do one side; then turn again to do the other side. This is slow work but necessary because fluid varnish, after applied, levels itself on the surface. It obviously can't do this on a vertical surface and it will run if you apply more than a very thin coat.

Brushes

Use a soft, natural-bristle brush which has not been used with paint before. Dislodge any loose bristles by working the brush back and forth across your hand a few times and then rapidly "painting" the edge of a table for a minute or so. Good brushes are quite expensive, but this job really requires the best. Bargain brushes will give you a bargain finish.

SETTING UP SHOP
The Dust Problem

The biggest problem in varnishing is dust, and the problem has two faces. The first is the dust already on the piece of furniture before you apply the finish coat. The second is the dust that falls on the wet surface after you have finished the application. Each speck of dust turns into a tiny bump on the surface. On glossy surfaces, these bumps spoil the appearance, and they can be felt on all surfaces when you run your fingers over the dried varnish.

The obvious answers are: (1) get all dust off the piece before you start; (2), work in an area that is as free of dust as you can make it, so there is little to fall on the surface. There is a third answer, and that is to be prepared to lift any dust from the new varnish before it dries.

Dusting the Piece Remove all sanding and other dust before you start, by vacuuming the entire piece with the drapery wand attachment of your vacuum cleaner. Then wipe the piece with a tack cloth just before starting the application.

Dusting the Work Area A dust-free work area is difficult to achieve, but you must try. The day before finishing the piece, vacuum the room, using the vacuum's tools to get dust out of corners, off of window sills, etc. If you have forced air heat, close the outlet to the room, because it can stir up dust. Keep the windows closed during application and drying. (Fortunately, most varnishes do not present a ventilation problem. Lacquers do.) Don't scurry around the room as you work. Walk and move slowly so you will not stir up any more dust than is necessary.

Temperature

Room temperature is important to drying and curing. The room should be above 70 degrees Fahrenheit.

A Working Light

To do the best job of varnishing, you must be able to see how the coats are going down and to see any dust that has settled on the surface. The best way to make this possible is to place a table lamp with its shade removed just beyond one end of the work. Then, when you look down into the work from a position opposite the lamp, you can see every imperfection because of the reflection of the light on the new surface. (This lamp trick is good when enameling or applying other finishes, too. It enables you to see when one area is not covered as well as the rest.)

Step 1: Preparing the Piece for Finishing

Before you apply a finish coat, you want to be certain that the surfaces of the piece are smooth and ready for it.

Sanding If you have not stained the piece, you can sand as much as you want. If the piece is stained, sand with great care, because if you sand through the stain and expose the wood beneath it, you will be faced with some problems. Patching stain to an even color isn't easy, and you might end up restaining the whole thing. The best way is to sand the stained surfaces lightly to knock off any tiny bumps. Apply the first coat and sand again.

Tack Rag The very last step, before you begin application of the final finish, is to go over the sanded piece with a tack rag to remove all vestiges of sawdust. Do this immediately before beginning the final coat. If you let the piece stand several days between staining and finishing, be sure to do another wipedown on the day of the final coat. Dust will have settled on the surface during the interim.

Step 2: The Sealer Coat

Furniture finishers sometimes think of the first finish coat as the sealer coat, and many recommend that the first coat be of varnish thinned with 1 part turpentine to 4 parts of varnish. This coat is brushed well into the surface, allowed to dry, and then sanded. This is usually recommended over water-based stains, but is not necessary with wiping stains. We are a bit leery of the procedure because of the thinning requirement, so we generally apply our varnish straight from the can unless otherwise directed by the manufacturer. This works for us because we usually employ pigmented wiping stains.

Place the can of varnish conveniently, so you can dip into it without traveling very far. Dip the brush into the liquid for one-third its length. Then lift the brush straight up without wiping it against the lip of the can.

Begin laying down the finish at the farthest point from you, and work from there toward you. The bare lamp should be opposite you to create a reflected surface. Apply this first coat across the wood grain. Brush on the varnish with deliberate, even strokes, and don't allow the strokes to overlap much. At the end of each stroke, lift the brush straight from the surface, dip it in the varnish again, and begin the new stroke on an unvarnished area.

Evening It Out When the entire surface has been coated, go back and, using just the tips of the bristles, brush lightly with the grain to smooth out the finish. Look for areas that seem to be heavy and run the tip through them to help level them. Be especially careful at the edges. It is easy to wipe varnish out of the brush by crossing over the edges, and this varnish will run down the sides. Avoid this by brushing with care near all edges.

Tipping Always remember that you are brushing the varnish on. You are laying down a fairly thick, even coat. You

want to work deliberately and avoid creating bubbles, and you want to even out any areas with too much or too little varnish on them by "tipping" — working across the surface with the bristle tips.

Pattern Approach You might like the "pattern" approach to varnishing. In this, you lay down stripes of varnish from one end to the other, with each strip as wide as the brush is. Then you move over, leaving a stripe unvarnished, and lay down another stripe. You end up with alternating varnished and unvarnished stripes in one direction. Next, you apply varnish across the work to fill in the previously unvarnished areas. This method helps create a smooth coat by spreading the first varnish stripes into the unvarnished areas.

Step 3: Levelling Out

Don't brush out the varnish as you would paint. Once the surface has been laid down, let it level itself and dry. Suspend your brush in a can of mineral spirits between coats to keep it pliable. Once you have stopped brushing, don't attempt to add more varnish or do additional brushing. If you suddenly see an area that doesn't have enough varnish, leave it alone. You can handle it by sanding carefully after the varnish has dried and by coating it properly the next time around.

Dust Specks If you are applying a satin finish, you probably won't see any dust specks in the new surface. If you are putting down a glossy coat, you now may be horrified to see a collection of little dust bumps in the new varnish. Don't panic. First, remember that this is a first coat and that sanding between finishes will take care of many of these bumps. Second, if some seem too big or really annoy you, lift them out using the tip of a very fine artist's brush. Do this deftly, trying not to disturb the varnish very much. If you decide to remove dust specks, do so before the drying gets very far along. This allows the varnish to level itself after the dust speck has been removed. If you wait too long, you may create a tiny crater when you lift out the dust speck because the varnish, once it has begun to dry, won't level itself.

Step 4: Varnishing Odd-size Surfaces

The previous instructions apply to nice big surfaces like table tops. But every piece of furniture has other surfaces such as rungs

and stringers, moldings, spindles, edges. Some of these will have to be varnished in a vertical (or other) position, and you won't be able to lay down a smooth coat. We recommend that you buy a smaller brush for this kind of work.

To varnish rungs, turned legs, spindles and other round work, apply the coating with short strokes across the work; then finish long strokes to even it out. Do not apply a heavy coat when doing round work because the varnish may run. Be content with light coats, and apply one coat more than for a flat surface.

Step 5: Varnishing Carved Pieces

Carved areas offer a special problem. When you varnish across them, you put too light a coat on the high spots and too much in the low spots. If you dab at them, you create bubbles in the finish. The best way is to smoothly brush varnish over the carving, and then go back with a dry brush (this means you don't dip it in the can after discharging the last load on the surface) and gently lift the varnish from the low spots. This is rather like wiping up the excess varnish. Wipe the excess from the

The patterned approach is one way to apply varnish. In this method, you have alternate varnished and unvarnished strips. Then fill in.

To prevent runs when you varnish round parts such as legs and rungs, apply less thick a coat than you do on a flat surface.

and look for both of these words in them, and look for instructions that tell you to wipe off the coat. Some good brand names are Deep Finish Firzite, Clear Rez, and Clear Minwax, but there are many others.

Application Procedures

As always, read the labels before using. There are minor differences between brands. Follow the specific instructions on the label to get the best results.

Step 1: The First Coat You don't brush or spray on a penetrating resin. You mop it on and keep the surface wet for perhaps half an hour (or more, depending on the brand) while the penetration of the resin takes place. Watch for spots where the resin has soaked in and apply more to these areas. When all the soaking and penetrating has taken place, wipe the surface clean with rags. Rub the surface down thoroughly, because any excess left on the

surface will later produce a shine you won't like.

Step 2: The Second Coat About three hours after this rubdown, apply a second coat in the same manner as the first, allowing the surface to stand for the required soaking time and then rubbing it down thoroughly with old rags. Allow the resin to dry and set as directed on the can. Finish the job by applying two coats of good paste wax.

HOW TO APPLY A TUNG OIL FINISH

The tung nut originated in China, but now there are tung nut groves in the southern United States. Oil from this nut is a penetrating oil that builds up on the wood during repeated applications to a glossy finish. The tung finish is durable and good looking. There are at least two furniture finishing systems on the market built around tung oil — Hope's and Formby's.

These systems use a refinishing mixture

that, when applied with fine-grade steel wool, removes the old finish without taking away the stain beneath it. Then you rub the tung oil into the finish with your bare hands. The heat of your hands helps the wood to absorb the oil. You should cover all surfaces of the furniture, including backs and undersides, to seal the wood against moisture.

The tung oil in these systems is not pure oil, but is a mixture designed to give good results. For this reason, you must follow

each maker's instructions to the letter. Observe the instructions for the number of coats, time between coats, and drying times.

These systems are very easy to use, and require much less work than other refinishing methods. You aren't likely to err as you work and the results are excellent.

The same systems can be applied to wood that has been stripped naked. In this case, use the stains in the system to restore the wood's color before applying the oil.

APPLYING THE OLD FASHIONED WAX FINISH

The wax finish isn't seen much any more, but it is an interesting way to treat wood, and you may need to know about it if you are restoring a piece that originally had a wax finish.

Actually, this method is not a finish in

itself, but a coating applied to a shellac finish. See the section on shellac for instructions on how to apply a shellac finish. Then apply two coats of fine paste wax, buffing each one thoroughly with the buffing pad in your electric drill. To renew the finish from time to time, apply another coat of wax.

Over a long period of time the surface will develop a pretty good wax buildup. Then it is time to get out the wax remover, take off all the old wax, and start over. A wax finish is rich looking, but because it is laid over shellac, it doesn't resist scratching and surface wear very well.

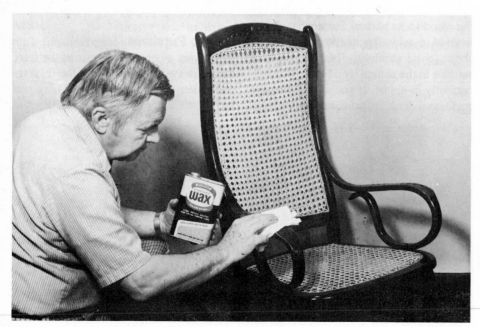

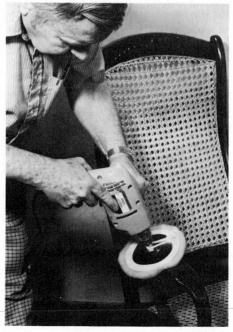

A good paste wax makes an excellent last step — though some experts tell you to avoid any wax and use only a lemon oil polish. We like the wax. Here a liquified carnauba wax is applied to the just-completed caned rocker.

Now the wax is buffed to a high shine with a lamb's wool buffer in the electric drill.

APPLYING A HAND-RUBBED OIL FINISH

Furniture people speak in reverent tones of hand-rubbed oil finishes. The classic hand-rubbed oil finish has warm, soft depth and is regarded as exquisite by antique buyers. However, once you have bought a piece of furniture with this type of finish, you discover the other side of the coin. The oil finish collects dust like a magnet and requires regular care to maintain its appearance. So, for the furniture restorer, the question is: do you want the undeniable beauty of an oil finish — along with the effort of maintaining it? If you really want a genuine oil finish, here is how to apply it.

Step 1: Staining the Piece

Stain the piece, but only use a water-based stain. This leaves the wood porous so it can soak up the oil that you apply later.

Step 2: Applying the First Coat

Make a mixture of one part distilled turpentine and one part boiled linseed oil. Just before application, heat the oil. Do not heat this mixture over an open flame! Instead, use a double-boiler technique. Place the can containing the mixture in a larger pan, and pour boiling water in the larger pan. The oil mixture will heat up in a few minutes. Brush the warm mixture generously over the wood to be finished. Allow it to soak into the wood for ten minutes or so. Then wipe off the excess.

Step 3: Polishing the Surface

Use a hard cloth, such as denim, to polish the newly oiled surface. This is where the hand rubbing comes in. You will have to rub hard until the surface takes on a warm glow.

Step 4: Scheduling Followup Treatments

The treatment must be repeated frequently. Here is a typical schedule you might want to follow: once a day for the first week, then once a week for the next month. Then finish once a month for the rest of the year. After the first year, you should do an annual refinishing. As you can see, achieving and maintaining the classic oil finish is time-consuming work, and you must be dedicated enough to complete what you start.

Alternative Method

Modern technology provides one alternative. You will find cans of so-called "oil finishes" at your hardware store. These are finishes which go on in one coat, require no more maintenance than any varnish finish, and yet give you the rich look of the hand-rubbed oil finish. Check the store shelves. Each brand has its own method of application, so read the label carefully and follow directions exactly. The modern one-coat oil finishes offer advantages over the classic method — they are less sticky, more durable and attract less dust. Their appearance provides a close imitation. But you have to face it: the modern finish is still only an imitation. If you want to say, "This is a hand-rubbed oil finish," you have to get the finish the hard way. We happen to be allergic to the kind of maintenance schedule an oil finish demands, so we don't use it; however don't let our allergies stop you.

HOW TO APPLY A SHELLAC FINISH

The tiny lac insects of India feed on the sap of trees and secrete a resinous substance that hardens on the tree branches. This substance is scraped from the branches and is used to produce shellac. It is interesting to note that all shellac you can buy is the natural substance. No one has, as yet, made a synthetic version of this finish, which has been used on furniture for hundreds of years.

Advantages

Shellac offers advantages and disadvantages. It dries quickly, is easy to apply, looks beautiful on furniture, and is flexible (which is why it has often been used on floors). Its main disadvantages are the fact that it blooms after absorbing water and that it is softened by alcohol and other chemicals. Thus, it shouldn't be used on tables or other surfaces on which drink glasses are likely to be set.

Each new coat of shellac softens the previous coat. This process results in an excellent bonding between the coats. Four or five coats build into a deep single coat because of this bonding. A shellac finish has a warm depth that is highly prized by furniture lovers.

How to Buy Shellac

It is essential to always use fresh shellac. Once the can has been opened, the contents will deteriorate within six months to such an extent that they will not dry after application. Even in cans that have never been opened, shellac deteriorates, which is the reason that many manufacturers date their products. When buying shellac, check the date, and do not buy the product if it has exceeded the expiration date. If you are offered undated cans, buy them only with the understanding that you will get your money back if the contents do not dry as they should.

The "Cut" The resinous shellac is dissolved in denatured alcohol, and the proportion of resin to alcohol is called "the cut." Thus, when you see a can marked "1-pound cut," it means that the contents consist of shellac cut at the rate of three pounds of shellac resin to one gallon of alcohol. The 3-pound cut, which is the right consistency to be used straight from the can for finishing floors, is the most common cut found in stores. The best cut to use for furniture finishing is the 1-pound, which brushes on easily and dries quickly.

The more shellac resin in the mixture, the thicker the coat laid down each time. It is true that with a 1-pound cut you have to apply more coats than with a 2-pound or 3-pound cut, but since brushing is easier, the 1-pound cut works best, particularly for novices and their early efforts. Later, after gaining experience, you may want to shift to heavier cuts.

You build a shellac finish coat by coat. As a rule, most finishers using a 1-pound cut would plan on three to five coats. Since shellac dries hard in half an hour (up to an hour in higher humidity and lower temperature conditions), you can apply these coats quickly, usually finishing the entire job in a day or two.

Types of Shellac Shellac comes in white and orange. White shellac is clear and is the one usually used in furniture work. Orange shellac tends to darken light woods, and will give darker woods a richer look.

Mixing with Denatured Alcohol

When you buy shellac, also buy the denatured alcohol you will need to thin it. Use the accompanying chart to find out how much alcohol to mix with each "cut" of shellac in the can to get the cut you need for your work. As you can see from the chart, you can start with any cut, so it doesn't make much difference which one your dealer sells. Look in the chart for the cut you bought. Glance down the left-hand column to the cut you intend to use. The chart indicates how many parts of alcohol to mix with the ingredients in the can to get the cut you desire. If you buy 3-pound cut shellac, and want to work with 1-pound cut, the chart shows that you should mix three parts of shellac with four parts of alcohol.

PROPORTIONS FOR SHELLAC CUTS

Shellac	Alcohol	Resulting Cut
2 parts 5 lb.	1 part	3 lb.
1 part 5 lb.	1 part	2 lb.
1 part 5 lb.	2 parts	1 lb.
1 part 4 lb.	2 parts	3 lb.
4 parts 4 lb.	3 parts	2 lb.
1 part 4 lb.	4 parts	1 lb.
5 parts 3 lb.	2 parts	2 lb.
3 parts 3 lb.	4 parts	1 lb.

Step 1: Applying The First Coat
Dip the brush one-third to one-half of its length into the shellac can. Flow the mixture onto the surface. As with varnish, you do not brush the coat on; you lay it down. Work slowly with the brush to avoid creating bubbles in the shellac, and be sure the brush marks overlap. Place a lamp without its shade beyond the furniture piece and opposite the side on which you stand. The reflection of the light will immediately reveal any areas that have not been covered. Without the light, it can be difficult to see these areas, especially on dark wood.

Step 2: Sanding the First Coat
The first coat will dry rough to the touch, even if the surface below has been thoroughly sanded. To even out the shellac, sand the shellac well, using a sanding block and an open-coated 4/0 or 5/0 sandpaper. The open-coated paper is necessary because shellac clogs the paper rapidly as you sand. As a result, even if you use open-coated paper, you should have a good supply on hand when you start sanding, for you will use it quickly. Sand until the surface feels smooth. You need not worry about sanding through the surface, because the next coat will fill in and bond to it. As long as you do not disturb the stain underneath, you will have no problem.

Step 3: Subsequent Coats
After wiping the sanded surface clean with a dry cloth, apply the next coat. This coat won't need nearly as much sanding, and each succeeding coat will require less. The final smoothing should be with a very fine (4/0 grade) steel wool. After this treatment, allow the piece to cure for 24 to 48 hours before applying a coat of paste wax.

Shellac should be applied carefully to avoid air bubbles. The material is laid down, as is varnish. Be sure that the brush marks overlap.

HOW TO CREATE THE FRENCH POLISH One of the finest finishes, often found on valuable antique pieces, is the French polish. This is a deep, lustrous, translucent shellac-and-linseed oil finish made by rubbing coat after coat of shellac onto the furniture surfaces. If you are working with true antiques, you should know how to apply it.

Overview
The furniture is first stained, then sanded. Next the entire piece is treated to a coating of boiled linseed oil, which is allowed to dry. Then use a pad lubricated with linseed oil to rub coats of shellac on the surface, until the surface finish is as deep and lustrous as you want it.

Making an Applicator Pad To make an applicator pad, use a lintless cloth (an old T-shirt which has been washed several dozen times is fine). Fold it into a 6x6-inch pad that is quite thick.

Step 1: Applying The First Coat
Saturate the applicator pad with 1-pound cut shellac and begin rubbing the furniture surface with a circular, non-stop motion. You will be able to see the pad depositing shellac on the oiled surface. Keep rubbing as long as shellac transfers. Then saturate the pad again with shellac and add a few drops of linseed oil for lubrication.

Rubbing on the Shellac The rubbing motion is the most difficult part of applying the French polish. In order to do it correctly, you must practice until you develop the knack. Start the circular motion with the pad held over the surface. Then lower the pad without pausing until it contacts the surface. The motion must be continuous, because if you stop even for a moment, the pad will become tacky. When it comes time to lift the pad from the surface for recharging, do this with a sweeping motion so that the pad "takes off" of the surface without stopping.

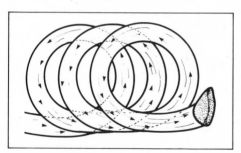

The success of a French polish depends upon the rubbing motion. To avoid blemishes, practice before you work on the wood itself.

Step 2: Adding Subsequent Coats
After one coat has been applied, allow it to dry and apply the next coat. There is no limit to the number of coats you can apply. We recommend 1-pound cut shellac for beginners, but after you have learned how to apply this finish, you can graduate to heavier cuts, even up to 5 pounds. The heavier the cut, the thicker each coat will be, and the sooner you will achieve the depth you want.

Step 3: Final Finishing

After you have applied all coats, dip a pad in denatured alcohol and wring it out so that it is no more than damp-dry. Whisk this cloth over the surface to eliminate excess oil and any pad marks that you might have left. Be cautious during this operation, because the alcohol can soften the shellac, and that's not what you want. This is a type of reamalgamation of the surface; it requires little more than a hint of the alcohol in order to work.

HOW TO APPLY AN ENAMEL FINISH

People sometimes think of enamel as the finish to use when you must cover up problem furniture surfaces, and it can be used for that purpose. However, enamels have been used on fine furniture for many years, and they produce fine finishes in their own right. An enamel really is a pigmented varnish, with the pigment supplying the color. The material acts like varnish, leveling itself after brushing and drying to a hard, glossy finish.

How to Buy Enamel

Modern enamels are the results of the paint chemists' wizardry, so you'll find alkyd-based enamels, latex enamels, and other formulations similar to those mentioned in the varnish section. All of these seem to be good for furniture finishing purposes. Enamels come in glossy, semi-glossy and flat. As a general rule, the glossy enamels are the best choice for finishing furniture. Semi-gloss enamels are satisfactory, but flat enamels shouldn't be applied to furniture.

Color Choice

When buying enamels today, you have an absolutely unlimited color choice, since your dealer can custom mix the color you want. The only problem posed by this amazing range of color choices is that the final decision can be difficult. You must look at small color chips, with only tiny variations from chip to chip, to make your selection. Our only advice is that it helps to have selected a color in advance and to bring a sample of the color in. Matching a sample is much easier than picking a color without a guide. The sample color can be from wallpaper, a fabric, even from a magazine or book illustration.

Overview

As a rule, the best enamel finish on good furniture consists of a first coat of enamel undercoat, followed by two coats of enamel. You sand between coats, and after the last coat has dried completely, you give it a good rubbing with pumice and water. The finishing is completed by a final coat of paste wax.

Step 1: Start with an Undercoat

You can find arguments both for and against applying an undercoat as the first coat. Most enamel makers specify the use of an undercoater on bare wood before the first coat of enamel is applied. Many furniture finishers say that if the wood has been prepared properly, the enamel itself, thinned a little, makes an ideal undercoat. However, it has been our experience that you get the best and most consistent results by starting with an undercoater.

Use an undercoater that is compatible with the enamel. Usually, the enamel maker markets an undercoater developed specifically for his product. All undercoaters come in basic white, but we have found it best to have them tinted to a color near that of the final enamel coat. After applying the undercoat, give it plenty of time to dry. Remember that local temperature and humidity conditions can seriously affect drying. If you live in a desert or low-humidity area, the drying time specified on the can will be more than enough.

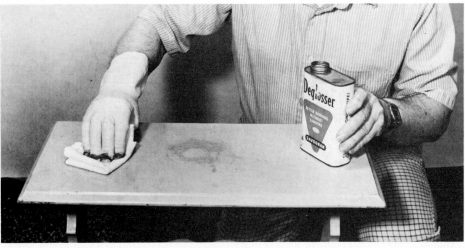

Applying enamel is similar to applying varnish. If you are recoating a piece already enameled, remember that the new coat will not adhere properly to the old glossy surface. Either sand the old surface or use a "deglosser" liquid on it so the new coat has tooth.

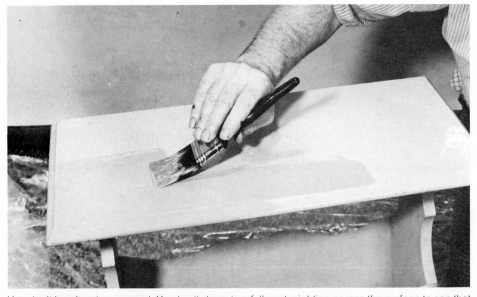

You don't brush out an enamel. You lay it down in a full coat, sighting across the surface to see that you are covering properly. Brush marks disappear as the enamel dries.

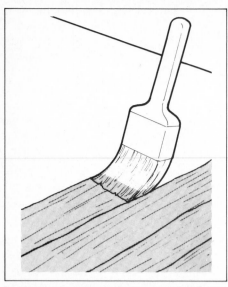

To apply enamel, first lay down a coat with long, full strokes. Make sure that you cover the entire surface of the wood.

When the surface is covered, go over the coat the other way, with the tips of the brush, to smooth out the brush strokes as you go.

If you live in a humid area — the ocean-side, for example — you might want to allow a couple extra hours.

Step 2: The First Enamel Coat Sand the dried undercoat with 4/0 paper, then apply the first enamel coat. Enamel should be applied like varnish. Lay the enamel on, but do not brush it out as if it were paint. Turn the piece so that you can work on horizontal surfaces. Enamel, like varnish, is self-leveling, but will only do this on a flat, horizontal surface. Apply full-brush stripes of enamel to the surface, working in one direction. Then go back and use the bristle tips to brush across the strips to make the coat even and smooth. Be careful not to wipe the brush on the edges, causing drips and runs.

Step 3: The Second Coat
Sand the first enamel coat after it has dried, and apply the second coat in the same manner as the first.

HOW TO APPLY AN ANTIQUE GLAZING You can buy antique glazing kits that contain the basic materials needed: a color enamel for the base coat, a glaze for the final coat, and a sealer. Antique glazing is a two-step process in which you first apply an enamel coat in a selected color, and then brush a glazing material of a different (usually darker) color over the enamel coat. The "antique look" is achieved by wiping this glaze before it dries, and the final results really depend on how you do this wiping. The idea is to wipe the glaze so that it shades from a light color in the center of a panel to a darker color at the edges, which is the way the finish would look if it had darkened its appearance due to age and wear.

Antiquers use a wide variety of wiping tools to achieve various effects: wadded paper towels, sponges, squeegees, rubber ink rollers, folded cloth pads — anything to both wipe and to create a pattern in the glaze. There are a number of wiping tools you can buy for such purposes as creating a wood grain effect.

Step 1: Preparation
Prepare the wood of the furniture for antique glazing just as for other finishes. If only the finish is severely damaged, it should be removed. If there is only minor damage, sand the old finish to smooth out chipped and broken areas and to provide tooth for the new finish.

Step 2: The Enamel Coat
Follow the maker's instructions for applying the enamel color coat. As you work, keep in mind that you are not painting the furniture; you are laying down a finish. Since this is an enamel finish with an overlay of glaze, everything we mentioned about application in the enamel section of this chapter also applies here.

Step 3: The Glaze Coat
You must sand between coats of enamel, and also sand the last coat of enamel before applying the glaze. Apply the glaze coat as directed. Most glazes are brushed on, allowed to dry for a time and, finally, wiped.

Step 4: Finishing
After wiping, the glaze is allowed to dry before the application of a sealer coat. The sealer coat usually is a clear urethane varnish, supplied with the kit.

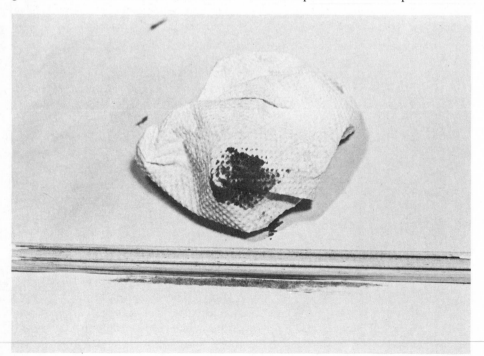

When you antique, first apply a base layer of enamel. Dry thoroughly. Then brush over the glaze coat and wipe the glaze away to highlight trim and outer edges.

10
Veneering

A veneer is a thin sheet of wood applied to the exterior surface of a piece of furniture to enhance its appearance. Usually, the veneer is a fine wood while the wood under it is of a common variety. The technique has been in use for over 3,500 years and perhaps longer.

Veneer woods originally were shaved by hand, so that the making of a veneer to cover a table was a long, tedious job and one that required great skill. Veneers today are ½8, ⅓2 and ¼0-inch thick, the latter being about as thick as four average sheets of paper. They are peeled from turning logs in continuous sheets by huge veneer knives. Watching the process, you are reminded of wrapping paper being pulled from a roll.

For a time, in the early part of the century, veneered furniture was considered by many people in this country to be a cheap imitation of good solid-wood furniture. They assumed that furniture makers saved money by using cheap wood and covering it with a thin sheet of good wood. Even today, you occasionally hear someone say disparagingly, ''Oh, it's veneered.''

These people don't know that veneering goes back almost as far as the production of solid wood furniture. They also don't realize that when a log is sliced for veneering, a whole new kind of woodgrain beauty results. You can easily see this by comparing a piece of solid mahogany furniture to a piece faced with a lovely mahogany veneer. Both are beautiful, but the veneered piece has gorgeous grain patterns that can be had only when the log is peeled across the grain.

Veneers, in furniture, are used for several reasons. One is the beauty of the grain produced by veneering. Another is that

Here are the veneer pieces cut out for application to the dresser. The larger pieces, for the faces of the big drawers, are still held together with masking tape on the underside.

some woods are too rare to be used in solid wood construction. One log of these woods might make several pieces of furniture in solid wood, but would produce hundreds of beautiful veneered pieces. A third reason is cost. You can make mahogany veneered furniture for less than solid mahogany furniture—the fact that gave rise to the idea that veneered furniture is cheap.

VENEERS IN FURNITURE RESTORATION

When we began to restore furniture, we discovered a number of uses for a knowledge of veneering. First, we found that old, severely damaged veneers often had to be replaced. The 1852 dresser we restored during the writing of this book was a good example of that. Next, we found that sometimes we could take a plain piece of sound hardwood furniture, the kind that was made for utility rather than appearance, and upgrade it to a beautiful piece by veneering all or part of it. Finally, we constantly faced jobs requiring repairs of existing veneers.

Veneering, we discovered, is fun, and it isn't difficult. We received a lot of satisfaction standing back to survey the work after applying a beautiful veneer to an old beat-up table top. We suddenly felt like very proficient craftsmen, and our first impulse was to call people over to see what we'd done.

Finding and Buying Veneers

Veneer woods generally are available through specialty mail order houses. Constantine, in New York, and Craftsman, in Chicago, are two major suppliers, but a number of others advertise in the do-it-yourself and furniture magazines. Send for the catalogs of as many of these suppliers as you can find. They all sell veneering supplies as well as the wood, and also sell speciality items such as pre-assembled chess boards or emblems. You also can buy decorative inlay strips to use in conjunction with standard veneers to make beautiful table and cabinet designs. With these, you can veneer a table top, for example, and inlay a strip made of rare and exotic woods around the edges. One friend buys ready-made jewelry and other boxes at a craft shop. She applies exquisite veneers — lovely woods such as teak, zebrawood, rosewood, purpleheart and ebony — to these to make beautiful gifts.

Reading the catalogs of veneer suppliers provides an education. You learn the prices, sizes of sheets and strips available, and also discover what butt, burl, crotch and swirl woods are. You find out about the different cuts — quarter, rotary and flat. And you also begin to learn to identify rare woods, a useful ability for the restorer.

Recently, a new thickness of veneer came on the market: the super-thin flexible variety. This has some remarkable advantages if you must veneer large surfaces. These veneers are sheets of real wood only ¹⁄₆₄-inch thick on a thin, very flexible backing. They come in 8-foot lengths, and 18, 24 and 36-inch widths — much larger sizes than you can obtain in the standard veneers. You can avoid all the matching and jointing that goes with the veneering of large surfaces when you use the new type.

Tools for Veneering

You won't need a lot of expensive tools to veneer. The most basic item is a veneer saw, a specialty device that isn't expensive. For measuring and as a cutting guide, you'll use a large carpenter's square and a combination square. A sharp craft or wallboard knife is useful, and so is a small plane for trimming edges. Most essential is a veneer roller, which turns out to be the same roller used for rolling wallpaper seams. These rollers are made of wood. Other rollers, such as those made of rubber, are apt to stain the veneer. Finally, keep some plain boards handy to use as cutting boards. We have found the best size to be a 36-inch length of 1x10 pine.

Glue

The basic glue for veneering is contact cement, although many veneer workers still use ordinary furniture glues. However, if you use the latter, the veneer must be clamped tightly during drying. Clamping large surfaces requires some specialized and expensive tools. If you use contact cement, no clamping is necessary because the cement bonds instantly. You can use ordinary contact cement sold in stores, but special veneering contact cement, sold by veneer specialists, is said to provide a better and more permanent bond. Contact cement is applied with a small paint brush, the cheap kind.

HANDLING VENEER

When delivered to you, veneers are thin and a bit brittle. They tend to tear easily from the ends along the lines of the grain. To avoid such tears, handle the material carefully. Store it flat, not rolled, in large flat cardboard cartons used for shipping pictures.

Veneer Preparation

Often, veneers come to you in a curly, buckled condition. This is especially true of burls and crotches. They look as though they had been wet and then had curled as they dried. It is easy to flatten veneers in this condition. Just sprinkle them generously with water, lay brown kraft paper over them (and between sheets of them), and put heavy weights on top of them. Let the sheets dry for 24 hours or so. Sometimes, if the buckles are severe, you may have to repeat this treatment several times before the sheets flatten out completely. Wait for a few days after flattening any veneer before using it. All veneer must be absolutely dry before you apply it to a surface. Damp (even mildly damp) veneer may shrink as it dries. If you have mounted the material, and shrinkage occurs, this shrinkage can cause cracks, splits and blisters.

Matching the Sheets of Veneer

One of the wonderful things about a sheet of veneer is that the grain pattern is repeated over and over again because of the way the log is peeled by the knife. It is this repetition of pattern that gives special beauty to veneered panels, for example, and table tops. It also calls for careful matching of grain patterns.

When veneer is delivered to you, it comes in pieces that range from 4 inches to perhaps 18 inches in width, and usually 36 inches or more in length. These sizes are determined by the size and condition of the tree they come from. If you buy a number of pieces, the dealer usually makes sure you get pieces that come from the same part of the original sheet. This enables you to match the grain when you lay the veneer down.

"Book Matching"

The most common phrase in matching of veneering is "book matching." This means that you lay down two pieces of veneer so that the pattern of the grain matches to create a pleasing pattern. Then you turn one piece, as you would the page of a book, over onto the other. The edge you turn is the edge that must be trimmed so that the two pieces fit together exactly.

Next, book match the sheets. Turn one sheet over on the other, like the page in a book. The edges closest to me will butt each other when the veneer is laid down.

The first task is to match the grain patterns in the veneer. We are using rosewood, which has a pronounced black grain design, and we searched through our sheets to find those that looked pleasing when placed side by side.

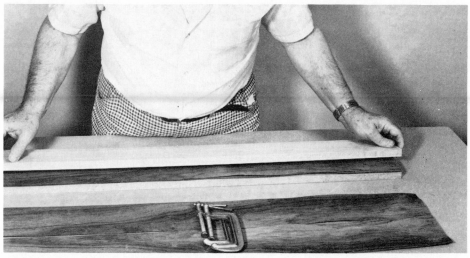

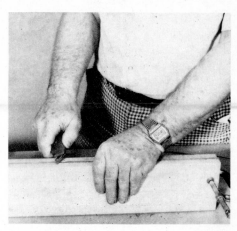

To trim the edges which are to butt together, you can make a veneer jig out of two long, perfectly straight hardwood boards. Place the veneer sheets between the boards with just a fraction of an inch protruding beyond the edge of the board. Clamp the boards solidly to hold the veneer in place.

Trim the protruding edges of the veneer pieces to the hardwood boards. This makes the edges straight and identical. Cut away the excess with a craft knife. Cut only against the grain of the veneer. Make small shaving cuts. Then sand smooth.

For example, if you turned the left-hand page over on top of the right-hand page, the edge on the left side after you finish turning is the edge that must be trimmed for matching. These edges, when glued down, should fit together so well that the seam or joint is practically invisible. There are two ways to trim these matching edges to achieve this perfect fit.

Using the Joining Jig One way to trim the veneer is to use a joining jig. This is a simple, homemade tool consisting of two perfectly straight hardwood boards. You fit the veneer between these boards, with the matching edge extending out slightly, as shown. Then trim the protruding edge until it is flush with the hardwood boards. To trim, use a small plane or a craft knife, or sand them until they are level with the hardwood face of the jig. When taken out of the jig, the two pieces should fit together perfectly.

Veneer Saw Method The second method, using a veneer saw, is the one we prefer, chiefly because over the years we have had consistently good results with it. In this method, you lay the matched pieces of veneer on a cutting board, just as they will appear on the finished pieces. Overlap the matching edge only as much as necessary for complete coverage. Place a hardwood or metal straightedge where the two pieces overlap. The straightedge is lined up along the edge to be trimmed, just far enough in from the edge so both pieces of veneer are cut. Using the veneer saw, cut the full length of the veneer, trimming away the edges of both pieces simultaneously. This results in perfectly matching edges that lay down beautifully.

Many people prefer to use a coarse sandpaper instead of a knife to cut the veneer down. The very best way is to use a small plane, if you have one. Plane only against the grain.

When you remove the jig and turn the veneer pieces back to their original position, the edges match perfectly. The grain pattern of the wood is good and when you glue the pieces they will butt perfectly and look like one piece of veneer.

Another way to match the edges is to use a metal straightedge and a veneer saw. The veneer in this picture is walnut burl. One piece is laid so it overlaps the other by a fraction of an inch.

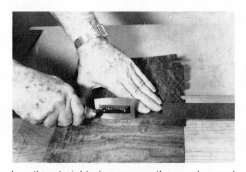

Lay the straightedge across the overlap and use it to guide the veneer saw. Hold the saw tight against the straightedge during cutting. If you are afraid the straightedge will slip, clamp it down before starting to cut.

VENEERING SECTIONS OF A DRESSER

On the 1852 dresser there are decorative veneer panels on the drawers and on the body. Originally they were done in a walnut burl, but over the years the veneer dried, cracked and peeled away. We would have preferred to save the old veneer, but much of it was missing, and what remained was so brittle and delicate that we decided a complete new veneering job was necessary. (This is the kind of choice a furniture restorer has to make all the time. The purist will tell you it is wrong not to save the old veneer and patch it. After all, it is 130 years old, an integral part of the furniture. Part of value of the piece depends on maintaining as much of the original wood as possible. If you decide to patch, see Chapter 5 for instructions.)

Having made the decision to reveneer, we then chose to replace the old walnut burl with a lovely rosewood veneer. We thought the coloring of the rosewood would add a positive dimension to the appearance that a walnut burl did not.

Step 1: Removing the Old Veneer

This proved to be quite a job. We used a sharp wood chisel. Some of the veneer lifted easily when the chisel was applied to its edge, but some hung on tenaciously. This latter came away quickly when we made chisel cuts into the veneer.

Step 2: Preparing the Surface for the Veneer

It is critical to have a perfectly smooth surface on which to apply a veneer. Even the tiniest bump or indentation on the surface of the base will show up through the veneer and spoil its appearance. First we sanded away all vestiges of old glue and veneer bits. Then we used a spatula to wipe a wood filler over the surface, in order to fill all marks and depressions. When the wood filler dried, we sanded again. This left a very smooth surface.

Step 3: Preparing the Veneer

We veneered the panels on the large drawers first. We looked through our sheets of rosewood veneer and laid out those that created an attractive matching pattern. The drawers panels were wide enough to require two pieces of matched veneer, instead of a single piece. This occurred because the rosewood veneer we were able to buy came only in 4-inch widths.

Remove the old dried and cracked veneer before applying new. The best tool for the job is a sharp, wide wood chisel handled carefully. Get under the old veneer, but do not damage the surface of the drawer. If you do, the new veneer will not lay flat.

In some areas, the old glue still held. To break through, hold the chisel vertically and tap to make cuts through the veneer. When you make several cuts near each other, the old glue will loosen and release the veneer. Again, try not to cut into the base wood.

To cover a few chisel marks and some old indentations on the surface, use a spatula to wipe a wood filler across the surface. Don't build up the old surface; just fill the dents.

After the filler has dried, sand again to make sure the surface is perfectly smooth.

Book Matching Having created the patterns we wanted, we next book-matched the veneer pieces. We turned the two pieces to be used on one panel in book page fashion and then trimmed the edges so they matched perfectly.

With the patterns and edges now perfectly matched, we laid the veneer down on the work bench, butted the edges, and applied a strip of masking tape to hold them together. The two pieces now became, for our purposes, one piece to be applied to the drawer panel.

Step 4: Preparing a Pattern

To help us in cutting panel pieces from the veneer, we made cardboard patterns of the different panels — the large drawer, small drawer, and dresser frame panels. We made these patterns slightly oversize so that when the veneer was glued down, we could finish the edges right on the dresser. This method has several advantages. First, when the edges are sanded in place, they blend directly into the side wood of the panel. If the panels were cut to an exact fit, this might not be the case. Second, these panels were not exactly the same size, varying as much as $1/16$-inch in overall dimensions. By cutting oversized patterns, we didn't have to make one for each panel, but only one for each type of panel.

Step 5: Cutting the Veneer

Now we placed the large drawer pattern over the prepared veneer. We positioned the pattern so that the design we had achieved during the matching of the veneer pieces was centered. Using the veneer saw, with a large steel combination rule as a straightedge, we cut the panel from the veneer.

Step 6: Gluing the Veneer

Using an inexpensive paint brush, we painted a coating of contact cement on the surface of the drawer panel, and also on the surface of the veneer. This was then allowed to dry.

Drying Time The usual drying time is about one hour. Do not apply the veneer while the cement is even slightly wet. The cement should be dry when you touch it and should not even feel sticky. If you wait two hours before applying the veneer, the bond will be even better. However, do not wait more than three hours or you will lose all bond.

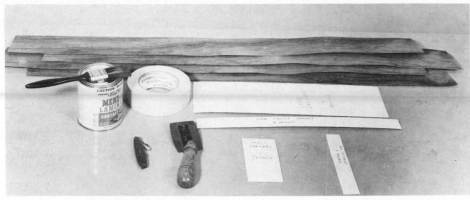

These are the veneering tools and materials: sheets of rosewood veneer, cardboard patterns of the areas to be veneered, contact cement, masking tape, a veneering saw and a small craft knife. You also will need some brown kraft paper.

Now that the edges of the veneer match perfectly, use a strip of masking tape to hold them together. Be sure the sheets butt perfectly as you tape.

Position the cardboard patterns of the pieces to be cut on the veneer. Carefully select the grain pattern and place the pattern over the part you want; then tape the pattern in place.

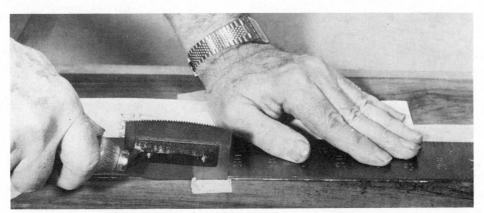

Make cuts through the masking tape. It's a good idea to practice making cuts both across and with the grain on scrap veneer before you cut your first veneer for application.

Apply contact cement to the drawer face. Use an inexpensive paint brush; evenly coat the entire surface.

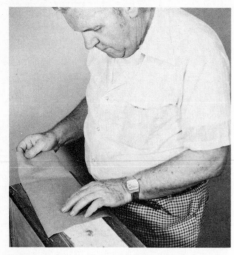

The contact cement has now dried for more than an hour. It is dry enough so that paper won't stick to it. Lay a piece of brown kraft paper down on the drawer face, to cover about two-thirds of the surface.

Lay down a second sheet of brown kraft paper, overlapping the first and covering the remainder of the drawer face.

Place the piece of veneer, cemented side down, on the kraft paper. Feel through the kraft paper with your fingertips to position the veneer exactly where you want it, with its edges matching the edges of the drawer face.

When the veneer is positioned, place your palm at one end to hold the veneer in place. Slowly pull out the sheet of kraft paper from the other end. This allows the two cemented faces to contact each other.

Still holding the first end down with your palm, rub the other end with your hand to assure good contact of the cemented faces.

Now pull out the second sheet of kraft paper and press the veneer into contact with the drawer face. The veneer is now firmly glued to the drawer.

Positioning the Pieces Do not simply set the veneer in place. Since contact cement bonds immediately, you will be unable to correct the alignment once the two surfaces touch. Instead, use the paper mask method described here.

When the cement has dried, cut out two pieces of brown kraft paper a few inches larger on all sides than the panels being glued. Place one of these paper sheets so that it covers about two-thirds of the surface to which the veneer is to be applied. Place the second sheet over the remaining exposed surface. This second sheet should overlap the first sheet by a couple of inches.

Now position the veneer panel on the brown kraft paper. Carefully feel the edges of the drawer panel through the kraft paper with your fingers and locate the veneer exactly where you want it — slightly overlapping each edge. You are working in the blind a bit here, since the kraft paper covers these edges, but you shouldn't have any trouble in placing the veneer correctly. You could cut the kraft paper to exact size, which would enable you to feel the edges better, but we have never found this necessary.

Removing the Kraft Paper Now place the palm of your hand on one end of the veneer and press down firmly. It is best to press the end of the veneer under the first piece of kraft paper, which covers two-thirds of the panel surface. With your other hand, grasp the other (second) piece of kraft paper and pull it out from under the veneer. This brings one end of the veneer into contact with the surface of the drawer panel. Discard the paper and, with the free hand, rub over the veneer so that it makes good contact with the drawer panel surface.

Next, pull the other sheet of kraft paper out and rub the veneer over the whole surface to bring it into contact with the drawer panel.

Removing the Masking Tape Finally, pull off the masking tape used to hold the pieces of the veneer together. Do this slowly and carefully so that most of the tape's adhesive comes off. Some of the contact cement will have worked its way under the masking tape and will now appear on the surface of the veneer. Use a soft cloth dampened in contact cement solvent to remove this. Use care in this operation. The solvent will loosen the veneer if it penetrates the wood; on the other hand, if any of the cement remains on the veneer it will interfere with later staining and finishing.

Step 7: Rolling the Veneer

Once the veneer is in contact with the panel, get your veneer roller and go to work. We have found that one of the secrets of veneer success lies in rolling the surface sufficiently. Apply plenty of pressure and roll every bit of the surface. In particular, be sure to roll all seams and edges. It is almost impossible to roll too much.

When you think you have rolled the veneer sufficiently so that every bit of it is in good contact, run your fingers lightly over the surface. If you feel any raised areas, roll again. If you applied even coats of cement to both sides and rolled enough, the veneer should feel smooth and level.

Step 8: Trimming the Edges

Allow the cement to set for a couple of hours, to make a firm bond. Then trim the edges of the veneer to match the panel underneath. The best method is to use the veneer saw and a straightedge laid down carefully and clamped in place. Be sure your saw cut is exactly at the edge or you may ruin the whole job.

You also can trim the edges with a sharp craft knife, but if you do, be sure to cut against the grain. If you cut with the grain, the knife may follow the grain, start to cut into the body of the veneer, and create ugly sharp spikes that you will have to repair. When using a knife for this purpose, make small peeling cuts rather than long cuts.

After the edge of the veneer is trimmed to match the edge of the wood under it, use fine grade sandpaper to finish the job. It usually is best to make a sanding block of the appropriate size, depending on the shape of the edges you are dealing with. In our project, we found that the edge of one of our hand sanders happened to fit perfectly along the edge of the drawer panels.

Round off the top of each edge very slightly, and also sand the sharp point of each corner just a little.

Step 9: Finishing the Veneer

Veneer should be finished like any other furniture wood. Sanding is vital. You may not always be able to see them, but there are saw marks in the surfaces of most veneers. When you get them, veneers have not been sanded at all and these saw marks

will show up all too plainly once the final finish is applied unless you sand thoroughly during finishing. Don't use a coarse paper, but start with a medium grade and graduate through several finer grades until the surface is smooth.

You probably will want to stain your veneer, but keep in mind that the stain should enhance, not hide, the beautiful grain. We feel that the purpose of a stain in this case is to bring out the color and the pattern of the wood. We lightly used a brown-red gelled stain on the rosewood of the 1852 dresser. We applied just a little and rubbed it thoroughly. This deepened the blacks and enhanced the reds of the veneer, but covered none of the pattern.

We used a clear polyurethane plastic finish on the 1852 dresser, and selected

Now pull off the masking tape. The butted pieces should fit tightly together. You can see the joint — but just barely. The finishing process will hide it completely.

Use contact cement solvent to clean all contact cement and any gum from the masking tape off of the veneer. Caution: Test the solvent on a sample of the veneer before doing this, especially when veneering exotic woods. In rare cases, the solvent may cause the coloring in the wood to run.

the satin finish. You might want a glossy finish on some veneers. Apply the finish just the same as on any solid wood.

We deliberately cut these veneer panels slightly oversize so they could be trimmed in place. Use the veneer saw and a straightedge.

After giving the contact cement a couple of hours to set, sand the edges. The edge of our hand sander was a perfect fit for this job. If it hadn't been, we would have made a small hand sander of the right size and shape from a block of wood.

Before finishing, sand the veneer face thoroughly to eliminate saw marks in its surface. Use coarse, then medium, then fine and very fine paper to get the veneer ready for a stain and the finishing coats of varnish.

11

Repairing Caning

In restoring old furniture, you frequently find it is useful to know how to recane. Cane backs, seats, side panels and decorative panels have been features of good furniture for generations. Cane looks good, adding a distinctive color and eye pleasing pattern to any piece. A typical caned seat in normal everyday use is durable, lasting 20 years or more, and comfortable.

WOVEN VS. PREWOVEN CANE

There are two types of caned surfaces — either woven or prewoven. Woven cane is worked right on the chair. When you look at the seat there will be a series of holes through which the cane is drawn. Prewoven cane seats and backs come "ready-made." A spline in a groove around the opening holds the section in place. The type of repair you make depends on the existence of the holes or the groove. Prewoven cane cannot be applied to a seat having holes; woven cane cannot be applied to a seat surrounded by a groove.

WOVEN CANE

Caning is not difficult, but it does take time. The seat of the rocking chair that we recaned in this chapter is a little larger than most, and required something over 22 hours of work. Fortunately, the work can be broken into as many sessions as you need, because you can stop at any time and pick up later just where you left off. Because you can develop sore fingertips if you are not accustomed to weaving cane, it probably is better to schedule sessions no longer than 4 hours long on any day.

HOW TO CARE FOR CANE SEATING

Unless the cane is cut or broken through rough use, it will give long service.

Shrinking Stretched Cane

Once in a while we find cane seats that have sagged a little. These can be shrunk back to normal shape using glycerine and water. Use the same mixture employed in caning — 1½ ounces of glycerine to a pint of warm water.

The procedure is as follows. Turn the

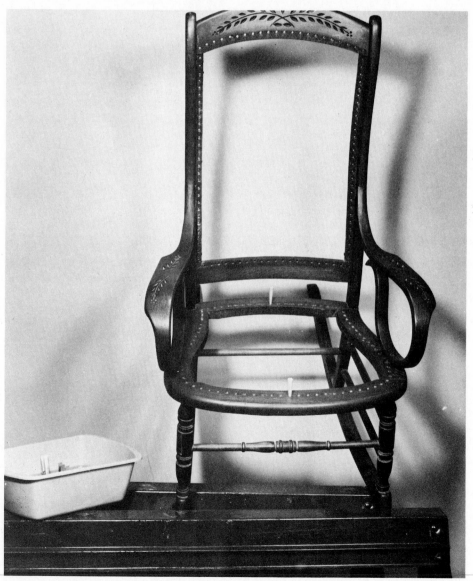

Repaired and refinished, the rocker is ready for caning. We set the piece up on metal sawhorses tilted against a wall, to bring the work to a convenient height. If you work in an uncomfortable position, you will end up with fatigue and sore muscles.

chair over, with the seat on a table. Put plenty of old newspapers under the seat. Now brush the glycerine and water solution on the cane generously, but as much as possible avoid getting it on the wood. (The wood will get wet. Just don't let it get too wet, and wipe off any water as soon as you can.) After a few minutes, the cane should be well soaked. Turn the chair right side up and allow it to dry. In most cases, the cane will shrink and tighten as it dries.

Another method is to apply towels soaked in the glycerine and water solution to the cane while covering any exposed wood with plastic wrap. After about 15 minutes, the wet towels will have soaked the cane and can be removed. With either method, you may have to soak the cane several times to remove all of the sag.

CANING TOOLS

Only very simple tools are needed for caning. You should buy about two dozen hardwood caning pegs when you order your supply of cane. These inexpensive pegs are used to mark the center strands on the work piece and to hold cane in starting holes until you tie it in place. An awl (we use a regular ice pick) is used to aid in inserting strands of cane in the holes. You'll need about half a dozen ordinary spring clothespins to hold the cane while it soaks. A bucket for soaking the cane, a standard cellulose sponge, and a scissors are the only other items you require.

Materials for the job include weaving cane of the proper size, binding cane, and glycerin, which is mixed in the water in which the cane is soaked.

SELECTING THE RIGHT CANE

We have found cane available in a number of local shops. It also can be purchased by mail from Squaw Alley, the Newell Workshop and others. Check the ads in do-it-yourself and furniture magazines for suppliers.

Cane Sizes

Cane comes from the rattan palm, which grows in the orient from India to Malaysia. The outer bark of the palm is cut into thin strips that range up to 18 feet in length and come in widths of from $1/16$ to $3/16$ inches. The normal hank consists of 1,000 feet of cane, but you can buy 500-foot hanks. Usually, some strands of binding cane, which is cane that is two sizes larger than the weaving cane, are included with

each hank. When you shop for cane, identify the wider strands in a hank before you buy it to be sure you have the binding cane you need. One or two long strands of binding cane are needed for each typical chair seat.

The size of the holes in the chair determine the size of the cane you will use. Cane comes in six widths and is generally referred to by name rather than dimension. The widest is called "Common" and the narrowest "Superfine." Look at the accompanying chart for the name of each size, the size of the hole, and the distance between holes.

Cane Quality

The best quality cane is smooth, bright yellow in color, and has a minimum of imperfections. As you draw a length of poor quality cane between your fingers, you can feel rough spots and weak areas. On any cane you will feel prominent lumps called "eyes" — places on the palm bark from which the leaves grew. On good quality cane, the eyes are smooth and unbroken, while on poorer quality cane, they feel rough and the cane may bend sharply at that point — a sign that it is cracked and may break during weaving.

In our experience, places that specialize

in caning materials tend to have better quality cane, chiefly because they know good quality and how to buy it. They may charge more, and may offer different qualities at different prices. Local shops, with no caning specialist on the staff, take whatever the supplier gives them and charge one price regardless of quality. Some of their cane is excellent in quality an some is not so good. You should examine the stock, running your fingers down several strands and looking for the eyes, and select the best.

Quantities

Most places sell cane by the hank. A typical hank would contain 60 to 80 strands in different lengths, enough to do 5 or 6 small seats and 3 to 5 larger ones. You may find some places selling cane by the pound, with the pound bundle being about the same as a hank. You sometimes can buy a half hank, but you cannot buy cane by the strand or in amounts other than the hank or half hank. Prices vary with the quality and with the market. At this writing, a hank costs from $9 to $14 (more for the select quality in long lengths).

Determining the Right Cane Size

First, measure the size of one of the holes

BUYING CANE

Cane comes in six widths from $1/16$ to $3/16$ inches. A standard hank has 1,000 feet of cane in strips up to 18 feet in length, enough to do an area about 24 by 24 inches. High quality cane is called "select", costs more, and is worth it. The size of cane you buy is determined by the size of the hole in the chair rail and the distance between the holes. Cane is generally designated by name (superfine is the narrowest, common the widest) rather than measurement. You will find variations in these names, and if you buy your cane in places where no one knows much about cane, you may find widths with the wrong names. We suggest you buy from cane suppliers who advertise in magazines and who know the business, or from local dealers who understand the material and how it is used. The chart below tells you the kind of cane to buy to fit your chair.

Note that the sizes of cane supplies are not critical and that you have some leeway. You can use cane a size smaller than specified, for example, for a given hole diameter — but not larger. The relationship of the cane size to the hole size is important because so many strands of cane must go through each hole. If the hole is too small, or the cane too large, you won't be able to fit the last strands through and you won't be able to finish the job.

Name of Cane	Hole size	Distance between holes
Superfine	$1/8''$	$3/8''$
Fine-fine	$3/16''$	$1/2''$
Fine	$3/16''$	$5/8''$
Narrow medium	$1/4''$	$3/4''$
Medium	$1/4''$	$3/4''$
Common	$5/16''$	$7/8''$

in the seat. An accurate way is to insert drill bits of known diameter. The bit that completely fills the hole — for example, a ³⁄₁₆-inch bit — tells you the diameter of the hole. Next, measure the distance be-tween the centers of several holes. (This should be consistent. However, you can find chairs with holes which are different distances apart, particularly on older chairs and those that were not factory made. When this happens, find the aver-age distance.)

Take these two measurements to the chart and determine the name of the cane you need.

PREPARING TO RECANE YOUR FURNITURE

If the piece has any old cane re-maining, remove that first. Study the way the cane was woven, if you can, just to help you get started on the new caning later. Save a piece of the old cane as a guide in buying the correct size of new cane.

STEP 1: READYING THE PIECE

Make any necessary repairs to the piece before caning. Clean the wood with a wax remover and, if refinishing is necessary, do that before you cane and allow the new finish to "cure" for a few days. We had to make repairs on the left arm of our chair and install one new rung. While the finish was generally in good shape, we had to refinish because of the repairs.

Cleaning the Holes

There is one very important step in getting an old chair ready for recaning: checking the cane holes. Often, wax, dirt and fin-ishing material accumulate in the holes, making them smaller in diameter. Since each hole will have to accommodate half a dozen or more strands of cane, small holes can become a problem. The easiest way to clean the holes is to fit a drill bit of the exact size of the holes into your electric drill and run the drill down into each hole. One pass will clean a hole completely, and cleaning all the holes on any chair takes only a few minutes.

The cane will be woven while it is wet, so the wood of the chair or other piece also will get wet during caning. We recom-mend that any piece to be caned be fin-ished in polyurethane varnish, tung oil, or other finish that isn't readily affected by water. Lacquer and shellac tend to absorb water and turn white.

STEP 2: PREPARING THE CANE

Be careful when handling dry cane; it may have sharp edges which can give you nasty cuts similar to paper cuts.

Cane is softened by soaking in a water and glycerine mixture before you weave with it. Use about 1½ ounces of glycerine to each pint of warm water, and allow each strand of cane to soak at least 15 minutes. You'll need a couple of quarts of this mixture.

Pull a strand from the hank of cane and form it into a coil about 6 or 8 inches in diameter. Now squeeze the coil into a bow and clamp the bow with a spring clothes-pin. Drop this clamped bow into the bucket containing the glycerine and water mixture. Remember to keep ahead of yourself as you weave. Begin by soaking 3 or 4 bows, and as you use these, form new ones and drop them into the bucket, so there are always several bows that are soaked, pliable and ready to be applied.

As you weave, the wet cane will dry out. Keep handy a cellulose sponge soaked in glycerine-water mixture so that, as the cane dries, you can remoisten it.

STEP 3: PREPARING THE SEAT

Carefully examine all of the holes on the seat to see that they are open, and that they have no sharp edges that might cut into the cane. Use a small wood file or fine sand-paper rolled into a tight tube to round any such edges. If it appears that the edges of the frame that contact the cane might cut, round them as well.

Before recaning an old chair, make sure the holes are free of dirt and old finishing material. The best way to do this is to redrill each hole with a bit that is the size of the hole. It only takes a few minutes to run the bit into each of the holes.

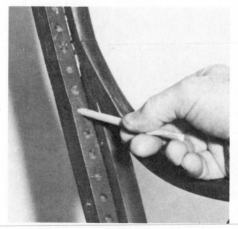

Roll a small sheet of sandpaper tightly to make a device for sanding any sharp edges on the holes. Sharp edges might cut into the cane.

The caning is gathered into loops held by spring clothespins and soaked in a solution of warm water and glycerine for at least 15 minutes be-fore use. (An hour is better.)

HOW TO WEAVE A CANE BACK OR SEAT

Once you have finished your preparations, you are ready to begin the caning procedures. Once you have identified the key holes in the pattern, the procedure divides into seven steps.

1. Lay down first cane strand, back to front.
2. Lay down first cane strand, side to side.
3. Lay down second cane strand, back to front.
4. Weave in second cane strand, side to side.
5. Weave in right to left diagonal cane strand.
6. Weave in left to right diagonal cane strand.
7. Apply binder cane to the edge of the cane.

PRELIMINARIES: COUNTING THE HOLES

Begin to plan your work by counting the holes across the back of the seat. If there are an odd number of holes, place a peg in the center hole. If there are an even number, put a peg in each of the two center holes. Now count the holes on the front rail and peg the center hole or holes on it.

If the seat is not square, but splayed or shield shaped — as our rocker is — the next job is to identify the corner holes. At the back of the seat, the corner holes are those at the far left and far right. At the front, because of the shape of the seat, there usually are several holes located on a curve and it will appear that any of them can serve as the corner. The correct corner holes are those directly in line with the corner holes on the back of the seat. To be sure, insert a dry strand of cane in the back corner hole and run it down the seat to the front. Keep the strand perfectly straight from front to back. The hole at the front with which it aligns is the one you designate as the corner hole.

On chairs with round seats, you locate the center hole on each side and at the front and the back. Strands running from the front to the back and from side to side form a perfect cross at the center of the seat.

STEP ONE: FIRST STRAND BACK TO FRONT

You have marked the center holes at the back and front with pegs. Take a strand of cane from the water, remove the clothespin, and run the strand between your fingers to remove excess water. At the same time, note the "direction" of the cane. You will find that the eyes on the strand face in one direction. This is hard to see, but when the cane is pulled through during the weaving process, the eyes will snag a little if they face toward the end you are pulling, and will not snag if they face away from that end. The caning is easier if you have identified the direction of the eyes and start each strand with the eyes facing away from the direction of pull.

Also, cane strands have a shiny and dull side. They should be woven with the shiny side facing up. Always check to see which is the shiny side before starting a strand.

If you have one center peg at the back, remove the peg and insert one end of the first strand in the hole so that it extends down below the hole about 4 inches. If you have two center holes, begin with the left hole. Re-insert the peg to hold the strand in place.

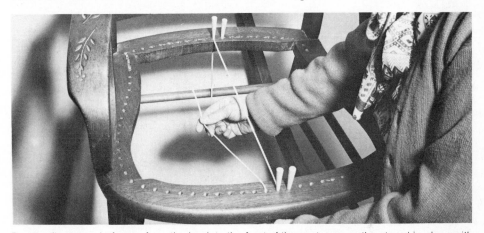

Run the first strand of cane from the back to the front of the seat; secure the strand in place with pegs. It should be strung a little on the loose side. The glossy side of the cane should face upward. After going through the center hole at the front, the cane is run up through the next hole to the left and strung to the back rail.

Count the holes in the front and back rails of the chair, and mark the center holes with pegs. This chair has an even number of holes, so two pegs are needed to mark the two center holes.

At the back, push the strand of cane down through the second hole and then bring it up through the third. Continue this procedure from hole to hole to the left of the center peg. When you have used most of the first strand, anchor the end with a peg. Make sure enough extends below the seat to allow tying off later.

This is as far as the first strand went. Test the tension by laying your palm on the woven strands. Under slight pressure, the cane should sink about ¾-inch. This will tighten up as you weave and as the wet cane dries.

Pull the strand toward the front. Remove the front center peg and insert the strand in the hole. Check to see that the shiny side of the cane is facing up. Draw the entire strand through the hole; then reinsert the peg. The cane should not be drawn tight, but should be slightly slack.

Now, at the front, move to the hole to the left of the one with the peg and cane in it. Feed the end of the cane up through this hole and toward the back of the seat. There, insert it into the hole to the left of the hole with the peg and cane in it. Pull the cane down through this hole until the second strand across the seat is at about the same tension as the first.

Continue this laying of the cane from front to back, always moving one hole to the left, until you get to the end of this strand, at which time you will have five, six or more strands across the seat. When you come to the end of the first strand, just make sure that at least 4 inches is below the hole. This is needed for tying off later. Insert a peg to hold this end of the strand in place.

Now get another strand of cane from the bucket. Insert its end into the hole next to the one where the last strand finished. Continue working to the left, hole by hole, until strands extend from each hole across the left side of the back rail.

If the seat is square or perfectly rectangular, you are now ready to go back to the center, and lay the cane to the right of the center peg, using the procedure just described. If the seat is splayed, however, you will note that there is some space at the side caused by the curvature of the side rail of the chair, as shown. To take care of this, you lay the next strand from one of the side holes in front of the back rail to the appropriate hole in the front rail.

The side hole used will depend on the curvature of the particular chair. The easiest way to determine it is to insert a strand in the front hole and run it toward the back, keeping it parallel with the last strand you put down. The hole it touches in the back of the side rail is the one to use. Your objective is to make all strands parallel to each other and the same distance apart. It generally is best to use a separate strand for the side holes, rather than running the strand from the back holes to them.

You may need two or even three side strands, again depending on the shape of the seat.

Once the side strands on the left have been placed, you can return to the center peg and lay the strands to the right of it. The side strands on the right side are handled just the same as those on the left.

As you lay these back-to-front strands, you should test the tension occasionally. As mentioned, the strands should not be tight. After eight or nine are in place, lay the palm of your hand across them. you should be able to press down lightly and note a sag of about ¾ inch. This may seem loose to you now, but as you continue weaving, the seat will tighten. If you make it too tight now, it will be difficult to weave later.

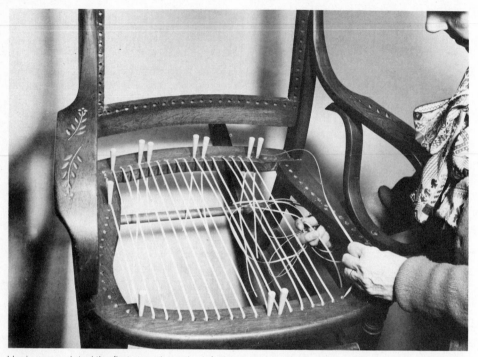

Having completed the first strands on the left side, we move to the right, laying the cane in the same manner.

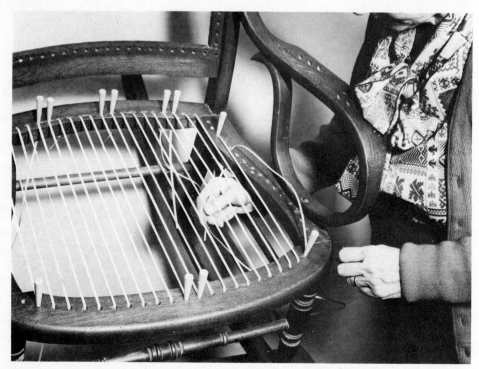

The shield shape of this seat has made it necessary to weave shorter strands at the left and right sides. When you must use strands that start along the side rather than at the back, employ the side holes that will keep the strands parallel with those already in place. In this case, the fourth hole from the back along each side proved to be the right one. Also, when inserting short strands, use a separate strand rather than continuing the longer strands.

STEP TWO: FIRST STRAND SIDE TO SIDE

Begin at the back holes. Insert a strand of cane in the back left hand hole; peg it in place. Then lay the strand across the top of the vertical strands and insert the end in the back hole on the right side. Always remember to check to see that the cane is laid with the shiny side up.

Move to the second hole from the back on the right side. Insert the cane up from the bottom into this hole, pull it through, and run it across the seat to the right side. Continue this procedure until you have laid in all of the horizontal or side-to-side strands. You should now have a perfect grid of back-to-front and side-to-side strands in place on the seat.

Tying Off

Before moving to Step Three, you need to know how to tie off the ends of the cane strands on the underside. The cane must be wet to tie a tight, flat knot, so moisten the loose ends well. First, push the loose end of the cane strand under and through an adjacent loop. This loop is formed by the cane running from one hole to the next.

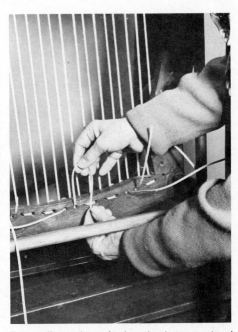

In Step Two of the caning process, lay in the first horizontal or side-to-side strands, starting at the back and working forward. Use the same technique of going into one hole and coming up through the one next to it that you used on the front-to-back strands.

Tying off consists of tying the loose ends of strands on the underside of the seat. Neat ties take a bit of practice. Begin a tie by pushing the end of the loose strand under an adjacent loop of cane.

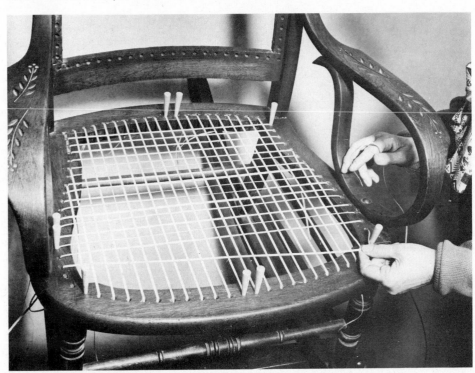

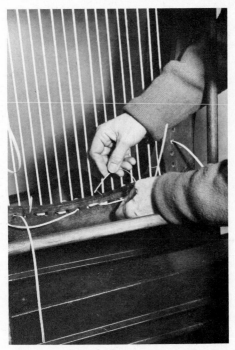

The strands laid down in Step Two simply lie on top of the vertical strands already in place. You don't weave at this point.

Pull the strand tight under the loop, making sure the cane is flat and untwisted. Then carry the loose end back over the loop.

Then bring the cane strand back under its own loop, pull the strand over, and back through the loop, and pull the knot thus formed tight. The knot should be tight and flat. Position it so that it does not cover the hole. It takes a bit of practice to make good tie-offs. Don't hesitate to take poor knots apart and retie them until you are satisfied with their shape.

You don't need to tie off each strand as it is put in place, but you should stop weaving and secure the loose ends every so often. If there are too many loose ends hanging down, they interfere with the weaving.

STEP THREE: SECOND BACK-TO-FRONT STRANDS

You are now going to repeat Step One. That is, you are going to put strands from back to front in the same holes that you did in Step One. The only difference is that you will position each strand so that it lies to the right of the strand already in that hole. Don't worry if the new strands won't stay to the right and tend to overlap a little. This will be corrected later.

As a general rule, it is best not to lay double strands over the short strands at the left and right sides. You can do it if you like, but it may cause some crowding during the later weaving.

STEP FOUR: SECOND SIDE-TO-SIDE STRANDS

Now install the second strands across the seat, but this time the strands are woven, and not just laid in.

Before beginning this step it is a good idea to moisten the cane already in place by wiping your wet sponge across it several times. This will help during the weaving process.

Insert the first new strand in the left

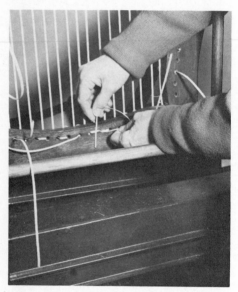

Now run the end under the loop again, making sure that the cane is flat and untwisted.

In Step Three, put in the second set of vertical strands. The second strands go through the same holes as the first ones did, but are placed to the right of the first ones. These also are simply laid on top of the other strands, with no weaving.

The cane tends to dry out as you work with it. Keep a sponge soaked in the glycerine-and-water solution handy, and remoisten the cane at regular intervals.

After pulling the end under the loop the second time, feed it through the loop it has formed and pull it tight. This makes a tight, flat knot. Moisten the cane with a sponge before tying off, since wet cane makes much better knots. Clip off the end close to the knot after the tie is finished.

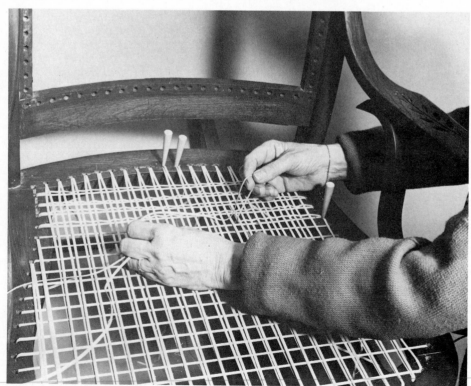

Here the work has progressed to Step Four, when the second layer of side-to-side strands are put in. Now, for the first time, you start weaving. Each new side-to-side strand is woven over the first and under the second strand in each front-to-back pair.

back hole, being sure that 4 inches of the strand extend below the hole. Now take the end of the new strand and work across the seat. The cane should go over each strand laid in Step Three, and under each strand laid in Step One. If you work from the left, as suggested, this means that at each pair of back-to-front strands you encounter, you go under the first and over the second strand. (Remember, you laid the second back-to-front strands to the right of the first.)

If, because of the shape of the seat, you laid short strands at either the front or back, these should be left single, and not doubled up. This would occur only if the seat were curved sufficiently at either the front or back, as it was at the sides.

When you finish Step Four, you have a grid of squares on the seat. You can take one of your hardwood pegs and adjust the position of the strands wherever the little squares appear to be irregular. Just put the peg through the hole next to any strand that is out of place and push with it until the strand is positioned properly.

STEP FIVE: FIRST DIAGONAL STRANDS

In this step, you will weave strands diagonally across the seat, beginning at the back right corner.

Insert a new strand in the hole at the back right corner and peg it. To check the track of this strand, first lay it across the seat in a straight diagonal line. Note the hole it touches at the front and put a peg in this hole as a marker.

In this weaving, the new strand will go *over* the pairs of side-to-side strands, and go *under* the pairs of back-to-front strands. After you start weaving, you'll find it becomes easy to identify the different pairs. Just start slowly and check each pair of strands carefully. Before you have finished the first diagonal strand, you will have gained the knack of weaving under and over the right pairs.

After weaving in the first diagonal strand, move to the hole to the left and weave the second strand parallel to the first, following the same procedure: under the back-to-front strands and over the side-to-side strands. Continue weaving until all diagonal strands have been woven in. Occasionally wet down the cane already in the chair with your sponge to make the weaving easier.

Remember to check the track of each

This is the seat at the completion of Step Four, with two sets of strands in running vertically and two running horizontally. Note that we have not yet put in the single strands near the very front or at the last row in back.

Step Five has progressed and the fifth diagonal strand is about to be woven in. Note the holes in the lower left. It was necessary to weave the same strand in and out of the same hole in both the first and second holes. This was done to keep the strands aligned and often is necessary at corners. When doing this, anchor the strand around a cross piece of cane under the seat before coming back out the same hole.

Notice that as we weave, the pattern of the cane is becoming visible and regular, aligning itself.

diagonal strand before you begin to weave it. Sooner or later, you will find one that doesn't match the hole at the other end properly. The solution to this is to use the open hole twice to keep your rows straight.

This is what will happen: you will weave one diagonal to its hole but will find that, when you move to the next hole, the new track is out of place. You must skip a row to keep the diagonal lines parallel. However, you don't really want to skip any rows. So you tie off the strand you just inserted, and instead of moving to the next hole, you bring the strand back up through the same hole. Now you weave the strand along its proper track. This usually occurs near the corners and creates no problem in the weaving if you follow these instructions.

Incidentally, when performing diagonal weaving, you handle the single strands near the edges just as if they were pairs of strands — over the side-to-side and under the back-to-front. The only difference is that you are dealing with one strand instead of two.

STEP SIX: THE SECOND DIAGONAL STRANDS

Now you weave another set of diagonal strands, but this time you start at the back left corner and weave the first strand from there to the right front corner.

The procedure is exactly the same as in Step Five, except that now you weave *under the side-to-side* pairs and *over the back-to-front* pairs. Just as in Step Five, you will find it necessary in some places to use one hole instead of two.

We always find this step a little difficult because you now have a lot of cane in place, and the weaving becomes harder. Here are some tips that seem to help.

1. Sponge the seat frequently to keep the cane moist, pliable and slippery.
2. Use your awl or ice pick to help fish the ends of the strands through.
3. The chair holes have now become crowded and inserting strands in them is no longer easy. If you insert your awl into each hole (carefully, so as not to spear or split any cane) and wobble it around a little, you will reposition the cane in the hole and make room for the new strand.

This last weaving step also is the most satisfactory because the final pattern of your cane seat begins to appear, and it

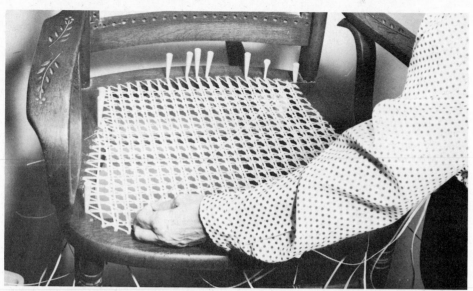

Now we start Step Five, weaving in the first diagonal strands. Start in the upper right corner, and peg the strand in the hole there. Then run the loose strand across the seat to determine its track.

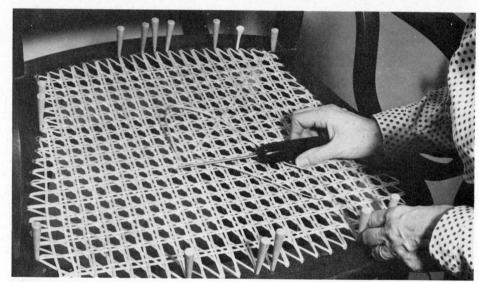

Weave the diagonal strands, going under each horizontal pair and over each vertical pair. Pull the strand tight after each weave.

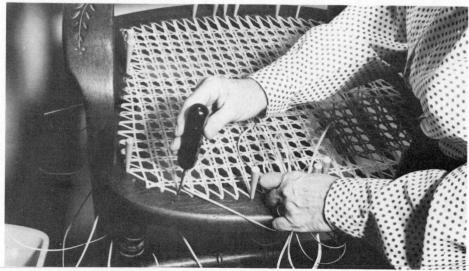

By now the chair holes are becoming crowded with cane. Carefully insert your awl or icepick into a hole and wobble it around. This compacts the strands already in the hole and clears space for the new strands.

grows with each new strand. You suddenly see the end of your work — and it looks good. One good thing about weaving strands of cane by this method is that the strands are more or less self-aligning. The regularity of the design and the precise shape of the holes in the seat require no extra effort on your part. They simply appear automatically as you weave one strand after the other according to the directions.

STEP SEVEN: APPLYING THE BINDER CANE

After the weaving of the seat has been completed, binder cane is applied around the perimeter of the seat to give a neat and finished appearance. Binder cane is identical to weaving cane in all respects, but is just one or (preferably) two sizes larger.

First, identify the binding cane in the hank of cane you purchased. It is bigger than the rest. Now measure off a piece that is long enough to go entirely around the newly caned seat, with a couple of inches to spare. Soak this piece of cane for 15 minutes in warm water and glycerine (double this time if the water is cold). The cane must be very pliable if it is to follow the contours and corners of the seat.

After it has soaked, insert about 2 inches of one end of the binding cane in the left corner hole at the back of the seat and peg it. Now lay the binder along the back of the seat over the holes. You are going to secure the binding cane in place by tying it down with regular weaving cane at each of the holes.

Take a long strand of regular weaving cane, one which has been well soaked to tie the binder in place. Tie one end of the cane securely under the seat and next to the left corner hole. Run the weaving cane up through the first hole, over the binder, and back down through the hole, thus making a loop over the binder cane. Pull this loop tight so that it anchors the binder firmly and tightly over the hole.

Next, under the seat, run the weaving strand to the next hole and repeat the procedure. Continue this for every hole until the entire binder along the back of the seat has been tied down. The binder now appears as a neat edging for the back of the seat, with tie-downs across it at every hole.

At the corner of the seat, turn the binding cane sharply, so that it now runs along the right side of the seat. Remoisten the

In Step Six, you weave the second diagonal layer. This one starts at the rear left corner. The same procedure is followed in weaving as in Step Five. The strand is woven under each horizontal pair and over each vertical pair.

And here we have the newly woven seat, neatly patterned and attractive.

In Step Seven, you install the binder cane. First, a couple of inches of the end of the wet binder cane are inserted in the left rear hole, and the cane is laid across the back rail, covering the holes.

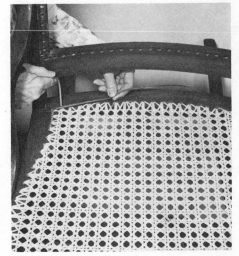

Now a length of weaving cane is used to tie the binder cane in place. The end of the weaving cane is tied to a loop under the rail. The other end is brought up through the second hole.

binder before doing this so that it is pliable enough to make this turn. Continue to tie the binder down through each hole.

The tricks to making a good looking binder edging are these.

1. Make sure the binder is centered over each hole before you draw the tie cane tight.
2. Hold the binder cane flat against the wood as you draw the tie cane tight.
3. Be sure the shiny side of the tie cane is facing upward before you draw it tight.
4. Keep both the binder cane and the tie cane well moistened as you work.

Work all around the seat, up to the last two holes. Here, pull out the end of the

binding that you initially inserted in the left back hole and run it along the left side for a distance of about two holes. It should be located over the holes. Now slide the end of the binder that you have been running around the seat under the binder cane from the back, so that the two binder pieces overlap. Cut the binder cane that runs from the back and that is on top, right over a hole. This will enable you to hide the cut end under the tie cane which comes through that hole. Continue the tying process along the left side until you have tied through the last hole. The binder is now finished. Tie off the tie cane.

STEP EIGHT: FINISHING THE WORK

The seat is now caned. Clean up the work

by clipping off any hairs which are visible on the cane. Use a single-edge razor.

Tightening the Tie-off Knots

Look the underside over carefully and pull all tie-off knots tight. Clip off any loose ends of cane to make the bottom as neat as possible. Flatten the tie-downs you have just made over the binder cane by tapping each loop flat with a small hammer.

Adding a Surface Finish

You can leave the cane unfinished, or you can apply a coat of shellac, lacquer or varnish as a protective coating. In some chairs you work on, you may find cane finished a darker color than natural. The replacement can also be a darker color; use a colored finishing material as a final coat.

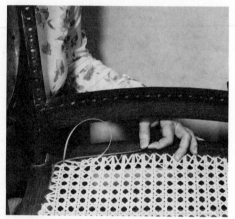

Now the cane is looped over the binding cane and run back down in the same hole.

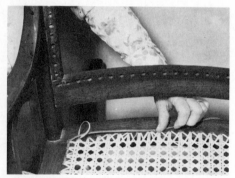

The weaving cane is pulled tight over the binding cane. Then it is moved to the next hole, where the same operation is performed again.

To make a neat binding tie at each hole, hold the binding cane flat and directly across the hole as the weaving cane is drawn tight.

The binding cane has been anchored all across the back of the seat and the binder is now running down the left side after being turned at the corner.

Here is the finished seat, with all binding cane in place. We are now ready to proceed with the chair back. The total investment, including purchase, repair, and caning was less than $50.

APPLYING PREWOVEN CANE SEAT OR BACK

Machine-made prewoven cane is frequently used in modern furniture and you'll find that some pieces dating back 50 years or more have it. This boudoir chair had been in the family for over 60 years. In the past, someone had tacked a pad over the opening rather than replacing the cane. We removed the pad, repaired the tack holes and refinished the chair before we installed the prewoven cane that the design required.

The only difference in appearance between the handwoven and machine-made cane is that the machine-made version has a more regular appearance, particularly near the edges. The installation, however, is totally different. Machine-made cane requires no weaving at all. It is laid in place and secured by a heavy-duty reed spline wedges into a groove around the outer edge of the seat or other caned area.

STEP 1: SELECTING THE MATERIAL

The machine-woven cane can be purchased by the running foot in widths from 12 to 24 inches and in different cane sizes. Take a sample of the old caning with you when buying so as to match the cane size. If none of the old cane exists, then choose a size that seems appropriate. Generally speaking, the larger the area to be caned, the larger the cane size. Smaller cane makes a smaller weaving pattern.

How Much to Buy

Measure the area to be recaned from groove to groove, front to back and side to side. Make the measurements from the outer lips of the grooves and add 2 inches to allow for wedging into the groove and trimming. Thus, if you are to cane a seat 18 inches by 18 inches, buy a piece of cane webbing 20 inches by 20 inches, minimum.

Buy a piece of reed splining when you buy the webbing, getting about 6 inches more than the running length of the groove on the chair. Grooves range from $\frac{1}{8}$ to $\frac{1}{4}$ inch in width, depending on the maker and the size of the caned area. The reed splining is tapered to a wedge shape for tamping down into the groove. Specify the width of the groove when buying the spline.

STEP 2: REMOVING THE OLD CANE
Tools

Tools needed for the removal of old webbing and the spline that held it in place include a hammer or mallet, 6 to 8 hardwood wedges (sold by caning suppliers), a heavy-duty pair of scissors, a sharp craft or wallboard knife, and two chisels.

The chisels are used to dig out the old spline, and to trim off the excess cane after the new webbing is in place. The best chisel for the trimming is a very sharp 1-inch wood chisel. The chisel used to remove the old spline may be hard to find — a very narrow ($\frac{1}{8}$- or $\frac{3}{32}$-inch) splined chisel with an angled blade. The reason for this size and shape is that it is driven

Someone tacked or nailed a panel over the opening after the cane seat broke. This created dozens of holes and nearly ruined the wood.

First, we filled the holes with wood filler. We then gave the entire chair a coat of colored varnish in deep red mahogany.

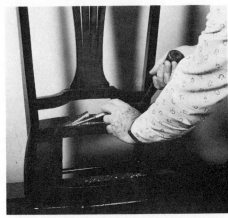

To remove the old spline from the groove around the seat, dig through the old spline and get a small chisel or narrow screwdriver under it.

Now that old spline has been removed from this boudoir chair, and the chair has been refinished, it is ready to receive new prewoven cane.

down into the groove and under the old spline. You can do the job with a screwdriver if no narrow chisel is available, but be careful because you don't want to damage or widen the groove.

If the chair to be recaned needs repair or refinishing, do the work before applying the cane.

Removing the Old Spline

In our chair, the old spline was glued and wedged into the groove. In these cases the glue, because it has been under no strain, usually holds pretty well. You can make the job easier by using an artist's brush to paint a warm-water-and-vinegar solution generously over the spline (getting as little as possible on the nearby wood), allowing the mixture to soak in. Repeated applications over a period of several hours are helpful in difficult cases.

To start, try to locate the point at which the two ends of the spline were joined. Usually, this is in the center of the back of a seat. Chisel down into the spline at this point and work the chisel under the spline. Tap the chisel in the direction of the groove under the spline and attempt to force it up and out. If you are lucky, the spline will pop out easily. If the old glue holds and the spline is tightly wedged, you'll have to work patiently with the chisel to get the spline out. As you work, be very careful not to damage the edge of the groove.

After working the spline out, clean the groove of all old glue and caning. The vinegar-and-water solution can be a help in this.

STEP 3: MAKING THE PATTERN

Now make a paper pattern of the area to be caned. Lay a large sheet of paper across the opening and hold it in place with masking tape. Use a heavy pencil to trace the groove. Then remove the pattern from the chair and sketch a line all around the tracing made by the groove, following the exact configuration of the pattern. This line should be a minimum of ¾ inch from the tracing; for safety's sake, make it an inch or inch and a quarter. Cut the pattern on this outline.

STEP 4: PLANNING THE ALIGNMENT

The trickiest part of applying cane webbing seems to be getting the webbing correctly aligned on the seat. First-time caners all too often end up with the webbing at a slight angle in the seat. Strive to lay the cane so that the lines of holes run straight from front to back and from side to side. If they don't, you'll end up with an odd looking seat. We have found two aids to solving the alignment problem.

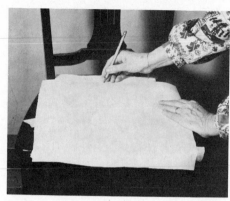

The first step is to cut a paper pattern. Use a pencil or felt-tipped pen to trace the pattern of the spline groove on the paper. Then, draw a freehand line all around the pattern about 1 inch out from the groove line. This will be the line on which you cut the webbing.

Next measure off the midpoint of the front of the seat and mark it.

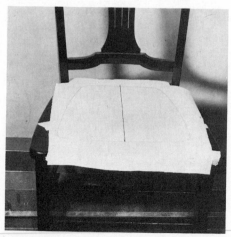

Align the holes in the webbing with the guideline on the paper pattern as you cut the webbing. The holes will run straight from back to front.

Pattern Guidelines

The first is to draw guidelines across the pattern, one from front to back and the other from side to side. These lines should be carefully drawn to show the horizontal and vertical axes, and should be used as a guide when cutting the webbing. Lay the

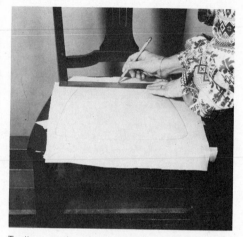

To line up the new cane on the seat, draw a guideline on the paper pattern. Measure off the midpoint of the back of the seat and mark it.

Finally, connect the two midpoints to make your guideline. You will use this line when cutting the cane webbing to fit the seat.

Also to assist in the alignment of the seat, run a piece of twine from front to back at the midpoint of the seat. Hold the string in place with masking tape.

webbing over the pattern, line up the pencilled lines with the lines of the holes in the webbing, and then cut the webbing, using a heavy scissors.

Seat Guidelines

The second help in aligning the webbing is to tape a guide string across the seat from front to back. Carefully determine the center of the seat and the exact front-to-back line. Then put a guide string between the front and back rails, under the area to be webbed. You can hold the string in place with thumb tacks or masking tape.

By using the guidelines on the pattern, you guarantee that the webbing will be cut straight. When you place the webbing over the opening, align it with the guide string, assuring a perfect front-to-back alignment.

STEP 5: SOAKING AND CUTTING THE WEBBING

The webbing should be soaked in a solution of warm water and glycerine (1½ ounces of glycerine per pint of water) for about an hour before cutting and before application to the seat. Soak the splining at the same time.

After soaking the cane, lay it on your pattern with the glossy side of the cane facing up. Line up the guidelines on the pattern with the holes in the webbing; cut out the piece for the seat. A heavy-duty scissors is the easiest cutting tool for this job. (A tin snip works fine.) Follow the outer edge of the pattern, the line you drew that is about an inch from the tracing of the groove.

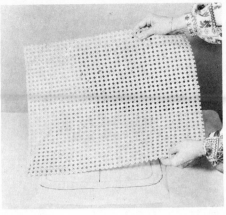

After soaking, place the webbing on the paper pattern.

Carefully align the holes running from the back to the front of the webbing with the guideline on the pattern.

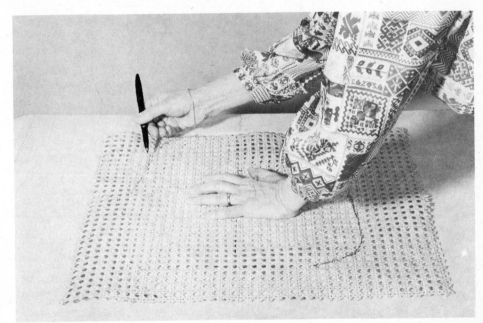

Transfer the outline from the pattern to the cane webbing by drawing with a felt pen. Remember that you will transfer the outer line on the pattern and cut on that line.

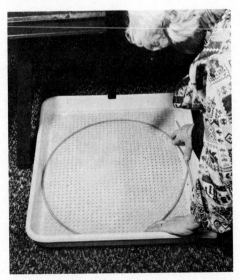

Soak the webbing for an hour in a warm-water-and-glycerine solution. Soak the splining at the same time.

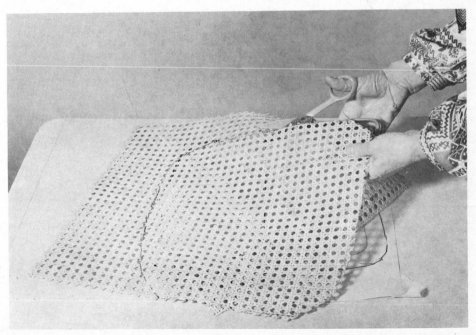

Now, with a heavy duty scissors, cut the webbing to size. The softened cane cuts easily.

STEP 6: INSTALLING THE WEBBING

Lay the moist webbing over the opening. Center it carefully and align it with the guide string you placed in the chair seat to be sure the hole lines run straight from back to front.

Now use the hardwood wedges to drive the webbing down into the groove. Begin by driving the first wedge into the groove at the center of the back rail. Work carefully so as not to tear the webbing apart. Now go to the front rail. Stretch the webbing across the opening so that it has a slight sag. This sag will be taken up as you wedge the webbing and also as the webbing dries out. Drive a wedge in the center of the front groove.

Continue by driving wedges in the center of each side, so that you then have four wedges holding the webbing in position. Visually check at this time to be sure the webbing is aligned and where you want it. This is your last chance to make corrections.

Now use another wedge and work your way around the groove, beginning at the center of the back, tamping the webbing down into the groove. When correctly tamped, the webbing should touch both sides and the bottom of the groove. Use as many holding wedges as you need to keep the webbing in the groove.

Keep the webbing moist as you work. Run a sponge soaked in the glycerine-and-water solution over strands frequently.

Note that you may have to shape the hardwood wedges to suit your work. The wedges you bought may be too thick for the groove if yours is narrow. Sand the wedges down to the size needed. Some caners make one larger wedge, 2 inches wide and 2 inches long, for working

Place the webbing on the seat. Sight through the holes to align it with the guide string you placed under the seat. Your caning pegs can be helpful in positioning the webbing.

To anchor the webbing, tap a hardwood wedge into the groove at the center of the back of the seat. Do this carefully so that the wedge doesn't tear the webbing. Keep tapping until the wedge hits the bottom of the groove.

Now move to the front and tap in a second wedge. The webbing between these two wedges should sag just a little. The sag will be taken up later as you work.

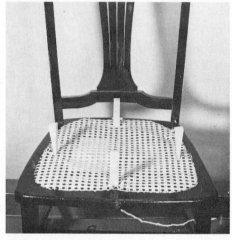

Complete the anchoring of the webbing by tapping in wedges at both sides. Take a good look before going on to be sure the line of holes in the webbing runs straight from front to back. This is your last chance to adjust them.

The next step is to lay a thin bead of glue in the groove just before you put the webbing in place on the seat.

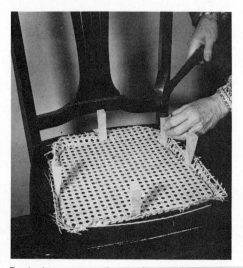

Beginning next to the anchor wedge at the back, work your way around the groove, tamping the webbing down into the groove. Always be sure the cane is tapped all the way in.

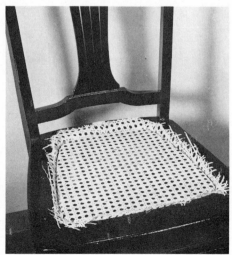

Here the webbing has been tapped into the groove all around the seat and the wedges have been removed. You are ready to install the spline.

around the groove, and use smaller 1 by 2-inch wedges for holding.

STEP 7: PREPARING AND INSERTING THE SPLINING

After all of the webbing has been grooved, prepare the splining. If the opening is square in shape, use a separate piece of splining for each side. If it is circular, use one continuous spline. The chair shown here was square in shape but had rounded corners, so we used a continuous spline.

The splining should be well soaked in the glycerine-and-water solution. It should be a little narrower along its bottom edge than the groove *after the webbing has been placed in it*. If the splining you have is too wide, you can shave it with a wallboard knife. Use a new, sharp blade in the knife for this work.

Cut one end of the splining at an angle. If the seat is square, angle the cut of the splining for each side, cutting so that the back and front pieces will overlap the side pieces. If you use a continuous piece of spline, the overlap will take place at the center of the back rail of the chair.

Now run a bead of good glue (such as white carpenter's glue or liquid hide glue) in the groove over the webbing. The glue will be forced up and out of the groove as the spline is tapped into place, so don't put in too much now.

Place the narrow bottom of the spline in the groove and tap it into place. Using a wooden block as a pad, hold the block over the splining and tap the block with your hammer. Work from one point along the groove and keep moving, tapping the spline in as you go. The spline should go into the groove until it is flush with the surface of the webbing.

STEP 8: FINISHING UP

After the splining has been seated firmly all around, and the end have been neatly cut at an angle, you must trim away the ends of the webbing sticking up along the outside of the spline. The easiest way is to use a very sharp 1-inch wood chisel. Place the chisel against the side of the spline groove just at the point where the webbing emerges. Tap it sharply to cut through the webbing. You can also cut the excess cane away with a very sharp knife.

Allow the new caning to dry overnight before using it. It can be left natural or given a coat of clear shellac, lacquer or varnish for protection against moisture.

You should miter the end of the spline to make a good fit. Here you see the end trimmed at a slight angle. The other end will be trimmed to match this one when you cut it after installing the spline.

Place the spline in the groove with the narrow side down; then use a wooden block (one of the hardwood wedges serves here) and a hammer to drive the spline into the groove until it is level with the top edge of the groove.

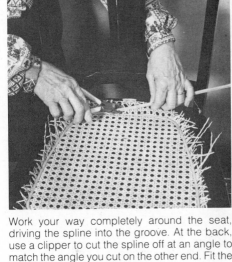

Work your way completely around the seat, driving the spline into the groove. At the back, use a clipper to cut the spline off at an angle to match the angle you cut on the other end. Fit the mitered spline ends over each other in a neat fit to hide the junction point.

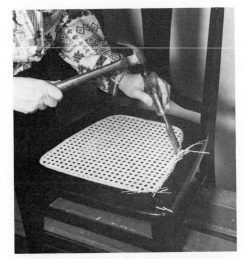

Using a very sharp 1-inch wood chisel, go around the seat trimming off the excess webbing. Insert the chisel into the groove, cutting down at an angle so the cane is trimmed off down in the groove. This way, the cut ends will be invisible.

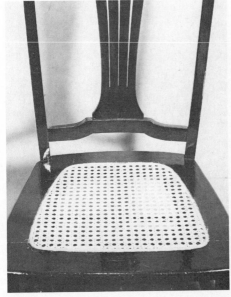

Here is the finished seat. Allow the cane to dry overnight before putting the chair to use.

12
Assembling and Finishing Furniture Kits

Scouting your attic and the garage sales to find good old pieces to restore is one way to acquire good furniture for your home. Another way is to buy unfinished furniture. And a third method rapidly growing in popularity is to build fine furniture in kit form.

For years, unfinished furniture has been the cheap way to add a bookcase, a night stand, or a chest of drawers to the home. Most of the unfinished furniture available was made of pine, spruce or other softwoods, and was of simple, inexpensive construction. Parts often were stapled in place, joints were sometimes ill-fitting, and design was dictated by the need for low price and ease of manufacture. This furniture could be finished to look pretty good. Its main reason for existence was to provide useful and inexpensive furniture, notably for young and growing families.

After hours of painstaking care, this is the finished butcher's table. The kit from which it was made is manufactured by Heath.

This secretary and plant stand are both manufactured by Bartley. Many of Bartley's pieces are reproductions of furniture found in Greenfield Village, Michigan.

This is the Heath Craft Woodworks rolltop desk, made of white oak. It would require about 100 hours of work altogether.

The Queen Anne dining room table, sideboard and cupboard, brandy stand table and arm chairs are from the Bartley Collection.

HARDWOOD FURNITURE

But in the past couple of years, a revolution has taken place in unfinished pieces. Hardwoods such as oak began to appear. Boxy designs began to be replaced by true furniture designs, some even based on good period pieces. For example, you can now buy round oak pedestal dining tables typical of tables produced just after the turn of the century, and the chairs to go with them.

Old-line furniture manufacturers such as Kroehler and Norwalk have added "whitewood" (the trade designation for unfinished furniture) pieces to their lines, and good furniture stores in major cities (for example, Homemakers, a division of John M. Smyth, and Marshall Fields, both in Chicago) have begun showing excellent unfinished hardwood furniture in a variety of pleasing designs.

It is true that good unfinished furniture has always been available, but only from specialized sources, usually by mail order. Many people have not been aware of this availability. Now the better furniture is within easy reach.

The prices on this new kind of unfinished furniture are higher than the pine boxes of the past, but the costs are still low enough to be attractive. The pieces add an interesting dimension to the do-it-yourself field because it is possible to put in some "sweat equity," — extra time in sanding, filling, staining and varnishing — and end up with a very creditable collection of furniture.

The market for unfinished furniture also has changed. *Business Week* magazine reports that buyers of unfinished furniture have a new profile. They are now middle-class, middle-aged white-collar workers who own their own homes and have incomes in excess of $17,000 a year. This group is not looking for cheap unfinished pieces. Instead, it wants something good enough so that with the investment of time and personal craftsmanship, the completed furniture is both attractive and valuable. Marketers suspect that there is another deep-rooted dimension to the movement: these buyers are looking for the glow of satisfaction that comes with creativity, and finishing good unfinished furniture seems to provide it.

KITS

Perhaps the most astonishing development in the unfinished furniture field has been the rapid growth of the fine-wood furniture kit, for which you will pay from several hundred to over a thousand dollars per piece. An outstanding example of this type of kit is made by the Bartley Collection in Lake Forest, Illinois. Heath, the well-known electronic kit manufacturer, of Benton Harbor, Michigan, also has a fine line of these kits.

For kits by these and others in this relatively new end of the business, you pay premium prices and receive kits with beautifully machined parts in solid, top-grade woods. Bartley furniture kits are authentic duplicates of items in the Henry Ford Museum or at Greenfield Village, Michigan, so with a Bartley piece you get both lovely antique design and fine woods.

Furniture kits have been available for a long time. Yield House, of North Conway, New Hampshire, has been offering high-quality pine furniture in kit form for over 30 years. So the idea isn't new. But broad public acceptance of the kit idea *is* new.

Paste Stains and Varnishes

One feature of all kit furniture is ease of finishing. Bartley pioneered the use of paste wiping stains and paste wiping varnish on its furniture. Heath followed suit, and we anticipate that more and more kit makers will do so in the near future. Both materials are applied in the same way as the jelled stains discussed in Chapter 8. The stains are incredibly easy to apply. They just wipe on with a cloth pad. There is no muss, no dripping, no overlapping of stain. If you can shine a pair of shoes, you can stain good furniture with a wiping stain and achieve a professional result.

The paste varnishes are equally easy to apply. The only difference between a paste varnish and a liquid varnish is that you must apply more coats of the paste varnish than the liquid to build up a good finish. While that may seem like a bit of a nuisance, the fact that the wiping is so easy and messless that you can actually do it in a living room more than offsets the time required.

SOURCES

Where to buy good unfinished furniture and furniture kits? Shop your local home centers, stores which specialize in unfinished furniture, and furniture stores. All three have become sources for the better

grades. Most furniture kit makers are mail order houses, so check the do-it-yourself, hobby and furniture magazines for their ads. Then send for their catalogs. The prices for the very good pieces won't be low. As for kit quality, we can personally vouch for kits from Bartley, Heath and Yield House, and believe that there are other kit makers trying just as hard to acquire satisfied customers.

GUIDELINES FOR FINISHING

Most unfinished furniture is delivered to you "machine" sanded. Some stores get carried away and say that this furniture is "ready to finish." The beautifully shaped pieces in furniture kits also have been sanded before delivery. But in our estimation, there is no such thing as a piece "ready to finish," if that phrase means, "ready to stain and varnish."

The really good finish that you want on any piece of furniture can be had only through a sound finishing procedure. This includes:

(1.) final sanding of the wood prior to the application of any stain;

(2.) careful application of the finish coats (enough to build up a sound and durable finish) and light sanding between coats;

(3.) allowance of more than ample drying time between all coats;

(4.) a final handrubbing to produce that warm and lovely final patina.

If you follow this procedure and put all the elbow grease into the sanding that you should, there is no reason why you can't achieve finishes as good as or better than any you see in the furniture stores. The bywords to guide you in this work are *patience* and *take your time*.

There are problem areas when working with kits or unfinished furniture.

Glue Problems

Beginners sometimes are not careful with glue. They apply too much and allow the glue to dry on the surfaces near joints. If that happens, you will not be able to stain and finish that area later. Never apply too much glue.

When you work with new, raw wood, it is *not* a good idea to wipe away excess glue that is squeezed out of joints. Wiping tends to spread the glue and to seal the wood surface. The best removal method is to let the glue dry and then carefully trim it away with a very sharp knife or single-edge razor blade.

If excess glue does get into or on the wood near a joint, you'll find out when you apply the stain, which won't have the same color on the glued area. To correct this, you'll have to sand the area and perhaps even shave the surface carefully to get rid of the glue. When the stain takes evenly, you know that all the glue is gone. However, it is best to avoid the problem in the first place.

You can avoid many problems if you use glue carefully. Don't apply too much, and clean away any excess before you stain. Clamp the drying pieces firmly.

Sanding Problems

Too many people aren't willing to take the time to sand properly. The result is a final surface that is rough and without that professional look. No doubt about it, when you must sand 15 or 20 pieces in a kit, the work is boring, and there is always the temptation to quit before the job is done. However, if you are assembling a kit, you must read the instructions carefully and follow those for sanding exactly. These instructions will have been tailored for the type of wood used in the piece.

The sandpapers and sanding instructions supplied with the kits we have seen were aimed at just the right amount of final sanding—neither too much or too little—with the correct grades of paper. Follow the instructions that come with your kit.

Too Much Sanding As we pointed out in Chapter 4, it is possible to sand too much. If you start with a medium grit paper on hardwood and work your way to a very fine paper, you can actually polish the surface of the wood to a point that it will not accept stain readily. To avoid this, don't sand raw hardwood with papers over 300 grit unless you intend to finish a piece naturally, with no stain or varnish. Oversanding on softwoods such as pine and redwood produces a surface fuzz that will interfere with the application of the final finishing material.

General Procedures As a general rule, begin with a 220-grit paper, and do final sanding with a 280-grit. If you must sand parts like tenons to make them fit, use a coarser paper (around 150-grit) to remove material faster, then finish with finer grades. Don't use a grade finer than 300 grit for finish sanding; save grades from 300 to 600 for sanding between coats and for the last handrub sanding.

How Much Sanding Is Enough?

As long as you don't use a very fine paper you can sand forever. You want all surfaces to be smooth, with all sawmarks and sanding scratches removed. You want the natural roughness of the end and cross-grains eliminated.

You will be able to see whether you have sanded enough when you apply your first coat of stain. If an area has not been sanded enough, it will appear a little rough and the stain will be darker here than on the rest of the wood. You will notice this particularly in shaped areas that run across the grain such as carved table edges.

As you stain, if you find an area that was not sanded enough, you can fix it. Wait until the stain has dried completely; then sand the rough area with a 180 to 220-grit paper. When the area is smooth, re-stain the spot. Apply the stain carefully to match the color of the wood around the area. You can use a cotton swab to apply the stain, which you then wipe off after a minute or so. You may need several coats to match the color of the rest of the surface.

Problems With the Fitting of Pieces

Wood is, in many ways, like a sponge. It absorbs water when the humidity is high and gives it up when the humidity is low. Wood used in furniture making—and in making kits—is kiln dried and delivered to the maker at a specific moisture content, and the pieces of a kit are shaped at this moisture level. They are made to fit together snugly and accurately.

As a rule, kit makers box their kits and store them under controlled conditions until the day of shipment. But during shipping and after they arrive at your house, the parts are exposed to a different set of climatic conditions. Usually, the parts absorb moisture from the air and swell slightly. If they were made to fit accurately in the first place, they now become just a little too big. Or if they are now exposed to high temperatures and low humidity, they may shrink a little and become just a little too small.

The instructions usually cover the problem and tell you what to do about it. The point is, don't get discouraged if the parts of your expensive furniture kits don't fit the way you thought they should. There is a good reason for the problem, and also a solution for it.

The pieces of fine wood kits are manufactured carefully, but because of humidity changes, you may have to do some sanding.

Once you have sanded the joint, dry fit the pieces. Work until the fit is satisfactory; then glue the pieces carefully.

Once the glue has dried, sand all the pieces thoroughly. No brand of unfinished furniture comes in a condition that is ready to stain. Your sanding should be thorough.

Defective Parts Rarely, when the pieces are cut, a mistake will be made. The piece will be too long, or too short, or too something. A little reflection will tell you that this problem wasn't caused by climate, but by a mistake in the plant. Kit makers generally tell you that they will replace any defective parts quickly and at no cost. Usually, a letter or a phone call to the maker will get quick results.

Problems with the Final Finish

Whenever we have checked out a final finish problem on a kit, we found that the kit assembler had glue or sanding problems (outlined earlier), or he substituted a different finish material for the one supplied or recommended by the kit maker. If you want to finish your kit in a different manner than described by the kit maker, it is a good idea to call him and discuss the change. Tell him the product you have in mind to use. He may be able to tell you of a better product, or of poor experience he has had with the one you want to use.

Don't hesitate to contact the kit maker, whatever your problem. Firstly, he wants you to be satisfied because you will buy more and your friends will buy when they see your good results. Secondly, you've spend a pretty good chunk of money on the kit, and have a right to expect good results in the assembly and finishing of it.

Problems in Your Own Work Area

As noted earlier, wood is like a sponge, and it changes size readily in different humidity conditions. If you work in an area with a high humidity during kit assembly, and then move the finished piece to an area of low humidity, you might expect problems.

In drier conditions, the finished piece may lose moisture. The parts may shrink and the joints may become loose. In more moist conditions, the joints on the finished piece may swell; this can, if the moisture change is great enough, crack the wood in the joint area. Large flat pieces, such as table and chest tops made of solid wood,

can warp if moisture conditions are severe. There are two ways to minimize these problems.

Controlling Humidity First, set up your work in an area that isn't extreme in humidity, neither very moist nor very dry. Ideally, the humidity of your workroom should be approximately the same as the humidity in the room in which the piece of furniture will be used. In a home with whole-house air conditioning, this presents no problems. In a home where window units are used to control the air in different rooms, or in homes without air conditioning—especially in parts of the country subjected to high humidity—there may be large humidity differences from one room to another, and from one season to the next. The best answer is to use a humidifier or a dehumidifier, as required, to control the air in your workroom while assembling the kit.

Protecting the Wood Second, you can reduce the amount of water absorbed and given up by furniture, thus limiting the expansion and contraction of the wood. This is accomplished by applying a good, sound coat of finishing material to all surfaces of the parts.

A sound finish coat means a coat built up through the application of a number of thin coats. If the finish coat is thick enough, moisture will pass through it very slowly, and perhaps not at all. This is not a license to make the final coat an eighth of an inch thick. A final coat that is too thick will probably crack and peel and do other terrible things. However, three or four coats of a brushed-on finish, or half a dozen wiped-on coats of a wiping varnish, make sense from the viewpoint not only of appearance but also of moisture absorption.

Obviously, it will do little good to put a sound finish coat on the exposed and visible parts of the piece, while leaving drawers, frame members and undersides uncoated. The uncoated parts can absorb moisture and cause problems. So it makes sense to coat all the wood to minimize moisture problems.

When you finish interior surfaces depends upon the construction of the piece on which you are working. We did not finish the Queen Anne's chair that we worked on here until assembly was complete. The finishing of the butler's table, however, proceeded in stages. We assembled it partially, then finished, then con-

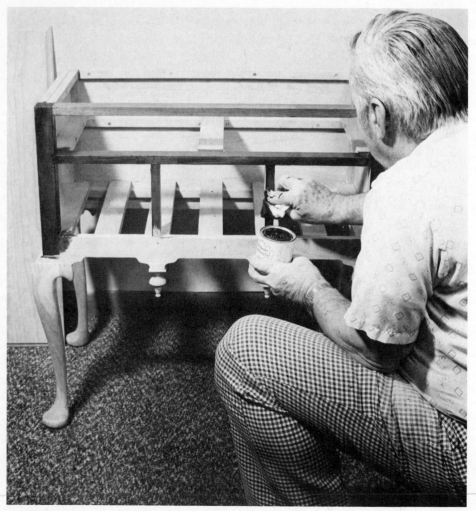

All surfaces should be finished. We finished the butler's table when assembly was completed. However, this low-boy has interior spaces that we finished before the top was installed.

tinued assembly. The same work order would apply to a dresser or a chest.

When finishing all wood areas, apply the same number of coats to each. Don't put five coats on a dresser top and only one coat on framing members or drawers. If you use a different number of coats, you set up a situation in which more moisture can enter one part than another. This is an open invitation to warping.

THE PROBLEM OF DRYING TIMES

Most of the materials you apply to furniture during the construction and finishing are liquid or semi-liquid, and need to dry. Manufacturers of these products, from glues and fillers to stains and varnishes, indicate the average drying times on their labels.

The problem is, there is no such thing as an average drying time. Drying depends heavily on temperature and humidity, and these vary radically from place to place and time to time. Therefore, use any drying times strictly as a general indication, and not as the gospel truth.

We have seen varnishes which dried completely in 12 hours at 77 degrees, and required as long as 30 hours when the temperature was below 70 degrees. That gives you some idea of the sensitivity of finishing materials to climatic conditions—a variation of less than 10 degrees in temperature can increase drying time by a factor of 2½ or 3. High humidity usually has an even greater effect.

Defining "Dry"

Perhaps the problem starts with the question, "What is dry?" If you read labels and literature, you find phrases such as *dry to the touch* and *new coats can be applied after X hours* and *dries dust free in X minutes*. These phrases suggest that there is more than one condition called "dry." In fact, there are about half a dozen identifiable stages, although actually, drying is a continuous operation. Different materials and different formulations act differently during drying, but here is a general description.

First, the material is liquid immediately after application. Then it gets tacky. When tacky, it doesn't come off if you touch your finger to it, but you will make one heck of a fingerprint by doing so.

Next the surface dries so that it is no longer tacky. This is the "dust-free" stage, which means that dust falling on the surface will not absorb into the finish material but will stay on the surface, where it can be brushed away later. At this time, it is also, "dry to the touch."

Material under the surface dries next, and when the full thickness of the coat is dry, you reach the first stage of true dryness. But this still isn't dry enough for sanding or for the application of additional coats.

Drying continues as the driers in the formulation evaporate from the material until the finish reaches what the Heath people, in their instruction manual, refer to as *bone dry*. This is the time for finish sanding or for the next coat.

There is another stage of drying, after the last coat has become bone dry. This final stage is sometimes referred to as curing. The finish continues to dry for days and weeks, slowly settling down to its final thickness. We think it is a good idea to wait for a week or so to apply wax or polish in order to allow ample time for this curing to take place.

The important thing to know about drying is that the surface should be bone dry before you sand it or before you apply the next coat. One of the most common of all errors on the part of finishers is the application of a new coat before the previous coat has dried sufficiently.

If you have doubts about whether the surface is dry enough, play it safe and wait. You can't go wrong by waiting; you can create problems by working on the finish or coating it too soon.

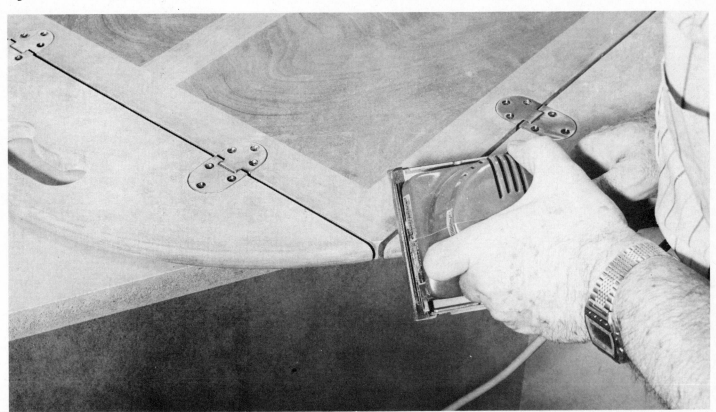

Give the detail work the attention that the piece deserves. Here we round the edge of the butler's table to match the curve of the leaves.

Note on some finishes Some poly-urethane and other finishes dry with such a hard surface that a second coat cannot grip the surface properly. The labels on these finishes tell you to apply a second coat *before* a certain time has elapsed. If you wait longer than the specified time, then the surface must be sanded to provide "tooth" for the next coat. This is typical of enamels and other very hard glossy finishes. This really isn't a problem, since you should sand between coats anyway. It just means that the sanding *must* be done and should be a little more thorough than you might otherwise do.

UPGRADING UNFINISHED FURNITURE

Top-quality furniture kits come to you with all pieces carefully cut, and all joints made to fit precisely. Less expensive unfinished hardwood furniture already assembled may or may not have had careful attention during assembly. As a rule, the cheaper the piece, the more likely you are to find such problems as poor joinery or ill-fitting drawers.

You can do an excellent job of upgrading the least expensive furniture if you want to take a little time. Here are some

places to check and some of the work you might do.

Joints

Joints may not fit tightly. You can use a wood filler for a quick upgrade. Or you may be able to take the piece apart and sand the components of the joint until they fit correctly.

Shaped Edges

Check tops of chests, tables, or other pieces that have shaped edges carved with a router. These edges usually have not been sanded at all, while flat surfaces probably have had at least minimal sanding. Spend some time sanding these shaped places so that they take the finish material nicely. Pay particular attention to those edges across the grain. They will absorb much more stain than the other parts and turn out darker.

The best way to handle staining of endgrain wood is to seal the wood either before or during staining. Before staining, a coat of thin shellac will work. During staining, lightly touch your stain pad to the top surface of the varnish, so that you get a mixture of stain and varnish on the pad. Apply this mixture to the endgrain.

Drawer Guides

Few inexpensive pieces have drawer guides. This isn't much of a problem with small drawers, but on big ones, which will hold a heavy load, the drawers may not work well for long without guides. You can buy ready-made metal guides or put in your own made from hardwood strips.

Better Hardware

The look of most furniture depends in part on the appearance of its hardware—drawer pulls, knobs or hinges. Inexpensive unfinished furniture usually has minimal hardware. You can replace wooden drawer pulls with brass or ceramic ones. Replace flat steel door hinges with more ornate brass models. Install casters in place of the steel glides many makers use.

Better Looking, More Serviceable Top Surfaces

When you buy a piece of furniture that is expected to do yeoman service—a table for children's use, for example—you can add years to its life by applying a plastic laminate to the top. Your home center has plastic laminates in stock or can order one for you. This material is applied like a veneer, with contact cement. Follow the instructions given in Chapter 10. Plastic laminates resist damage from just about everything and look good as well.

If the unfinished furniture you buy is of a hardwood that has no grain, color or character, you might consider applying a veneer of mahogany, cherry, walnut or other fine wood to the large, flat areas such as the top, sides, or drawer fronts. This can turn good but nondescript furniture into something worth having for a· long time.

THE FINAL WORD

Today, unfinished furniture is available in a range of prices, designs and materials, and if you are in the market for furniture, a shopping trip to discover what's out there is worthwhile. You'll see inexpensive bookcases and other simple pieces in particle board and softwoods; you'll also see well-made breakfast and dining sets in hardwood. The selection will range all the way up to museum reproductions in magnificent hardwoods.

This furniture is no longer inexpensive. It now offers a whole gamut of prices, designs and woods. Check it out.

One mark of the better kits is the fine quality of the hardware. If your kit is inexpensive, upgrade it by replacing lesser pieces of hardware with fine brass ones.

Glossary

Abrasive Any material used to wear away, smooth or polish a surface, such as sandpaper used to smooth wood.

Alligatored finish Any finished surface that shows cracks caused by aging and drying.

Antiquing A decorative finish process. A basecoat is covered with a glaze, another paint, stain or varnish, that is partly wiped or brushed away to reveal some of the base-coat color.

Breathing mask A device to cover the nose and mouth and prevent inhalation of dust or other material in the air.

Clear finish Any of a number of wood finishes that allow the wood grain to be seen.

Coloring stick A type of colored wax crayon that will hide small scratches in finished wood.

Denatured alcohol A solvent used to thin shellac.

Distressing A finishing process that adds dents, scratches, burns and other indications of wear and age to furniture for decorative reasons.

Dowel A wood pin frequently used to join two pieces of wood. The dowel fits into holes drilled in each piece; this creates a dowel joint.

Fasteners Nails, screws, brads and other items that are used to join two items or to secure hardware to furniture or millwork.

Flitch A sheet of veneer.

French polish A shellac finish applied in many layers with a rubber. The surface is sanded between coats with fine, oiled sandpaper. The final coat is often polished with rottenstone and oil.

Grain The growth pattern in the tree. The grain will look different in different trees and as a result of different sawing techniques.

Graining A specialty finish used to create the impression of wood grain with paint. Imitation wood grain.

Graphite powder A ground soft carbon material that is a dry lubricant.

Hardwood Wood that is cut from deciduous (leaf-shedding) trees. Although all such wood is designated as hardwood, some types are actually physically soft and easy to dent.

Lac beetle An insect that secretes a fluid which is made into lac flakes, the basic ingredient in shellac.

Lacquer A clear or colored finish material that dries to a hard, glossy finish. Usually applied with a sprayer, lacquer dries too quickly for smooth application with a brush.

Lacquer/shellac sticks Sticks of filler material used in the repair of surface damage to furniture. The filler must be melted onto the damaged surface and then trimmed smooth.

Linseed oil A finishing oil made from pressed flax seeds. An ingredient used in paint (oil-base) and varnish.

Mortise and tenon A joint in which one piece has a square or rectangular projection that fits snugly into a similarly shaped hole in the second piece.

Oil finish A clear finish produced by rubbing an oil, such as linseed, into bare or stained wood. The oil is rubbed to a soft, glowing finish.

Paint A pigmented varnish (oil-based) material that will completely cover and hide the surface to which it is applied. Newer formulas combine rubber (latex) and water.

Polyurethane A varnish to which plastics have been added. It creates a durable finish.

Pounce bag A cloth bag containing chalk dust or other powder that leaves a dust mark on any surface on which the bag is hit

Pumice A lava rock abrasive, pumice is ground into a powder for a polish.

Raising the grain A process of damping the surface of wood to bring up or lift small fibers for final smooth sanding.

Rasp A rough sided tool designed to dig into and wear away material such as wood.

Reamalgamated finish A previously alligatored or roughened finish that has been made level by rubbing the surface with solvent that melts the finish and lets it dry smooth.

Respirator A filter device worn over the nose and mouth to remove irritants—dust and toxic matter—from the air.

Rottenstone A fine powder abrasive made from crushing decomposed limestone. Rottenstone and oil are used as a fine finishing polish.

Rubbing varnish A finish material designed to provide an unusually high gloss when polished with rottenstone and oil.

Sanding block A padded wood block around which a piece of sandpaper is wrapped for hand sanding of a surface.

Sanding sealer A thinned shellac or other lightweight clear finish applied to wood to prevent the raising of wood grain by stain, filler or final finish material.

Sandpaper A coated abrasive—usually flint, garnet or aluminum oxide glued to a paper, cloth or plastic backing. It is used for smoothing or polishing woods.

Shellac A final, clear finish material created by dissolving lac flakes in denatured alcohol. A five pound cut of shellac is made by dissolving five pounds of lac flakes in one gallon of denatured alcohol. A one pound cut is one pound of flakes in a gallon of alcohol.

Softwood Wood that comes from logs of conebearing (coniferous) trees.

Spline A thin piece of wood used as a wedge. In a worn joint, a spline may be inserted into a cut to enlarge a dowel or a tenon so that the section will fit more tightly into the joint hole or mortise.

Stain Any of various forms of water, latex or oil based transparent or opaque coloring agents designed to penetrate the surface of the wood to color (stain) the material.

Tack rag A piece of cheesecloth or other lint-free fabric treated with turpentine and a small amount of varnish to create a sticky or tacky quality so the rag will pick up and hold all dirt, dust and lint that it touches.

Tooth A slight roughness created by light sanding of a smooth surface. The tooth allows a new application of a high gloss finish to adhere to a previously laid down high gloss finish.

Toxic Poisonous

Tung oil A water resistant finishing oil/varnish ingredient made from crushed tung tree seeds. Tung oil dries more quickly than linseed oil.

Varnish A durable clear finish made of a

mixture of resins, oil and alcohol or other volatile spirits. Varnish dries to a hard, smooth surface.

Veneer A thin sheet of wood applied to another piece of wood. Fine wood veneer is used in furniture.

Wood filler Liquid, paste, putty or plaster materials designed to fill in holes or grain lines so that final finishes may be applied to a smooth surface.

Index

PRODUCT SOURCES

The following is a listing of sources for products, materials, tools and kits discussed in this book. The list is by no means comprehensive, and is intended to serve as a starting point when these items prove difficult to find in your own area.

Most of the companies listed do business by mail and publish catalogs for which you can write. Some charge a fee for these, but we have found the price worthwhile in most cases, for they can be highly instructive and are fun to read.

Two important places to look when hunting for an elusive product, or when trying to find something as difficult as a match for a piece of antique hardware, are the Yellow Pages and the small ads in do-it-yourself and other specialized magazines.

CANE AND CANING SUPPLIES
Barap Specialities
635 Bellows
Frankfort, MI 49635
Cane and Basket Supply Co.
1283 S. Cochran Ave.
Los Angeles, CA 90019
Francis Cane and Rush Supplies
16402 Gothard St., Unit 6
Huntington Beach, CA 92647
Go-Cart Shop
PO Box 52
New Bedford, MA 02742
H.H. Perkins Co.
PO Box AC
Amity Station
Woodbridge, CO 06525
Jack's Upholstery and Caning Supplies
Oswego, IL 60543
Jim Dandy Sales
Box 30377

Cincinnati, OH 45230
Morgan
1123 Bardstown
Louisville, KY 40204
The Newell Workshop
128 Drawer
Hinsdale, IL 60521
Savin Handicrafts
PO Box 4251
Hamden, CO 06514
Squaw Alley, Inc.
106 W. Water
Naperville, IL 60540
TIE
PO Box 1121
San Mateo, CA 94403

HARDWARE
Colonial Castings
73 Westwood Drive
North Dartmouth, MA 20747
Horton Brasses
Berlin, CT 06037
The Renovator's Supply
Millers Falls, MA 01349
Squaw Alley, Inc.
106 N. Water
Naperville, IL 60540

FINISHING MATERIALS
General Finishes
Box 14363
Milwaukee, WI 53214
Minwax Co, Inc.
72 Oak St.
Clifton, NJ 07014

KIT AND UNFINISHED FURNITURE
The Bartley Collection
121 Schelter Road
Prairie View, IL 60069
Cohasset Colonials
Cohasset, MA 02025
Colonial Reproductions
Georgetown, MA 01833
Craftsmans Corner
4317 41st Street
Des Moines, IA 50302
Ellsworth of Willoughby
4010 Harmann
Willoughby, OH 44094
Ferguson's Country Store
Hwy. 65
St. Joe, AR 72675
Furniture-in-the-Raw
8 Rene Street
Brooklyn, NY 11211
Georgia Chair Co.
456 Industrial Blvd. SW
Gainesville, GA 30503
The Heath Company
Benton Harbor, MI 49022
The Hardwood Craftsman, Ltd.
811 Morse Ave.
Schaumburg, IL 60193
Indiana Wood Specialty Inc.
PO Box 4133
810 E. Louisana St.
Evansville, IN 47711
Mastercraft/Bailey & Sons
PO Box 239
Clarks Summit, PA 18411
Old Mill
Route 100
Weston, VT 05161
Old Timey Furniture Co.
PO Box 1165
Smithfield, NC 27577

S. Bent and Bros., Inc.
65 Winter St.
Gardner, MA 01440
Tennessee Hardwood
810 Maine
Woodbury, TN 37190
Wambold Marker
21101 Superior
Chatsworth, CA 91311
Yield House
North Conway, NH 03860

KNOBS, Antique Wooden
Andy Elder
Dublin, NH 03444

MARBLE
Door Store
3140 M St. NW, Georgetown
Washington, DC 20007
Vermont Marble Co.
101 Park Ave.
New York, NY 10017
and also
640 Pearson,
Des Plaines, IL 60016

NAILS, Antique
Tremont Nail Co.
PO Box 111
Wareham, MA 02751

TOOLS
American Machine and Tool Co.
Royersford, PA 19468
Arco Products Corp.
110 West Sheffield Ave.
Englewood, NJ 07631
Frog Tool Co., Ltd.
700 W. Jackson Blvd.
Chicago, IL 60610
Silvo Hardware Co.
107 Walnut St.
Philadelphia, PA 19106
Toolcraft Corp.
Plainfield Street
Chicopee, MA 01013

TRIM AND SUPPLIES
P. E. Guerin, Inc.
22 Jane St.
New York, NY 10014
The Renovator's Supply
Millers Falls, MA 01349
Storehouse
3106 Early St. NW
Atlanta, GA 30305
Sturbridge Yankee Workshop
685 Brimfield Turnpike
Sturbridge, MA 01566
Sugar Hill Sampler
Sugar Hill, NH 03585
Unfinished Wood Furniture
4728 Wilmington Pike
Dayton, OH 45440
Yield House
North Conway, NH 30680

VENEERS
Flitchcraft Veneers
Box 12195
Pensacola, FL 32590
H.L. Wild
510 E. Eleventh St.
New York, NY 10009
Homecraft Veneer
Box 3
Latrobe, PA 15650

Missouri Walnut Co.
Station A, Box 66
St. Joseph, MO 64503
Morgan
1123 Bardstown
Louisville, KY 40204

WOODS, FINE
Albert Constantine and Son, Inc.
2050 Eastchester Rd.
Bronx, NY 10461
Craftsman Wood Service
1735 West Courtland
Addison, IL 60101
Green Mountain Cabins
Chester, VT 04143
H.L. Wild
519 E. Eleventh Street
New York, NY 10009
Missouri Walnut Co.
Station A, Box 66
St. Joseph, MO 64503
N.H. Fellows and Son
Pittsfield, VT 05357
Rogers Iron Mine Woodworking Co.
Iron River, MI 49935
John Rowell
Tunbridge, VT 05077
Weird Wood
Box 190
Chester, VT 05143

WOODWORKING SUPPLIES
Albert Constantine and Son, Inc.
2050 Eastchester Road
Bronx, NY 10461
Barap Specialties
835 Bellows
Frankfort, MI 49635
Birchwood Casey
7900 Fuller Road
Eden Prairie, MN 55343
Craftsman Wood Service
1735 West Courtland
Addison, IL 60101
Minnesota Woodworkers Supply Co.
925 Winnetka Ave.
Minneapolis, MN 55427
Morgan
1123 Bardstown
Louisville, KY 40204

Contributors, picture credits

We wish to extend our thanks to the individuals, associations and manufacturers who graciously provided information and photographs for this book. Specific credit for individual photographs is given below.

Capital letters following page numbers indicate: T, top; B, bottom; L, left; R, right; C, center.

Armstrong Cork Company, Liberty Street, Lancaster PA 17604 *(p. 30)*

Bartley Collection, 121 Schelter Road, Prairie View, IL 60069 *(p. 149 T, BR)* **Monte Burch**, Rt. #1, Humansville, MO 65674 *(p. 44)*

Forest Products Laboratories, PO Box 5130, Madison, WI 53705 *(p. 31)*

Heath Company, Benton Harbor, MI 49022 *(p. 149 BL)*

Metric Conversion Charts

LUMBER

Sizes: Metric cross-sections are so close to their nearest Imperial sizes, as noted below, that for most purposes they may be considered equivalents.

Lengths: Metric lengths are based on a 300mm module which is slightly shorter in length than an Imperial foot. It will therefore be important to check your requirements accurately to the nearest inch and consult the table below to find the metric length required.

Areas: The metric area is a square metre. Use the following conversion factors when converting from Imperial data: 100 sq. feet = 9.290 sq. metres.

METRIC SIZES SHOWN BESIDE NEAREST IMPERIAL EQUIVALENT

mm	Inches	mm	Inches
16 x 75	⅝ x 3	44 x 150	1¾ x 6
16 x 100	⅝ x 4	44 x 175	1¾ x 7
16 x 125	⅝ x 5	44 x 200	1¾ x 8
16 x 150	⅝ x 6	44 x 225	1¾ x 9
19 x 75	¾ x 3	44 x 250	1¾ x 10
19 x 100	¾ x 4	44 x 300	1¾ x 12
19 x 125	¾ x 5	50 x 75	2 x 3
19 x 150	¾ x 6	50 x 100	2 x 4
22 x 75	⅞ x 3	50 x 125	2 x 5
22 x 100	⅞ x 4	50 x 150	2 x 6
22 x 125	⅞ x 5	50 x 175	2 x 7
22 x 150	⅞ x 6	50 x 200	2 x 8
25 x 75	1 x 3	50 x 225	2 x 9
25 x 100	1 x 4	50 x 250	2 x 10
25 x 125	1 x 5	50 x 300	2 x 12
25 x 150	1 x 6	63 x 100	2½ x 4
25 x 175	1 x 7	63 x 125	2½ x 5
25 x 200	1 x 8	63 x 150	2½ x 6
25 x 225	1 x 9	63 x 175	2½ x 7
25 x 250	1 x 10	63 x 200	2½ x 8
25 x 300	1 x 12	63 x 225	2½ x 9
32 x 75	1¼ x 3	75 x 100	3 x 4
32 x 100	1¼ x 4	75 x 125	3 x 5
32 x 125	1¼ x 5	75 x 150	3 x 6
32 x 150	1¼ x 6	75 x 175	3 x 7
32 x 175	1¼ x 7	75 x 200	3 x 8
32 x 200	1¼ x 8	75 x 225	3 x 9
32 x 225	1¼ x 9	75 x 250	3 x 10
32 x 250	1¼ x 10	75 x 300	3 x 12
32 x 300	1¼ x 12	100 x 100	4 x 4
38 x 75	1½ x 3	100 x 150	4 x 6
38 x 100	1½ x 4	100 x 200	4 x 8
38 x 125	1½ x 5	100 x 250	4 x 10
38 x 150	1½ x 6	100 x 300	4 x 12
38 x 175	1½ x 7	150 x 150	6 x 6
38 x 200	1½ x 8	150 x 200	6 x 8
38 x 225	1½ x 9	150 x 300	6 x 12
44 x 75	1¾ x 3	200 x 200	8 x 8
44 x 100	1¾ x 4	250 x 250	10 x 10
44 x 125	1¾ x 5	300 x 300	12 x 12

METRIC LENGTHS

Lengths Metres	Equiv. Ft. & Inches
1.8m	5' 10⅞"
2.1m	6' 10⅝"
2.4m	7' 10½"
2.7m	8' 10¼"
3.0m	9' 10⅛"
3.3m	10' 9⅞"
3.6m	11' 9¾"
3.9m	12' 9½"
4.2m	13' 9⅜"
4.5m	14' 9⅓"
4.8m	15' 9"
5.1m	16' 8¾"
5.4m	17' 8⅝"
5.7m	18' 8⅜"
6.0m	19' 8¼"
6.3m	20' 8"
6.6m	21' 7⅞"
6.9m	22' 7⅝"
7.2m	23' 7½"
7.5m	24' 7¼"
7.8m	25' 7⅛"

All the dimensions are based on 1 inch = 25 mm.

NOMINAL SIZE (This is what you order.)	ACTUAL SIZE (This is what you get.)
Inches	Inches
1 x 1	¾ x ¾
1 x 2	¾ x 1½
1 x 3	¾ x 2½
1 x 4	¾ x 3½
1 x 6	¾ x 5½
1 x 8	¾ x 7¼
1 x 10	¾ x 9¼
1 x 12	¾ x 11¼
2 x 2	1¾ x 1¾
2 x 3	1½ x 2½
2 x 4	1½ x 3½
2 x 6	1½ x 5½
2 x 8	1½ x 7¼
2 x 10	1½ x 9¼
2 x 12	1½ x 11¼

WOOD SCREWS

SCREW GAUGE NO.	NOMINAL DIAMETER Inch	NOMINAL DIAMETER mm	LENGTH Inch	LENGTH mm
0	0.060	1.52	3/16	4.8
1	0.070	1.78	¼	6.4
2	0.082	2.08	5/16	7.9
3	0.094	2.39	⅜	9.5
4	0.0108	2.74	7/16	11.1
5	0.122	3.10	½	12.7
6	0.136	3.45	⅝	15.9
7	0.150	3.81	¾	19.1
8	0.164	4.17	⅞	22.2
9	0.178	4.52	1	25.4
10	0.192	4.88	1¼	31.8
12	0.220	5.59	1½	38.1
14	0.248	6.30	1¾	44.5
16	0.276	7.01	2	50.8
18	0.304	7.72	2¼	57.2
20	0.332	8.43	2½	63.5
24	0.388	9.86	2¾	69.9
28	0.444	11.28	3	76.2
32	0.5	12.7	3¼	82.6
			3½	88.9
			4	101.6
			4½	114.3
			5	127.0
			6	152.4

Dimensions taken from BS1210; metric conversions are approximate.

BRICKS AND BLOCKS

Bricks

Standard metric brick measures 215 mm x 65 mm x 112.5. Metric brick can be used with older, standard brick by increasing the mortaring in the joints. The sizes are substantially the same, the metric brick being slightly smaller (3.6 mm less in length, 1.8 mm in width, and 1.2 mm in depth).

Concrete Block

Standard sizes

390 x 90 mm
390 x 190 mm
440 x 190 mm
440 x 215 mm
440 x 290 mm

Repair block for replacement of block in old installations is available in these sizes:
448 x 219 (including mortar joints)
397 x 194 (including mortar joints)

NAILS

NUMBER PER POUND OR KILO

Size	Weight Unit	Common	Casing	Box	Finishing
2d	Pound	876	1010	1010	1351
	Kilo	1927	2222	2222	2972
3d	Pound	586	635	635	807
	Kilo	1289	1397	1397	1775
4d	Pound	316	473	473	548
	Kilo	695	1041	1041	1206
5d	Pound	271	406	406	500
	Kilo	596	893	893	1100
6d	Pound	181	236	236	309
	Kilo	398	591	519	680
7d	Pound	161	210	210	238
	Kilo	354	462	462	524
8d	Pound	106	145	145	189
	Kilo	233	319	319	416
9d	Pound	96	132	132	172
	Kilo	211	290	290	398
10d	Pound	69	94	94	121
	Kilo	152	207	207	266
12d	Pound	64	88	88	113
	Kilo	141	194	194	249
16d	Pound	49	71	71	90
	Kilo	108	156	156	198
20d	Pound	31	52	52	62
	Kilo	68	114	114	136
30d	Pound	24	46	46	
	Kilo	53	101	101	
40d	Pound	18	35	35	
	Kilo	37	77	77	
50d	Pound	14			
	Kilo	31			
60d	Pound	11			
	Kilo	24			

LENGTH AND DIAMETER IN INCHES AND CENTIMETERS

Size	Inches	Length Centimeters	Inches	Diameter Centimeters*
2d	1	2.5	.068	.17
3d	1¼	3.2	.102	.26
4d	1½	3.8	.102	.26
5d	1¾	4.4	.102	.26
6d	2	5.1	.115	.29
7d	2¼	5.7	.115	.29
8d	2½	6.4	.131	.33
9d	2¾	7.0	.131	.33
10d	3	7.6	.148	.38
12d	3¼	8.3	.148	.38
16d	3½	8.9	.148	.38
20d	4	10.2	.203	.51
30d	4½	11.4	.220	.58
40d	5	12.7	.238	.60
50d	5¾	14.0	.257	.66
60d	6	15.2	.277	.70

*Exact conversion

PIPE FITTINGS

Only fittings for use with copper pipe are affected by metrication: metric compression fittings are interchangeable with Imperial in some sizes, but require adaptors in others.

INTERCHANGEABLE SIZES mm	Inches	SIZES REQUIRING ADAPTORS mm	Inches
12	⅜	22	¾
15	½	35	1¼
28	1	42	1½
54	2		

Metric capillary (soldered) fittings are not directly interchangeable with imperial sizes but adaptors are available. Pipe fittings which use screwed threads to make the joint remain unchanged. The British Standard Pipe (BSP) thread form has now been accepted internationally and its dimensions will not physically change. These screwed fittings are commonly used for joining iron or steel pipes, for connections on taps, basin and bath waste outlets and on boilers, radiators, pumps etc. Fittings for use with lead pipe are joined by soldering and for this purpose the metric and inch sizes are interchangeable.

(Information courtesy Metrication Board, Millbank Tower, Millbank, London SW1P 4QU)